The Vietnam War from the
Rear Echelon

The Vietnam War from the Rear Echelon

An Intelligence Officer's Memoir, 1972–1973

Timothy J. Lomperis

University Press of Kansas

All photos are from the author's private collection.

Published by the University Press of Kansas (Lawrence, Kansas 66045), which was organized by the Kansas Board of Regents and is operated and funded by Emporia State University, Fort Hays State University, Kansas State University, Pittsburg State University, the University of Kansas, and Wichita State University

Library of Congress Cataloging-in-Publication Data
Lomperis, Timothy J.
  The Vietnam War from the rear echelon : an intelligence officer's memoir, 1972–1973 / Timothy J. Lomperis.
      p.   cm. — (Modern war studies)
  Includes bibliographical references and index.
  ISBN 978-0-7006-1809-5 (cloth : alk. paper) 1. Lomperis, Timothy J. 2. Vietnam War, 1961–1975—Military intelligence—United States. 3. Intelligence officers—United States—Biography. 4. United States. Military Assistance Command, Vietnam—History. 5. Vietnam War, 1961–1975—Campaigns. 6. Vietnam War, 1961–1975—Peace. 7. Vietnam War, 1961–1975—Personal narratives. I. Title.
  DS559.8.M44L66 2011
  959.704'38—dc23   2011022661

British Library Cataloguing-in-Publication Data is available.

Printed in the United States of America

10 9 8 7 6 5 4 3 2 1

To Ana Maria
for her love and support, as always

Contents

(A photo section follows page 85)

Preface

"What Did You Do in the War, Daddy?"

April 1973 . . . the U.S. consulate in Can Tho . . . washing my hands in the bathroom . . . a big black ant falling into the sink . . . the memory returns.

Can Tho is in the Mekong Delta of South Vietnam, and I was trying to return to the capital city of Saigon. Like the ant who was stuck in the sink, I was stuck in the diplomat's office, being held against my will, and desperate to break out. I was being held because I couldn't tell my captor that I was on an exercise for my colonel back in Saigon and was under strict orders not to divulge my mission to anyone who was not part of the drill. In truth, I was a little confused myself about my trip to Can Tho, but I was certainly not going to let the diplomat in on this. For all I knew, I was on a secret mission to end the war. I had heard rumors. But the diplomat was not in the know, and I told him I wasn't talking—and he told me I wasn't leaving his office until I did.

I turned off the water to give the ant a chance to scramble out of the sink. Maybe I could think of a way to follow the ant. The little fellow started to scramble furiously up the steep porcelain surface of the sink. I was impressed! The big black ant steeled my resolve.

★   ★   ★

"What did you do in the war, Daddy?" is the question that every returning war veteran anticipates, or dreads. In my case, it was more complicated, and I have been stalling. I mean how do you tell a child about watching ants crawl out of a sink as if it were a war story. In truth, I never saw any combat, heroic or otherwise. I was a REMF (rear echelon mother f—cker) in the Vietnam War and served in the Army in the capital city of Saigon. In fact, I served for two tours in 1972 and 1973. So, I *was* in the war and have a story to tell; but it is a complicated one, and there was a lot I had to sort out in my mind and soul. But now I am ready. Since this book will be the formal answer to this question, most directly I dedicate this venture to our two children, Kristi Cain and John Scott Lomperis, and to both present and future grandchildren who might want to know, the present ones being Kristi and Greg's Katie and Jake. I also dedicate this to my wife, Ana Maria, who has been urging me to undertake a project like this for some time—ever since we first met in graduate school after I returned from my "tour of duty." As always, her love and support have been vital.

The immediate provocation for this project, however, came from Mike Briggs, the editor in chief of the University Press of Kansas. Since I am a scholar of the Vietnam War, Mike has had me review manuscripts for his press, and over the years at the annual meetings of the American Political Science Association we would chat about some of these works in particular and about the war more generally. At one such meeting in Chicago in 2008, we were talking about the siege of An Loc during the Easter Invasion of 1972, and I told him, "You know, Mike, I was there in Saigon during that siege; and, I tell you, An Loc was a little too close for comfort for me!"

"Well," he said, "have you thought about writing about your own experiences?"

Completely taken aback, I told him I would think about it. Two hours later, I came back to his booth, and said, "You know, I think I would like to do this." The stalling had come to an end.

While I was stalling, I became a professor of political science specializing in international security and Asian studies. My focus has been on the Vietnam War. I have published two academic works on this war: *The War Everyone Lost—and Won: America's Intervention in Viet Nam's Twin Struggles* (first published in 1984 and revised in 1993) is a political history of the war from international and national perspectives; and *From People's War to People's Rule: Insurgency, Intervention, and the Lessons of Vietnam*[1] (published in 1996) is a more analytical work comparing Vietnam to seven other insurgencies in order to establish some lessons. A third book (published second, between the other two) took me into new scholarly terrain. *"Reading the Wind": The Literature of the Vietnam War—an Interpretive Critique* (published in 1987 with co-author John Clark Pratt, who provided a bibliographic commentary) is a two-tiered account of a conference sponsored by The Asia Society in 1985 on the literature of the Vietnam War (novels, plays, poetry, and film). At one tier, I reported on the papers presented and critiqued them; and at the other, I commented on the interpersonal drama of the conference itself in which I was a participant. The juxtaposition of two separate but interwoven narratives that I employed in that book has helped me in setting up the basic approach for this memoir. I have also been inspired by the creativity of John Clark Pratt's own *Vietnam Voices*, in which he tells the story of Vietnam through placing nonfictional and literary accounts of the history of the war side-by-side. He calls it a "collage," and I think it worked very well.[2]

To give the fullest account of what I did in the war, I have decided to answer this question in three arenas. This, then, is my collage. I first provide a context of the war itself in the two years that I served in Saigon; namely, of the Easter Invasion in the spring of 1972, of the Paris Peace Agreement of January 1973, and of its immediate aftermath until August, when I left. I do not intend to add much here to the rich historiography of the war other than to shed some light on a "secret plan to end the war" in which I participated. About this historiography, let me profess a Hippocratic oath of at least intending to do no harm. I do, however, offer some conclusions that have escaped me in my previous writings. What I missed is what I will call my "Two-by-Two War Thesis." On the ground in Vietnam, Washington fought two different wars, and so did Hanoi. In Washington's case, in the Easter Invasion of 1972, there was General Abrams's MACV war and President Nixon's war of the two Linebacker bombing campaigns. These two wars upended each other and only compounded the tragedy discussed below. In Hanoi's case, it ran a conventional military campaign in the north of South Vietnam, and more of a guerrilla war in the south. By the Easter Invasion, however, the southern war was a pretense and posed no obstacle to, or support of, Hanoi's invasions of 1972 and 1975.

The second arena is the mid-level perspective of the rear-echelon war in Saigon. This was the level of mediation between the meta-level strategic decisions and politics between the two war capitals of Washington and Hanoi, on the one hand, and of the troops battling in the field on the other. The commanding height of this war was MACV (Military Assistance Command, Vietnam) Headquarters, sometimes called Pentagon East, a sprawling installation just north of Saigon and literally across the street from the Tan Son Nhut airport. This was the REMF war, a war of Americans running a military logistical infrastructure and decision-making bureaucracy dedicated to making the war work. Thus, MACV was tasked with figuring out how to translate the war policy made in Washington into something approaching a military and political victory on site in Vietnam. Those of us who lived in this world—REMFs (Rear Echelon Mother F—ckers)—did our military staff work alongside a civilian world that went on surviving in an urban life where some sort of society and economy hummed along. This lens through which I viewed the war will be the main focus of this work. This level has been largely neglected in the literature. Macro accounts of strategy and diplomacy abound, as do individual memoirs of combat. The value of this level is that it is where one can view the concrete complexities of the war, and where some of the impenetrable obstacles that were making the venture hopeless come into view.

I view the Vietnam War as much like a Greek tragedy, with a protagonist who makes a heroic attempt to cheat fate, despite its inevitability. If there is an overall thesis to this book, it is that it was in 1972 and 1973, in the twin events of the Easter Invasion and the Paris Peace Agreement, that the war's tragic fate was sealed, a view that can be most clearly seen at this REMF level. This, at least, is what I saw, and it is the story that I will tell.

Methodologically, this perspective lands us in the middle of the "level-of-analysis" question in political science; namely, at which vantage point, or level of activity (at the level of the international system, the nation-state, or institutions within a state), are actions most critically determined?[3] Kenneth Waltz, one of the giants in the theory of international relations, has been adamant in insisting that systemic forces at the international level are almost exclusively determinative of international events.[4] Naturally, a chorus of dissent has risen up from his peers. Illustrative of this group is the argument of Jack Snyder that foreign policy behavior really arises from the structure of domestic politics within a nation-state and from the nature of the different winning political coalitions that emerge from this structure.[5] In this work, at first blush I side with Waltz in that I will argue that the outcome of the Vietnam War was ultimately determined "off-camera," at a level far above the theater in Vietnam, but this overarching perspective misses the flesh-and-blood story on the ground that brings the tragedy of the war into poignant relief. And it is here where one can fully understand the forces that made

Vietnam a tragedy, regardless of what determined the event's outcome. Hence, I end up siding with Snyder and others who argue that the understanding of behavior comes more from lower levels—in the case of this work, from the level of REMF Land.

In the discipline of history, one of the earliest of these mid-level perspectives that was able to show how the British Raj operated day-to-day in India was Robert Eric Frykenberg's history of Guntur District.[6] More recently, an excellent work that shows the early vitality of the Roman Empire, and its slow deterioration, is a similar mid-level perspective by Stephen Dando-Collins in his history of Julius Caesar's Tenth Legion.[7] Indeed, Jeffrey Race's analysis of the war in Long An, the bellwether province in the Mekong Delta, which I consider one of the most insightful works on Vietnam, was also written from this mid-level vantage point.[8] My hope is that this book will follow in the insightful vein of this mid-level analysis.

The third arena is both an individual and a generational one. I am part of the Baby Boom generation that cut its teeth on the "Bad War" of Vietnam. Rather than unite us, like the "Good War" of World War II did for our parents' generation, this war tore us apart. We encountered this war differently, viewed it differently, and came out differently into a completely splintered generation. As part of this larger story, I will relate how all of my experiences in Vietnam affected my worldview and life choices. Hopefully, these reactions will be a window on how this war penetrated the souls of this not lost, but very alienated, generation. In my own case, what these pages will portray is that of a Lutheran missionary kid from India born with an expatriate's faith in the essential goodness of America and its institutions. Part of this youthful idealism accepted the Manichean, black and white view of the world—especially in the Cold War—where we as the "children of the light" were fighting the "children of the darkness" (naturally, Communists of any stripe). I grew up on morning prayers for all the missionaries held prisoner in Communist China, after all. I joined the fight in Vietnam as a crusader in this noble cause. My tours in Vietnam during these crucial two years, however, were disillusioning and tumbled me into a despair that changed the direction of my life—ultimately, I think, for the better.

In addition to the theme of the Vietnam War in general as

a Greek tragedy, Jonathan Shay has written of Vietnam as an individual tragedy for its veterans. In comparing the post-traumatic stresses of contemporary GIs to Achilles, he writes, "his tragedy was that events—simply what happened—created the desire to do things that he himself regarded as bad." Thus, his "noble character [was] brought to ruin—*moral ruin in his own terms.*"⁹ While I strove with others to avert this general tragedy in Vietnam, along with everyone else, we failed. In this general failure, however, I avoided a personal one. This I owe to the way my faith kept hold of me, and to the people of faith who surrounded me, even in Vietnam.

Like my commitment to the historiography on the war, I have tried to be true to the basic sequence of events in this personal account. For thematic purposes and narrative coherence, however, I must confess to two exceptions. I have put my secret exercise at the end of the section on my tour of duty in Vietnam, even though the event actually took place in April 1973. Since this event was the dramatic "conclusion" to my tour, I felt it belonged in the concluding section of my time in Vietnam. I also made an important trip to the coastal town of Tuy Hoa that was part of my "Alice" story. Alice was married in April 1972, and I tell the story of my trip to Tuy Hoa with Alice and her new husband right after the account of the wedding, even though the trip occurred in February 1973, shortly after I became a civilian. The significance of this trip did not depend on when it took place, and I thought it best to keep the Alice events together.

With this personal focus in the account of the REMF war in Saigon in 1972–1973, I am intending to primarily relate to my fellow Baby Boomers and to our generational trauma, even as I am trying to explain it all to my grandchildren—and to their grandchildren as well. To more contemporary readers, the relevance of Vietnam to Iraq and Afghanistan will rise as an unbidden ghost. Indeed, in the agonizing strategy review of Afghanistan in the fall of 2009 undertaken by the new Obama administration, Vice President Joe Biden warned that if President Obama succumbed to the military's request to send more troops, "We're locked into Vietnam."¹⁰ Since the president did, in fact, succumb, the question arises: if Afghanistan has hence become Vietnam, what was Vietnam anyway? Presumably, answering this question will hold the key to understanding Afghanistan as well. Though I have other purposes to this book than answering this question, by the end of reading this volume, readers should gain a good grasp of the reality of Vietnam. As to what the proper parallels and possible lessons, might be, however, I leave to the discretion of the readers.

For those who need further background on Vietnam to follow this memoir, I have added at the end of the book a list of acronyms and expressions of "Nam Speak," as well as a basic chronology of both my life and of the Cold War and Vietnam. In chapter 1, I have also included a brief overview of the history of the war until my arrival in-country. For those who are impatient to plunge into my story, they can skip over this background and begin on page 14, and refer back to this background material as the need arises.

The memoir divides into four phases. The first recounts my journey to Vietnam. Chapter 1 covers my civilian path into the military in 1969, and chapter 2 outlines the two-and-a-half-year progression of military training Stateside that culminated in my deployment to Vietnam. The second phase tells of my military career in Vietnam from the Easter Invasion when I first arrived in March 1972, through the Paris Peace Talks and Christmas Bombing, to the Paris Peace Agreement of January 27, 1973. Following a two-week Christmas leave in India with my parents, the memoir continues with the third phase, my tour as a civilian intelligence liaison officer from February 1973 to August 1973, when I returned home. Interspersed in these two tours are two portraits of life in Saigon. Chapter 5 presents the structure of society in Saigon, while chapter 9 draws out more of my life in this city, though there is overlap between these two city chapters. The final phase relates my decision to come home and recounts my subsequent struggles to come to terms with my involvement in the Vietnam War. In so doing, I make a shocking discovery that enables a spiritual journey to a final reconciliation with this involvement.

It takes a lot of encouragement to see a project like this to the finish. In addition to proposing this book in the first place, Mike Briggs has stayed with me all the way through the process offering encouragement and providing sage advice. I am also particularly grateful to Robert Jervis of Columbia University for blessing me in this venture. This is not really a book of political science (my field), so to get such enthusiastic support from such a prominent political scientist was legitimating. My two life mentors in this business have also implicitly guided me: Sam Huntington, of Harvard, in spirit (since he passed away in 2008); and Ole Holsti, at Duke, with numerous e-mails.

I seek a wider audience in this book than in my previous academic writings, and I have received the benefit of feedback from a broader cross-section of readers. All of them have helped with numerous refinements. Among my academic colleagues, I wish to thank JD Bowen, Eloise Buker, Jean-Robert Leguey-Feilleux, Father John Padberg, Steve Puro, Father "J. J." Mueller, and Tom Shippey from Saint Louis University; John Clark Pratt from Northern Colorado University (and my co-author on *"Reading the Wind"*); Lauretta Frederking from the University of Portland; and Patti Weitsman from Ohio University. I owe a vote of thanks as well to the following friends: John Tegenfeldt (the best man at our wedding), David Morris, Mary Lowry, Larry and Mary Kuster, Mike Kinsel, and Paul Gausmann (a Lutheran pastor who is Bill Gausmann's son). Even my gym buddies Steve Schilson (a fellow Vietnam veteran) and John Warmington read parts of it. Family members also chipped in enthusiastically with reactions, and I want to thank my daughter Kristi and son John, as well as uncles and aunts Gus and Lee Larsen, Russell and Carol Lomperis, and John and Lois Sibole (from the "greatest generation"); my sisters Anne and Sue Lomperis; sister-in-law Rosa Boeschen (a published novelist); cousins Andy and Tom Larsen, Linda and Judy Lomperis, and Janet and Steve More; and nephew Karl Olson and niece Julia Lohla.

Finally, I owe much more than thanks to my wife Ana Maria, who has been my most effective critic and ardent supporter, reading each draft and encouraging me on. In this project, she did a masterful job editing the final draft of the manuscript. Indeed, she has been my life partner through all my projects. Apropos of this book, I met Ana Maria when I returned to graduate school in the fall of 1973. At the Johns Hopkins University School of Advanced International Studies, she met a very sullen Vietnam veteran who would only answer, "yup," to her persistently friendly "you were in the Army, weren't you?" questioning. Eventually, I mellowed, and she helped me make my reentry into the "world." I could not have come to the personal conclusion in the Epilogue of this book without her truly divine intervention in my life.

I have been a bit of a "workplace" person, and this is the first book that I have written at home. I surrounded myself in a home office with books, memorabilia, pictures, and letters of my time in Vietnam. Whenever I entered this lair, the memories swept me across the ocean and back in time to this vivid epoch of my life. Our Stray Rescue Lab puppy, Sunshine Sparkle, was my constant companion, and disturber, that brought me back to the present.

I am deeply indebted to the support of my home institution, Saint Louis University. Wynne Moskop, my department chair, helped arrange for my sabbatical leave in the spring of 2010 and ensured that my responsibilities were kept to an absolute minimum. Ellen Carnaghan, the director of graduate studies, assigned me an absolutely top-drawer graduate research assistant, and even increased her hours to help me get this project in on time. This top-drawer graduate student is Elizabeth Szabo, whose assistance has been vital. She has been enthusiastic about this project and tireless in the long hours she has spent in the library and on the Internet tracking down all the little fact-checking and whole cloth "research projects" I sent her on.

This book is not neatly categorized—either as a memoir or as a history or political analysis of the Vietnam War. Understandably, it has received a thorough vetting. Three experts reviewed the initial prospectus and were instrumental in steering me away from substantial pitfalls in my subsequent writing of the full manuscript. Dale Andrade, a historian at the U.S. Army's Center of Military History; Frank Snepp, a former high-ranking official at the U.S. embassy in Saigon during the war; and James H. Willbanks, a professor at the U.S. Army's Command and General Staff College at Fort Leavenworth, Kansas, and a Vietnam veteran who served as an adviser during the Easter Invasion, have all written their own acclaimed accounts of the war, and their experience afforded me wise counsel. Mike Briggs himself and Professor David Anderson, at California State University, Monterey Bay (a Vietnam veteran and scholar on the war like myself), screened the full manuscript, and provided the final suggested focus to the work that was invaluable in writing the last revision.

At the University Press of Kansas, I also wish to thank production editor Jennifer Dropkin and my copy editor Kay Kodner, who took the roughage of my prose and refined it into something beyond my capabilities.

With all of this help and support, the writing of this book has been a pleasure.

Timothy J. Lomperis
Chesterfield, Missouri
Thanksgiving 2010

Part I

Getting There

South Vietnam (Central Intelligence Agency, *South Vietnam Provincial Maps*, September 1967; in the author's possession)

Prelude to the War's End:
The Years 1972–1973

One of the key periods in the Vietnam War occurred during 1972 and 1973, and these were the years I spent in Vietnam. It began with the Easter Invasion in March 1972, shortly after I arrived in-country. It ended with the Paris Peace Agreement of January 1973—and its tragic aftermath, an aftermath whose foregone conclusion was already becoming clear by the end of the year. This period was not marked by the more historically celebrated turning point of the Tet Offensive of 1968 or ended by the final Ho Chi Minh campaign culminating in the fall of Saigon in April 1975, but it signaled the denouement to this war, the prelude to the end.

There was plenty of drama in these two years. The Easter Invasion was a major follow-on offensive to Tet, and it was beaten back by the South Vietnamese military and American air power. The secret negotiations that became increasingly public reflected this strength—and the Christmas Bombing at the year's end confirmed it and drove home the Paris Peace Agreement of January 27, 1973.

I was a mouse in this cockpit of history. I had trained in the Army for two and a half years before arriving in Saigon in March 1972. I served first as an intelligence briefer to General Creighton Abrams, the MACV commander, and then I worked for the B-52 Arc Light Panel (the panel of General Army and Air Force officers that selected the B-52 targets to be struck each day) that was in the Air Intelligence Division of MACV. After the peace agreement, I stayed on as a civilian intelligence liaison officer and was dispatched on a secret mission to "end" the war.

This is my memoir of this drama, but I need to set the stage for it to be clear. In this account, I present the history that brought Vietnam to the impasse of these two years, the basic deal upon which the fortunes of the South Vietnamese depended, and some necessary analysis on why this deal could not work—an analysis, then, that illumines the contours of the tragedy of these years. Finally, there is my own fitful journey to the Saigon of 1972 and 1973, where I first

4   got caught up in this tragedy and from where I ultimately made my escape.

American involvement in Vietnam rose from the ashes of the dramatic French defeat at Dienbienphu on May 7, 1954. Dienbienphu was a remote village in northwestern Vietnam along the border with Laos. It lay astride the route to Luang Prabang, the capital of Laos, seemingly the objective of a campaign by the Viet Minh (the Communist revolutionaries under Ho Chi Minh) to widen the war by overstretching the resources of the French. The French had yearned for such a "set piece" battle and decided to place a garrison in the village as a blocking force to engage these advancing columns. In a fifty-five-day siege, the Viet Minh, with a generous supply of equipment and advice from the Chinese, shattered this outpost of 15,000 French Union forces, which included elite "Paras" (paratroopers) and Foreign Legionnaires. When Washington, after some dithering, spurned a desperate French plea for a military rescue in a plan called "Operation Vulture," this redoubtable little garrison fell. For its defenders, it had been "Hell in a very small place."[1]

Deciding not to intervene to save French colonialism did not mean the United States was abandoning all of Southeast Asia to Communism. To the contrary, at the Geneva Accords of July 1954 that attempted to solve the Indochina "question," U.S. Secretary of State John Foster Dulles resolved to foster a modern democratic nationalism against this new threat. The British, Dutch, and Americans had granted independence to their Asian colonies shortly after World War II as they sought to promote a new democratic nationalism under the rubric of "development" and "nation building."[2] The French alone had insisted on retaining their colonies in Indochina (the three Vietnamese colonies of Tonkin, Annam, and Cochin China, as well as the kingdoms of Cambodia and Laos). The United States had provided military assistance to the French in their war to regain these colonies after their loss to the Japanese in World War II. This support, however, was to assist France as an ally of the North Atlantic Treaty Organization (NATO) and to bolster the containment doctrine against Communism after Communist forces under Mao Zedong won their civil war in China against the Guomindang (nationalists) in October 1949.

As colonialism receded in Asia in the 1940s and 1950s and in Africa in the 1960s, the new struggle in the international arena was the standoff between the Soviet Union and the United States in Europe, and the struggle in the emerging postcolonial Third World for global "hearts and minds." This latter struggle was between a Communist call for revolutionary mobilization against the persistence of Western colonialism and a Western call for evolutionary development that would build nations of representative democracy and free enterprise.

The U.S. foreign policy that orchestrated this struggle was containment. The author of this policy was George F. Kennan, an American diplomat stationed in the Soviet Union. The focus of his famous "X" article outlining this policy was on the "sources of Soviet conduct," but he warned that this struggle was likely to be worldwide as the Soviet Union would seek to expand its influence in "rapidly shifting points."[3] The centerpiece of this policy was the NATO alliance in Europe. But Dulles envisioned a worldwide ring of containment treaties around the Soviet Union. From NATO, Dulles developed CENTO, the Central Treaty Organization, focused on Turkey and Pakistan. He also attempted to create METO, the Middle East Treaty Organization, built around Jordan, Egypt, and Lebanon, which foundered over Nasser of Egypt's Arab nationalism and the question of Israeli membership.

For Southeast Asia, Dulles had in mind a Southeast Asia Treaty Organization, or SEATO. He refused to sign the Geneva Accords and instead signed off on this new treaty in 1954. The United States, Pakistan (also a member of CENTO), France, Britain, Thailand, and the Philippines joined this alliance. This treaty document stipulated that the states of the former French Indochina were to be considered part of the SEATO treaty area and, hence, were to enjoy the provisions of "common defense" in this treaty. This guarantee became the centerpiece of the U.S. justification for its intervention in Vietnam.

Though the United States refused to sign the Geneva Accords (as did the fledgling government of South Vietnam), Dulles promised not to disturb their provisions. These accords called for the withdrawal of French forces and independence for the colonies of Cambodia, Laos, and Vietnam. Vietnam was to be temporarily divided at the seventeenth parallel until nationwide elections could be held within two years. Cambodia and Laos had traditional monarchs who presided over these new countries. In Vietnam, however, the victory over the French was exclusively a Communist one, and no one expected a non-Communist alternative to emerge in the South—certainly not in Emperor Bao Dai, the playboy prince whom the French nurtured as a pliant cover for their rule, nor in Ngo Dinh Diem, the Catholic recluse who had been called home from a Catholic monastery in New Jersey to assume the mantle of presidential office, presumably until the Viet Minh could make arrangements to assume full national power.

But Diem surprised everyone. Certainly with behind the scenes help from the CIA, he energetically consolidated power by breaking up the Binh Xuyen (a mafia-like organization operating widespread "business" interests in Saigon, an obligingly corrupt police force, and a set of French colons and military personnel) and buying off the Cao Dai and Hoa Hao sects (two religious offshoots with large followings in the Mekong Delta and in the region surrounding the nearby city to Saigon of Tay Ninh). After these struggles, Diem declared the South to be an independent republic. Since the North refused to hold elections on its side of the seventeenth parallel under Western standards of "genuinely free elections," he refused to hold them in the South, and in 1956 two separate countries were born from this disagreement.[4]

This unexpected "Cold War success" in Southeast Asia led to some euphoria in Washington. A group of liberals—Senators John Kennedy, Lyndon Johnson, and Mike Mansfield along with Justice William O. Douglas—formed a group called the Friends of Vietnam and hailed President Diem as the George Washington of Asia. Diem's success also surprised the regime of Ho Chi Minh in Hanoi, and it lost ground in the South in the late 1950s. In order to recoup its position, in late 1959 Hanoi announced the resumption of "armed struggle" in the South and began to infiltrate Southern Communist cadres back to the South who had fled to the North in 1954. In December 1960, the Communists announced the formation of the National Liberation Front to liberate the South from Diem's rule. Though created by Hanoi, it was supposed to be a Southern organization, and all the forces and organizations that came under it became known as the Viet Cong.

By 1960, the war was on. At this stage, it was a guerrilla war, what the Communists called a "war of national liberation." It was just the war that the incoming American president, John F. Kennedy, recognized as the new arena of struggle in the Cold War. Realizing that the process of nation building would have to take on the challenge of guerrillas who would try to twist these efforts into Communist revolutions, his adviser Walt W. Rostow called insurgent movements the "scavengers of modernization."[5] Exactly how to deal with these scavengers, however, was proving to be a problem. President Diem was not keen on having a large number of American troops in his country. He also did not seem eager to permit the development of political institutions independent of his control. Kennedy sent study group after study group to Saigon and they all kept returning with contradictory reports. Meanwhile, Viet Cong forces mounted wider-ranging attacks in increasingly larger formations. Washington countered with more military advisers and equipment. By 1964, there were over 20,000 U.S. military advisers in-country.

The assassination of President Diem on November 1, 1963, was a game-changer. Effectively, this was the end of civilian rule in South Vietnam. In Saigon, the event triggered an interregnum of chaos as nine successive coups d'état failed to bring some semblance of stability until the flashy Air Force General Nguyen Cao Ky seized power with the more stolid Army General Nguyen Van Thieu in February 1965. To further complicate matters, Buddhist militants and protesters mounted a national campaign against the regime. When they managed to turn the sympathies of the First ARVN (Army of the Republic of Vietnam) Division in the northern city of Danang, only the insertion of U.S. Marines between hostile units prevented a major armed clash.[6]

The Viet Cong took advantage of these political distractions, and mobile columns of battalion-sized Communist forces began to chew up ARVN units in the countryside, particularly in the Mekong Delta. From small-scale guerrilla attacks, Communist forces had moved into phase two of Mao Zedong's strategy of people's war—the strikes by mobile columns that Mao called the "war of maneuver"—and appeared poised to move into the final phase three of a frontal conventional assault on the centers of the Saigon regime's power.

Two attacks by North Vietnamese patrol boats on U.S. destroyers operating in international waters off the coast of North Vietnam in August 1964 led Congress to pass the Gulf of Tonkin Resolution authorizing the president to take all necessary measures to restore

8   peace in Southeast Asia, "including the use of armed force." As a casus belli, these attacks were caught up in a controversy that lasted for decades. Some questioned whether the attacks even took place. Others noted that the North Vietnamese patrol boats may have mistaken the U.S. destroyers for South Vietnamese saboteur vessels. With access to classified documents on the incident, Edwin Moise, a prominent historian of the Vietnam War, has concluded that the first attack did take place, but the second did not.[7]

In any case, events then started moving in several directions at once. The Communists, for one, picked up their pace considerably for their attempted takeover of the South. From a regimen of infiltrating individual replacements down the Ho Chi Minh Trail, in the fall of 1964 the Armed Forces High Command in Hanoi began sending entire combat units into the Southern battlefields. The United States, in turn, moved from its low-level advisory effort to the dispatching of its own combat units, with a division of U.S. Marines splashing ashore in Danang to defend a major U.S. air base in March 1965. By July, the new Commander of U.S. Forces in Vietnam (COMUS MACV), General William C. Westmoreland, had come up with his own strategy to exploit the massive U.S. troop buildup and win the war. His, too, was a strategy of three phases. The first one, of an estimated six months, was to "halt the losing trend" by bringing in enough air and ground combat units to reverse the disastrous string of Viet Cong victories in the field. The second, projected for another six months, was to move Communist forces away from populated areas so that pacification measures could be undertaken. The last phase, of somewhat more indefinite duration, mentioned as lasting another year to a year and a half, would be to push main force Communist combat units completely out of the country, consolidate pacification gains, and permit the emergence of a stable republic in the South.[8] By the end of 1965, there were 175,000 U.S. forces in Vietnam, a level that rose to 375,000 at the end of 1966. This force level topped out at 543,000 in 1969.[9]

Westmoreland's strategy was designed to enable politics in Saigon to stabilize around an emergent democratic system. In 1966, elections were held for a Constituent Assembly, which fashioned a Second Republic for the Government of Vietnam. This amounted to a presidential system on a Gaullist rather than an American model, since the president had the power to declare emergency powers and suspend the National Assembly. In any case, presidential elections were held in 1967. Since Communists refused the precondition of laying down their arms, they were not allowed to participate. The military rallied behind Ky's deputy, Nguyen Van Thieu. Mr. Thieu won the election and became the first president of South Vietnam's Second Republic.

While Thieu consolidated his hold on national power, the war in the countryside increasingly turned into a slug-fest between American combat troops and North Vietnamese regulars, what Guenter Lewy called, "the big unit war."[10] This marauding combat in the countryside drove much of the rural populace into the relative safety of the cities. Almost overnight, South Vietnam was becoming urbanized. The Communists made a massive bid to turn all of this around by launching the Tet Offensive in January 1968 that lasted until May. Tet is the Vietnamese New Year holiday. It lasts about a month, and it is supposed to be a time for parties, friendship, and gift-giving, not a time for work—or war.

In multiple and contradictory ways, Tet was a fundamental turning point of the war. Because of the conflicting pulls of these "multiplicities," however, nothing was yet inevitable. To begin with, it was an all-out shock offensive that struck every provincial capital almost simultaneously. All available Southern Viet Cong combat troops were deployed, with regular North Vietnamese troops ready for "mopping up." The offensive was everywhere beaten back, though Communist forces made some spectacular penetrations (for Western media footage) into Saigon, and they held out in Hue for a prolonged battle. This first Viet Cong wave was decimated, and North Vietnamese forces pulled back from engaging American and ARVN troops. More than a military defeat, the Tet Offensive essentially ended any hope of a Southern revolutionary movement making a bid for power. The Communist effort passed almost completely to Northern hands, whose forces were much more that of a conventional military machine supported by the same sort of foreign industrial suppliers that provisioned the South Vietnamese forces.

This significant transition escaped the attention of the American electorate because the timing could not have come at a more awkward time—right in the middle of a presidential campaign. Scenes of carnage and destruction from this offensive pulsed the TV screens of every living room in America. Public opinion, though fluid, shifted

10 decidedly toward favoring an end to the fighting. Through March, public support remained at 45 percent, but Johnson's approval rating for handling the war plummeted to 26 percent from an earlier 40 percent.[11] Senator Eugene McCarthy, from Minnesota, nearly won the New Hampshire Democratic Primary on a crusading antiwar platform. After this showing, another antiwar figure, Senator Robert Kennedy, declared his candidacy, and on March 30 President Lyndon Johnson withdrew from the race. With the assassination of Senator Kennedy in June, the Republican candidate, Richard Nixon, though a hawk on the war, campaigned on a platform to end the war. Nixon won the election in a close contest with the Democratic standard bearer, Vice President Hubert Humphrey.

Meanwhile in South Vietnam, the defeat of the Communists at Tet bought some time for President Thieu to consolidate his position. Domestically, a process of electoral politics was developing in the National Assembly. Buddhists who had led a protest movement against Diem in the early 1960s were generally alienated by the Communist attacks on civilians during Tet and formed their own voting bloc in the legislature, and they did well in the senatorial elections of 1970. Thieu himself won reelection in 1971, after inducing his two opponents to withdraw from the race. This was hardly an American model of democracy, but the Vietnamese president was patterning himself after French President Charles De Gaulle (who made a practice of calling for single referendums on his rule, rather than facing real electoral opponents) instead of George Washington.[12]

Perhaps Thieu's biggest domestic success was the passage of the Land Reform Act in March 1970. This provided "land to the tiller" by redistributing over 2.5 million hectares of land in three years, reducing the tenancy rate in rural Vietnam from 60 percent to 10 percent and allowing a real middle class to arise in the countryside, particularly in the populous Mekong Delta where half the country lived.[13]

The anchor to Thieu's political power, however, lay in his ability to deliver and retain American support. The term "Vietnamization" became the key, but to the Vietnamese and the Americans it meant two different things. In this difference lay the heart of the classic tragedy of the Vietnam War. The policy itself was clear enough. With the defeat of conventional Communist forces in the Tet Offensive, the United States would gradually withdraw its troops as

ARVN forces were increased and provided the training and equipment to continue the fight against the Communists on their own. The meaning of this arrangement turned into a definitional divergence that inevitably became a tragedy in the events of 1972 and 1973. To Washington, Vietnamization ultimately was the way out of Vietnam. To Saigon, it ultimately preserved the umbilical cord to America.

Under the rubric of this policy, the United States sought to achieve the fulfillment of the nation building of South Vietnam by putting in place an institutional infrastructure and a potent military force capable of sustaining the country's independent sovereignty and economic prosperity in the postcolonial global system. Naturally, as a SEATO ally, the United States would not leave without security guarantees. For the Vietnamese, the very nature of this nation building, particularly the military dimensions to it, seemed to guarantee a fundamental continuation of this commitment. That is, the military that the United States was bequeathing to the Vietnamese was an American one in all but the manning of Americans themselves in these uniforms. It could not exist without the steady lifeline of equipment, training, and parts from the military-industrial economy of the United States. President Nixon, in proclaiming this vision, reassured Thieu that, if the North Vietnamese rose to militarily challenge this "arrangement," the United States would retaliate against Hanoi in force. This was Thieu's umbilical cord. But achieving the goal of self-sufficiency would take a lot of time, and a very long cord. And time was not something that Nixon could command.

There were two dimensions to this tragedy. One was the issue of nationalism, or really the lack of it in the South. By the heroic act of throwing the French colonialists out of Indochina in the siege of Dienbienphu, the Communist Viet Minh had seized the high ground on this issue. This was particularly true since other nationalist groups had chosen to leave the country during World War II for American protection in South China. It wasn't just Dienbienphu; the Communists also had remained in-country during the war and fought both the Japanese and the French. There are many features to traditional Vietnamese nationalism, but its essence falls under the term *mat nuoc,* "lose the waters." The term "waters" refers to the two river deltas, the Red River in the North and the Mekong River in the South, which form the boundaries of the Vietnamese father-land. The idea, of course, is to *not* lose the waters, either to mis-governance or foreign occupiers, and thereby to protect Vietnamese identity. The non-Communist nationalist groups had committed the crime of deserting these waters in their hour of need.

The Communists, then, in the follow-on struggle against the Americans had this legacy of defending the fatherland; and in Com-munism they had a blueprint for the future. This is not to say that the Communists had everything going for them in the South. For one thing, their atheism had thoroughly alienated the Catholics, who were highly organized and represented about 15 percent of the population. After some flirtation with the Viet Cong, by the time of the Tet Offensive the Buddhist majority had become highly skeptical of the Communists, as had large sections of the urban population. All of the major trade unions, for example, were strong supporters of the government. Thieu had also managed to win over the major-ity of the two sects: the Cao Dai of Tay Ninh and the Hoa Hao of the Mekong Delta. The Communists did not own the issue of na-tionalism in the South like they did in the North.

But the Saigon regime never made a full-press effort to turn this issue into a fundamental cause for its war effort. Its leaders lacked the connection to this history, and their ideas about a modern state and society for Vietnam were an inchoate mixture of French phi-losophy, the politics of a strongman Gaullist republic, Confucian rectitude, American democracy, and Japanese prosperity.[14] It is in-teresting to note that Robert Brigham, in his study of ARVN, found little evidence of attempts to instill in the soldiers any sense of na-tionalist dedication. Vietnamese civilians feared that nationalism in the military would create a separate caste, while the military regime saw in it too much of a motivation for yet another coup. As one of-ficer put it: "They forbade us to do much political training because they did not want an army of nationalists."[15]

The well of support upon which the South Vietnamese drew to sustain their effort came not from their own society but from their American benefactors. In a sense, they chose this dependence because the United States' miracles of technology, its prosperous economy, and its position as the leader of the Free World marked it out as the model of the future. Thus, the Vietnamese were flattered, honored, and vitally dependent psychologically on the attention the Americans were paying them and their country as a laboratory for the American strategy of nation building in the Third World. They were thus participating in this American-dominated future. If the local history of Vietnam seemed to belong to the Communists, when Saigonese looked to the larger global stage, the American star seemed everywhere ascendant, and they drew their strength from being hitched to it.[16]

As the Americans attempted to turn over the destiny of South Vietnam to the Vietnamese through Vietnamization, the umbilical cord of American support was still vital, not just materially but psychologically as well. The basic deal was this: absent a motivational nationalism in South Vietnamese society, the South Vietnamese critically depended on the attentive constancy of this American support. Shortly after Senator Robert Kennedy announced his opposition to the Vietnam War and his intention to negotiate a peace and withdraw all American troops, Tran Ngoc Chau, a neutralist South Vietnamese politician and opponent of the military regime, rebuked Kennedy for this speech: "When you took over the war, you took on a responsibility towards us, and you must recognize that responsibility."[17]

This dimension of the lack of nationalism in the South did not guarantee the tragedy of the Vietnam War by itself, but it served to set it up for the other dimension that locked in the tragic consequences: the lack of constancy to this vital support. No one has done a better job in explaining how and why this support unravels than Andrew Mack in his prescient article, "Why Big Nations Lose Small Wars." He attributes this development to "the politics of asymmetric conflict." The asymmetry lies in the wills of the two sides. The small country, resisting the intervener, is totally committed to the war because its homeland is being fought over. The intervener, however, has a small war on its hands but also a host of other issues, such as a commitment to NATO, concerns about oil supplies in the Middle East, other Communist insurgencies in Cuba and Central America, and the buildup of Soviet missiles. Hence, there is an asymmetry of wills that can compensate for the small country's lack of conventional military prowess. Because of these competing concerns, the Big Nation's domestic politics becomes a second arena to the Small War. Although the Small Nation is unlikely to defeat the Big Nation militarily in the first arena, over time it can win its victory in the vulnerable second arena. To Mack, this vulnerability is pronounced in a parliamentary democracy in that eventually the continuation of this Small War will inevitably become a divisive issue between the contending political parties. With the war then hostage to political partisanship, overall public support for the war will drain away.[18]

Nixon's plan of Vietnamization was to avoid this development by winning before the inevitable partisanship set in. He launched an incursion into Cambodia in April 1970 to throw Communist forces into disarray and give the handover more time to solidify. Instead, he stirred up a hornet's nest in both Indochina and the United States. With American and ARVN troops on the prowl in Cambodia, the North Vietnamese widened their war effort through large-scale conventional operations in both Cambodia and Laos. The antiwar movement launched nationwide protests, which received a tremendous impetus with the killing of four protesters by National Guard soldiers on the campus of Kent State University.

After the Cambodian incursion, Nixon began his troop withdrawals in earnest. From over 473,000 troops in-country in 1970, by 1972 there were only 45,600 left, and very few of them were in combat units.[19] The Communists used this period to rebuild, and supplies and equipment from Moscow poured into Hanoi. By the time I arrived in-country in 1972, everything was about to explode into another offensive as Vietnamization faced the acid test.

When I flew into Vietnam (see page 41), I came with a background that differed from that of most of my peers. I was born in India during the opening years of the Cold War, when England was releasing the prime jewel in its empire: the British Raj in India. My parents, Clarence Lomperis and Marjorie Larsen, were married in Calcutta in April 1946 in the midst of pro-independence riots. Indeed, they had to postpone their wedding because the church had been torched. I was born in March 1947, in the last months of British rule; it was also the year of George Kennan's "X" article that articulated a case for the foreign policy of containment. Subsequent events included the Marshall Plan in 1948 and the Berlin Air Lift in 1949. I was a Cold War baby.

My parents were Lutheran missionaries who were saving souls for Christ, not scoring points in the Cold War. Yet they were firm believers in the goodness of America, as were virtually all of their missionary colleagues, essentially because of their belief that the United States was a Christian nation and the final bastion against the spread of godless Communism. There was even a low-grade Communist insurgency right in our backyard in the new province of Andhra Pradesh.

The Cold War came to Asia in October 1949 with the fall of China to Mao Zedong's guerrilla war. In the heyday of Christian missions at the turn of the century, there were 7,000 missionaries in China, the largest number in Asia. Lutheran missionaries were well represented both in China and India and also in substantial numbers in Japan, Taiwan, Malaya, and New Guinea. It was a pretty tight community with a lot of intermingling during furloughs in America as well as on trips from field to field. I grew up in the early 1950s praying for all the missing missionaries thought to be imprisoned in "Red China."

Three events in 1956 awakened me to the Cold War in the larger world. The Hungarian Uprising and the pictures of Soviet tanks crushing the crowds in Budapest confirmed the image of Communist tyranny suppressing cries for freedom. In this year, President Eisenhower swept into a second term. "I liked Ike" because he was a World War II hero and general, and I thought he was just what the Free World needed in the titanic struggle against evil. The Suez Crisis was baffling to me. It muddied the waters of the Manichean world of black and white. The Egyptian president Gamal Abdel Nasser had nationalized the Suez Canal owned by a British and French consortium. British and French forces seized control of the canal, and Israeli troops took advantage of the Egyptian defeat by seizing the Sinai Peninsula. In a fit of anticolonialism, the United States forced its allies to return the canal to Egypt and the Israelis to give back Sinai.

My devotion as a Cold Warrior rested on three legs. Two of them were solid, but the third one was squishy. One of the strong legs was my belief that the United States was a force for good. For one thing, all the missionaries around me were Americans (well, there were some Canadians)—and what they were doing was good. And America itself, of course, was good. Not having lived in America, I knew this was true through the patriotic books my mother read me about George Washington, the "midnight ride of Paul Revere," and Honest Abe and his call that America was "the last, best hope for the world." All of this was axiomatic. My mother quietly took me aside and told me that even the Democrats shared in this goodness—a stunning thought! The other strong leg, the polar opposite, was the belief that Russian and Chinese Communists were bad. In our own Andhra Pradesh, there was a bit of a festering Communist insurgency that targeted both police stations and the Christian community. This evil, then, was both generic and almost personal.

The squishy third leg was Third World nationalism. This was a puzzle to me. In Asia, how this fit in with the Cold War was anything but axiomatic. I thought America supported the rise of nationalism in Asia out of the ashes of colonialism. I also felt Communist attempts to twist this development to their own cause was a perversion of true nationalism, which, of course, was a force that ideally emerged from American independence as its best model. In my "later years" in high school, I was deeply ambivalent about colonialism and felt that the exceptionalist American experiment represented something different. My Dad, however, thought the British had been supportive of Christian missions and helped to carry the Cross to heathen lands. The British did have a good record in our Guntur District of Andhra Pradesh, but their record was decidedly more mixed in the rest of the Indian subcontinent. They had based their rule more on political and economic interests and felt these interests were best served by leaving Indian culture and religion alone. Inserting Christianity into this imperium upset the balance; and, officially, the officials of the British Raj opposed the evangelization of the Empire, even as unofficially the issue caused a great deal of anguish.[20]

Regarding the British, I grew up in the southeastern coastal town of Chirala in Andhra Pradesh on the edge of the turbulent seas of the Bay of Bengal. My earliest playmates were a set of English boys that lived on the other end of the town in a residential cantonment for families of an English tobacco company. Theirs was a world completely aloof from Indian society. None of them knew the local language, Telugu, for instance. In contrast, we missionary kids all did, so I had Indian playmates as well. The language in these households was strictly English, whereas in our household, though we had servants like the English, we always spoke in Telugu to them. The Indians—the servants, the local minister of the Indian congregation, the schoolteachers of our school—all lived on the "Mission

Compound" in what we liked to think was a model Indian Christian community. The British cantonment had no resident Indians; it was purely British. We were not colonials. We were different.

When we came back to America on furlough, or home leave, in 1957, we stopped off in Aden, still a British colony at the time. After shore leave, we returned to the mother passenger ship on a skiff. On board were a pair of drunken British sailors who had assaulted a local police officer on shore. Over huge local protests, the sailors were allowed to board our skiff and return to the ship scot-free. This was not a pretty sight for a ten-year old. And the memory angered me when Communists in India lumped American missionaries into this same colonialist epithet.

In the early 1960s a set of unusually contentious elections for major officers were held in our local church, the Andhra Evangelical Lutheran Church. The position of treasurer and all of the institutions were still in the control of missionaries, but the other elected positions were now in Indian hands. Not wanting the disputes to end up in the civil courts, some missionaries, my father included, attempted to intervene. I don't know what they attempted to do in Saint Matthews Church (the central parish of the church), but the intervention provoked an outrage among the delegates. I watched from the upstairs verandah of a bungalow just across from the church as some Indian delegates poured out from the church chanting, "white missionaries with black hearts." The missionaries were eventually let through the jostling crowds, but I was deeply shaken by what I had seen.

That evening, I was at the table when several of the missionary men were rehashing these dramatic events. Most felt that things had gotten way out of hand and that the church was not ready for complete Indian control. Though no one had any proof, there was a voiced suspicion that activists from the Communist "agitation" (as it was sometimes called) had penetrated groups of delegates to turn it into an antimissionary attack. The board secretary of the Home Mission Board in New York was there, and he was singled out for some "extra jostling." He was still visibly unnerved at the dinner. The upshot of this incident was that the Mission Board in New York decided on a course of gradually turning over all responsibilities to Indians and correspondingly withdrawing all of the missionaries in increments from the Andhra mission field. This transition to independence and nationalism was not easy. It was a preview of Vietnamization.

Whatever the ambiguities in the transition from colonialism to nationalism, Communism remained beyond the pale to me. Its perfidy was revealed in the twin treacheries of October 1962. For American audiences, these were the notorious "Thirteen Days" of the Cuban Missile Crisis. Despite repeated assurances from Soviet leaders that they had no offensive intentions in the newly Communist state of Cuba, the United States unveiled, at an emergency meeting of the United Nations Security Council, unmistakable photographic evidence of the installation of nuclear missiles in Cuba capable of devastating the entire Eastern Seaboard of the United States. In the wake of the revelation of these treacherous photographs, Communist China launched surprise military attacks on India in Kashmir and the Northeast Frontier Agency (NEFA) in response to long-simmering border disputes. Naturally, it was the "good old USA" that forced the Russians to withdraw their missiles from Cuba. The United States also rushed massive amounts of military assistance to India that enabled Indian troops to halt the Chinese advances.

The truth of these collective treacheries was further implanted in my soul by a series of readings I undertook in high school while in search of a life credo. Two books, in particular, stood out for me. One was Arthur Koestler's *Darkness at Noon*, which laid out the treachery and brutality of the Stalinist purges of the 1930s in the Soviet Union. Directly building on this work was the second book, George Orwell's *1984*. The chilling success of the brainwashing in "Room 101," whereby the rebellious protagonist, Winston Smith, ends up loving Big Brother, forever set my soul against tyranny. My father, probably wittingly, reinforced what I was reading by calling my attention to all the accounts of the brainwashing of American POWs in the Korean War.

As I searched, one reading that troubled me personally was William Golding's *Lord of the Flies*. The story relates the descent into barbarism of a group of English schoolboys who survive a plane crash on a remote island. They form into two groups that have competitive views on how to effect their rescue. From competition their differences descend into hostility and finally to what amounted to tribal war. The key transitional moment in this descent—and the moment that troubled me—was when the first boy was killed. One of the protagonists, "Piggy," delivered a soliloquy in which he noted the severe moral line crossed, a path of no return, when someone willfully kills a fellow human being and then becomes habituated to it. Killing, whether done for individual or collective purposes, is still a personal act in which the person doing it is never the same again. This issue would come back to haunt me again and again.

I came to the United States in 1965 to attend Augustana College in Rock Island, Illinois. America was my homeland, and I was thrilled with the chance to live on my own in the land of my dreams. For the most part, I was not disappointed. I found college courses and professors intellectually challenging. I joined a fraternity, played on the tennis team, and was active in student government. Soon I was fully immersed in college life, and sometimes I forgot that I was not a native. I played down being from India and spoke of home more in terms of my relatives in Rockford and the Chicago suburbs. At parties sometimes I would blank out when the conversation turned to favorite TV shows that I never heard of, like the Howdy Doody Show, but these moments were few, and I had tolerant friends. It became something of a joke: "Look at Lomperis here, he grew up in India. I mean how weird is that!" Because I didn't look like it, or act like it. I was blending in, and far more successfully than in my later career in the Army.

Two clouds cast shadows on this sunny time. The first one was a little diffuse, and intellectual. I noticed that some of my professors and the more intellectual-minded of my peers had an almost romantic attraction to Marxism. The big draw was Herbert Marcuse and his *One-Dimensional Man,* which blamed consumer capitalism for draining the humanistic soul out of the authentic "man." I did not see any evil in capitalism, and two of my uncles in Rockford, both of whom I admired, were enthusiastic apologists for it. From my vantage point in India, the class struggle was remote, and I just did not see much evidence of this exploitation in the America I was slowly coming to know. Any disparities in America paled in comparison to the rigid separations of India's hierarchical caste system. What became clear to me is that the Communism that folks liked at Augustana was abstract and academic. In India, I grew up with Communists all around me, and what I saw were its far more troubling features of atheism and tyranny. Communism was something I had experienced personally, and it repelled me as something morally and politically evil. I was indignant at the beliefs expressed by some that, even if Communism could not work in "advanced capitalist societies," in countries emerging from Western colonialism Communism was a legitimate way of establishing independence from the previous era.

This first cloud definitely irritated me, but the second cloud led me to a state just short of despair. In the years I was in college, 1965 to 1969, Vietnam dominated the TV network news shows. Formal and informal debates and teach-ins on college campuses raged throughout these years. The issue quickly became polarized into pro- and antiwar camps. I was a budding Asianist, and I approached the war from an Asian perspective. This was a perspective that seemed to be completely ignored. The prowar folks were intent on killing Communists wherever they were to be found. But there were nuances to Vietnamese history that went a little deeper than simple Communist and nationalist or capitalist distinctions. The antiwar folks, on the other hand, were all about the massive slaughter of innocents by the evil military-industrial complex. Their preoccupation focused on dismantling the American war machine so that it could no longer pursue its immoral wars. But there were Communists on the ground in Vietnam who were slaughtering the innocents as well.

In all of this, no one seemed concerned about the Vietnamese themselves. The problem, at least at Augustana, was that there were no Asian area specialists on the faculty. I did take an Oriental philosophy course as well as one on world religions, both of which I enjoyed very much. I remember being especially drawn to Daoism. The secret societies of the sect and its emphasis on the individualistic ethic of the Sage Warrior appealed to the rebel in me.

At many of these debates, I would take up the cause of the "average Vietnamese" who yearned for a life compatible with their values. If capitalism was not compatible with these values (which I doubted), neither was any kind of Communism forced down their throats. My exhortations irritated some of the antiwar faculty whose arguments had very little to do with Vietnam or Communism but were all about the immorality of U.S. foreign policy and the militarism that served it. One of these favorite professors derided me dismissively, saying, "Look, Tim, this war has nothing to do with Vietnam, or the Vietnamese. I don't really care about them. This has do with an America that has lost its soul, and Communism is not the evil that you say it is, so just let the Vietnamese become Communist." His admiring groupies burst into applause. I asked him if he minded if the Vietnamese became Communist, even if they didn't want to. No, he said, he did not. We were at complete loggerheads.

As I look back on it, the essential divide between my antiwar peers and professors and me was that we viewed the war from opposite ends of the street. At Augustana College in the nation's heartland, they viewed America fundamentally as a peaceful society cajoled into wars only when ominous threats imperiled national survival, like in the two world wars. Living at home on the ground, their vision was so wrapped up in day-to-day politics that they did not look upward, or across the oceans, to the essential "goodness" of America internationally, as I did. Instead, we were in a faraway war in Vietnam that seemed to have no bearing on their everyday lives except for the troubling disturbances on national TV news shows and reports of local casualties. And this war was enabled by an American war machine that somehow seemed responsible. As for all the international causes of Communist treachery and expansion, when even a Cold War in Asia posed no nuclear threat (as it did in Europe), my peers just could not bring themselves to see danger in any of this. From my side of the street, however, the story of Communist tyranny, violence, and treachery was mother's milk to me. A global sweep of Communism was a looming and truly evil force held at bay only by the American Sir Galahad. The misplaced brief against presidents and the Pentagon seemed petty to me in the overarching historical necessity of this global crusade. And it was not as if there was no one with me on my side. I had plenty of friends, among what President Nixon called the "silent majority," but the media hounds were riveted to the histrionics of the peace movement. Later, when I got more into the war and Sir Galahad fell off his perch, I began to see and understand the other side of the street more—but not to the point of embracing Peace Now. To me, Peace Now contributed to the cavalier abandonment of Vietnam by the United States that forced me to betray my Vietnamese friends.

In my senior year (1968–1969), all everyone wanted to do was get married and get out of the draft. Of the fifteen seniors in my fraternity, half were either married, engaged, or pinned six months after graduation. Of these same fifteen seniors, only two of us entered the military. I was dismayed at this small number. None of them saw military service as any kind of a duty, and no one wanted to go to Vietnam. Personally, I had my reservations about the essence of the military profession; but, as a good Lutheran, I believed in military service as a political obligation to the state. More than this, if none of my friends cared about the Vietnamese, and if even the larger American public did not care about a Vietnam turned over to godless Communism, in my heart of hearts I did care about these issues.

As I got closer to graduation, I contacted my draft board and asked what my chances were of making it into graduate school in the fall. I had just been through one of the most humiliating days of my life at the Armed Forces Entrance Examination Station (AFEES) in Chicago. Stripped down to my underwear and walking haplessly from station to station with a pitiable brown bag containing my watch and wallet, I had just been declared fit for military duty. With such declared physical fitness, my draft board told me my chances of going to graduate school were zero. I enlisted in a 120-day Delayed Entry Program so that I could start military life at the exalted rank of a Private First Class(or PFC). On October 6, 1969, the 120 days were up, and I was sucked into the "Green Machine" . . . the U.S. Army.

Nixon's "Secret" Plan and How I Got to Vietnam

Richard Nixon ascended to the presidency in 1969 having cam-paigned on the promise that he had a "secret plan" to end the war. He later admitted that he never had a secret plan,[1] but he did have a strategy. The strategy had five pillars, and the centerpiece was Viet-namization. The success of this process became the rationale for the second pillar, the phased withdrawal of American troops. The number of troops in-country peaked at 543,000 shortly after Nixon took office, and his electoral pledge was to end the war and bring the troops home. The third pillar was a plan to bolster the Thieu regime so that there would be no Communist government in the South in the wake of a U.S. troop withdrawal—at least not until af-ter a "decent interval." The aim of the fourth pillar was to conduct secret negotiations where rational deals could be struck away from the public talks that had been set up in Paris by former President Lyndon Johnson, which had deteriorated into propaganda postur-ing for the media. Away from the glare of the klieg lights, Nixon hoped to secure a stable political arrangement in the South and to achieve, with great public fanfare, the goal of the fifth pillar: the release of all American POWs.

To achieve this strategy, he relied on four instruments. General Creighton Abrams, in serving as General William C. Westmoreland's deputy, had focused on improving the fighting qualities of South Vietnamese forces. In confirming Abrams as Westmoreland's suc-cessor as COMUS MACV, he charged him with this central mission and thus put in place his first instrument. The next two instruments were Nixon's diplomatic package: the carrot of the negotiating and charismatic skills of his national security adviser and later secretary of state, Dr. Henry Kissinger; and, as his stick, the liberal use of the ultimate American weapon in Vietnam, the B-52 bomber, during lapses in the professor's diplomatic charm. The final instrument was the measure of public support Nixon hoped to gain by these other three instruments, which would give him the time to convince the

North Vietnamese to settle on a compromise peace.[2] This process started out well: by October 1969, 71 percent of the American public approved of Nixon's handling of the war in contrast to Johnson's nadir of 26 percent approval during the Tet Offensive of 1968.[3]

I entered the Army that fall believing in this plan. To my peers, I was somewhat of a supporter of the war, but probably more because I wanted to experience history than out of any fanatic dedication to this cause. Burned in my mind as well was the advice of my World War II–era uncles: never volunteer for anything. I compromised by agreeing to enter the Army and just let things happen. If history intended me to go to Vietnam, that was destiny. If not, well, so be it. In the cynical 1960s, if you supported anything relating to "the establishment," the external persona you projected could be no more than languid. Underneath, I was conflicted, as the Cold Warrior in me seethed with the moral compulsion to just get over there. But military life tossed up complications.

My military life had a dramatic beginning. I made my entry into the Green Machine on a "path of no return" as I engaged in the historically divisive war debate that split the soul of the Baby Boom generation. In my very first week in the army in October 1969, war protesters made a move to attack Fort Dix in New Jersey (irreverently named "Fort Ding-a-ling" because of all the congressional investigations that had allegedly softened the training). Our platoon of fifty men was called up to reinforce the MPs at the gate. None of us even had uniforms, and only half had military haircuts. We were all given trench coats and hats to provide a modicum of military appearance. We were also issued metal legs from our very own bunk beds and told to clobber any hippies that got through the MP lines. We were bussed to the gate and dropped off in a parking lot behind it. Fortunately, we were out of view of people on the other side of the gate. By the grace of God, our services were not required on that day. Someone smarter than all of us had thought to fly in a couple of helicopters that hovered over the crowd and tilted their rotary blades so that a storm of wind, noise, and debris engulfed the protesters. They panicked and fled, and our commanding corporal breathed a huge sigh of relief, saying, "I don't know what you swinging d—ks would have done if the hippies had actually come through." We didn't either.

Later during Basic Training, I was given a three-day pass for a high score on the Army Physical Fitness Test (APFT). I ambled to a coffeehouse in Philadelphia hoping to reconnect with my civilian peers and enjoy the Kingston Trio–type music in vogue among these coffeehouse troubadours. If I could encourage a smile out of a young lady, that would have been a plus, too. Though I was in "civvies," and therefore hoped to blend in, I forgot about my telltale haircut. After an initial smile from one of these young maidens, she froze and confronted me, "Oh, my God, you're a pig! There's a soldier in here, people!" The mellowly crooning guitarist suddenly snarled, "Get him out of here. I can't sing with a pig in the room!" I felt a volcanic rage rise up within me, but before I could concentrate this torrent into action, three very large gentlemen grabbed me and literally threw me out with an even choicer epithet. As I picked myself up, I knew a Rubicon had been crossed, and I was on the other side of the great cultural divide of my generation. I wasn't really hurt, but the epithet remains etched in my soul: just by being in the Army, I was judged as a "male chauvinistic, mother-f—king, baby-killer." There was no place for me in this America.

As I soldiered on in this prolonged period of military training, my adventures continued. After the three-day pass to Philadelphia, I came to the rescue of my captain when he was sharply questioned in a general assembly about the legality and morality of the war, and I pointed out our commitments to Vietnam under the SEATO treaty. This did not endear me to these questioners. In AIT (Advanced Individual Training, the follow-on training to Basic) at Fort Leonard Wood in Missouri, I rescued my fellow trainee Richard Pettus from drowning during a nighttime bridge-crossing exercise in February. He was traumatized, and I helped him get a Conscientious Objector discharge by writing a letter of recommendation for him attesting to the validity of his religious convictions. Also at Fort Leonard Wood, my unit was quarantined because of an outbreak of spinal meningitis, which was due to the fact that our cooks were starving us during some very cold weather. After we performed suspiciously poorly on a physical fitness test, an inspection revealed that the cooks were stealing our food and selling it to local farmers. Since they were disciplined, we did not see them again. For a while, we were fed very well.

Having had enough of being subjected to sergeants, who, I came to realize, were capable of getting me killed, I hastily volunteered for Officer Candidate School (OCS). I reasoned that at least as an officer I would be responsible for my own death, should I have the misfortune of being shipped to Vietnam. This blessed training took place at Fort Belvoir, Virginia. The post provided us with a bird's-eye view of all the antiwar demonstrations going on in Washington, D.C. I escaped the East Coast hippies with my officer's commission and promptly landed in the unwelcome laps of the West Coast hippies at the Defense Language School in Monterey, California.

The training at OCS, frankly, was very good, but it touched off some moral crises. For one thing, my long conversations with Richard Pettus in AIT had affected me more than I realized. Richard had studied for the Catholic priesthood and discovered he had mixed feelings about celibacy and the authority of the church. Joining the army, for him, was an act of atonement for this failing to his church, but the training triggered a latent pacifism in him. Needless to say, he was somewhat confused in his thinking as he struggled with this discovery. But I was convinced his struggle came from the soul, and I was able to write a very strong letter in support of his application for a Conscientious Objector discharge—which he was granted. I was also surprised at how I could have reached such a level of theological intimacy with a Catholic, of all people. I confess to having grown up in an environment of considerable prejudice against Roman Catholics.[4]

Strangely, one of the things that I relished about military life was its physicality. In college, I felt I was unfairly pegged as an egghead; I did play on the tennis team, after all. But OCS at Fort Belvoir was based on an engineering curriculum and was heavily quantitative, which, for a history and political science major, was maximally boring. There was no chance that I would be considered an egghead here. Academically, I did very poorly. But I shone in physical training (PT). Throughout all our military training, we were given the standard military PT test. It seemed to have been designed just for me. I had some upper body strength, and I was quick on my feet but not fast. Most of my peers were either meaty bears or speedy cougars, but not both. There was also a dexterity event in the grenade throw. This is the one event in which I was most likely to have the top score. I loved throwing that grenade. It reminded me of all the throwing-rocks-at-trees we had done as kids. For the bears, there was the 150-yard man carry, running (really, more like stumbling) with a man of equal weight on your shoulders, and the horizontal ladders, seeing how many rungs you could swing hand-over-hand in a minute. For the cougars, there was the 40-yard low crawl, slithering on your stomach in a sand pit, and the dodge, run, and jump, a zigzag obstacle race. Finally, of course, there was the mile run. I never did well in this because I hated running in combat boots and I always ended up with shin splints. Anyway, at the end of these tests, taking all the events together, I would usually end up on top. In fact, I was the PT honor graduate in my graduating OCS class.

One of the physical activities that I particularly relished was pugil sticks. These were sticks, more like clubs, with cushions on the ends, and you tried to knock an opponent to the ground in a simulation of bayonet combat. For some reason, something happened to me when I got in these "arenas," I just couldn't be beat. At Fort Leonard Wood, I even knocked my DI (Drill Instructor) to the ground. To me it was just great sport. Later, in OCS at Fort Belvoir, however, we were taken to a field with straw figures and given real bayonets to make our thrusts, accompanied by rousing cheers to shouts of "What is the spirit of the bayonet?" "Kill! Kill! Kill!" This hit me hard morally, and I lost all enthusiasm for pugil sticks. There was an issue here for me: I was prepared to kill if I had to, but I was going to be damned (which I felt literally) if I was going to glory in it.

This "spirit of the bayonet" business brings up, as a sidebar, the issue of the proper role of passion in warfare. In all accounts of traditional warfare, as two hostile forces faced each other across a field in the morning sun, both sides engaged in rituals of shouts, chanting, and singing to whip up their martial spirits and unleash almost orgasmic charges. This ritual over the spirit of the bayonet is certainly a primordial residue of this incantation, as is the more modern guttural cry, "Hooah!" But the central point here is that these are communal or unit rituals designed to bring soldiers to their colors and to the cohesion that is their battlefield strength. The objective of all militaries is to merge individuals into cohesive units that will respond to disciplined commands and thus to obtain the benefits of unit synergies that are far more potent than the undirected rage of individuals. Soldiers must be tempered to follow the disciplined commands of their officers and not run off in fits of temper that can destroy the integrity of a unit formation.

In discussing Achilles in the Trojan War, Jonathan Shay describes the phenomenon of giving in to these personal rages as going "berserk," a sort of rage that transcends all moral bounds. The military point of all collective societies is that in exchange for the moral sanctioning of violence by individuals for the collective good of social survival, all collectivities impose moral restraints on this individual conduct. These mostly have to do with proscriptions against individuals using the cloak of collective sanction to pursue private acts of violence (like murder) that have nothing to do with the preservation of the community. Indeed, such individual acts sabotage the central fabric of the community itself. Achilles was acting as the champion of the Greek cause in his individual combat with Hector, eldest son of the Trojan King Priam. After killing Hector following the prescribed rules of individual combat, however, he violated all moral rules by dragging the body behind his chariot in front of the city walls of Troy, mutilating the corpse in front of the grief-stricken Priam. Achilles had gone berserk. This was all the more loathsome because, earlier, after Hector had killed Patroclus, the dear friend of Achilles, in a similar individual combat, Priam had personally returned the body of Patroclus, along with the borrowed armor of Achilles, to Achilles.[5] Indeed, the special danger of summoning this individual blade of the bayonet to the collective defense of the community is that its sparkling glint can entice the owner into a berserker rage.

Occasionally, of course, these individual rages can merge into collective breakdowns of military discipline into berserk massacres. The most notorious of these in Vietnam was the My Lai massacre of March 1968, in which Charlie Company of the Americal Division, commanded by Army Captain Ernest Medina, moved into the hamlet of My Lai in southern Quang Ngai Province (in MR 1) with orders to burn and destroy the village. A platoon under Lieutenant William Calley took this command literally as a license to kill, and 175 to 200 villagers were gunned down. That the hamlet was situated among a knot of villages sympathetic to the Viet Cong, and from which Medina's company had suffered several casualties from snipers and booby traps, may explain, but certainly did not excuse, such slaughter.[6]

This menace continued to haunt me as my OCS training continued. We were not very far into our program when Nixon launched the Cambodian Incursion in April 1970, which triggered a round of passionate national protests, including one at Kent State University in which four students were killed. This, in turn, triggered an even larger protest in Washington, D.C. Our OCS curriculum was interrupted for a week of training in riot control, as our whole OCS regiment was put on standby for duty. I must say that this was very good training, as we learned several different marches for clearing streets and moving mobs away from central gathering points as well as sensitive objectives of crowd assaults. But here again the issue of the bayonet returned as the "last measure" order (before actually firing) was to "fix bayonets." As much as I viewed hippies and the war protest movement with revulsion, these were, after all, my peers and fellow citizens. I utterly recoiled at the prospect of actually using a bayonet against college students, ponytails or not. Fortunately, I was spared such a moment of crisis by the professional competence displayed by the Eighty-second Airborne Division from Fort Bragg, North Carolina, in handling these protests peacefully. The two battalions of the OCS regiment at Fort Belvoir, Virginia, were not needed.

Nevertheless, when we resumed normal training, I was paralyzed with the anguish I had felt over this issue. I went to see the chaplain about whether I could continue. My encounter with this particular man was so incredible, even miraculous, that I have come to believe that he was an angel sent from Heaven directly to me. As it turns out, he was a brother Lutheran. More than that, he was a Missouri Synod Lutheran, a conservative brand of Lutheranism that hews to a scriptural line in answer to "life's persistent questions."[7] I grew up in the more liberal Lutheran Church in America. Since the chaplain was a Missouri Synod Lutheran, I was not surprised when we went over Martin Luther's less idealistic views of warfare than Catholic Just War doctrine: that wars, at best, are sometimes necessary; but, when deemed necessary, Christians may serve in these wars as soldiers.

Although I could accept this basic Lutheran view, I was still troubled by the passion for killing instilled in our training. While I could appreciate the general imperative for having a motivated military force, individually I recoiled from both the hurt I would inflict on other people and the damnation that might stab through my soul. What shocked me was that the good Lutheran chaplain told me the place to turn for this was Lao Ze's *Dao De Jing,* the core scripture of

30   Chinese Daoism. In reading through this brief but profound text, I was struck not only by the centrality it placed on the cultivation of the inner life but also by its recognition of the importance of societal obligations as part of a spiritual life. This included warfare, and many of the "chapters" dealt with the moral challenges of soldiering. Lao Ze's basic message was to avoid violence whenever possible but to never lose your humanity when violence became necessary. There was much of a Lutheran approach in the *Dao De Jing*. The phrase I remember most was: "Conduct your triumph as if it were a funeral." This was a great comfort to me, and I was able to go on, as a newly minted "Daoist Lutheran." In this crisis, though, something had shifted under my feet. I still saw the Cold War as necessary, as something thrust upon us, but I had lost something of my earlier messianic vision for this struggle.

It faded further at our OCS graduation ceremony on September 25, 1970, in a surprise incident. As it happened, my mother was in the United States to help one of my sisters with the transition from college to nursing school, and so she was able to come to this ceremony and fulfill the ritual of pinning the gold bars of my commissioning as a second lieutenant onto my uniform. This familial insertion into my military life, I think, was unsettling for both of us. The graduation address was by Brigadier General Gerhardt Hyatt, the deputy chief of army chaplains and, what else, a Missouri Synod Lutheran. Unlike my OCS chaplain, this reverend was much more conventional. He thanked us several times for stepping up and being willing to die for our country. Frankly, I would not have put my motivations for military service in such bald terms, and, in my mother's presence, this was unsettling. My mother was surprised to hear my name called out as the Physical Training Graduate, and I was surprised to hear her tell the good general, when she pinned on my gold bars, that his speech was insulting and that she did not want to see "any of these fine young men die for our country." The general and I did not say anything, but I was secretly proud of my mom. Indeed, in her rebuke, the seeds of further limits to my military commitment were sown.

If part of growing up is the dispelling of youthful illusions, OCS disabused me of some of my military visions. In OCS, we were evaluated on academics, physical training, and leadership. This last category was demonstrated mostly in the field exercises we went on after classes in the afternoons (and sometimes at night) and on the weekends. Here my performance was erratic. Moves and actions that were planned ahead of time, and that followed recognized procedures, I could handle and lead: clearing danger areas, setting up ambushes. But actions that were surprises or required quick-thinking responses were definitely not my forte. All of these individual exercises culminated in a full week of field exercises at Camp A. P. Hill in the boonies of Virginia. In this week, we were kept constantly on the move, both day and night, getting virtually no sleep and very little food. The day usually began with fixed missions and different types of maneuvers spelled out. As the day wore on, the training cadre would deliberately throw in complications and surprises to see how we responded to the pressure.

It reminded me of what I had studied about Julius Caesar and Alexander the Great. Julius Caesar was a master logician and planner, and able to inspire heroic levels of activity from his men. Hence, he would often surprise his adversaries with the speed of his marches. But he always knew where he wanted to be, and planned his battle sites carefully. Alexander the Great could do all of this, but his true genius lay in the uncanny ways in which he could react to the unexpected and extricate his men from disasters with quick-thinking maneuvers. In Bactria (modern-day Afghanistan), he encountered Scythian horsemen whose spears had a longer range than those from the phalanxes of the Greeks. As these horsemen circled around the phalanxes in a clockwise motion, Alexander had his men break out of the phalanxes, get in closer despite the risks, and hurl their spears against this motion (or counterclockwise), throwing the Scythian formation into disarray as the horses went down. In military parlance, this is called a "meeting engagement."

At Camp A. P. Hill, something that added to the confusion was that we were all constantly being reassigned. Over the course of the week, we were to have had opportunities to lead, and serve, at all levels up to company and battalion ranks. One moment we would be a private on a patrol, then a corporal as a squad leader, then an RTO (radio traffic operator) for a platoon leader or company commander, then a platoon leader or company commander. The problem was that ongoing operations were very different at these various levels, and it took some adjusting to move from a private to a platoon leader. My particular problem was that I would get too wrapped up in my immediate situation and not keep an eye on the larger movements. Unfortunately, my pattern was to be disoriented when I first changed positions, and then I would find it hard to catch up before being reassigned again.

Still, I had some fun with the Julius Caesar–type moves. I could move troops across terrain, set up ambushes, and motivate slacking soldiers. I especially enjoyed setting up ambushes. I once set up an ambush in a patch of poison ivy. No one thought anyone would be stupid enough to set up in poison ivy, so I really caught people unawares and registered quite a number of kills. (Whenever you fired off your dummy rounds, the cadre would point to people and declare them killed.) But I suffered mightily for the stupidity of this brief moment of glory.

My moment of truth came when I was made a platoon leader of about forty men. We were ordered to sweep into a village and clear out Viet Cong from the hooches. The Intel people told us that our arrival would be completely unexpected, but they did not tell us that there was a steep hill up to the village. Platoons are divided into two sections, so I had one section wait at the bottom of the hill in the trees while I took the lead section up the hill into the village. Here I learned the peril of not paying attention to details. What I had not noticed was that the Intel report about this ignorance of our arrival was two days old. In other words, it was perishable intelligence. Sure enough, when we were halfway up the hill, machine gun fire raked us from the top of the hill. I froze for far too long. Mercifully, I realized running back down the hill was precisely the wrong thing to do, even though it was the immediate instinct I was fighting. I ordered a charge up the hill to take out the machine gun, but my delay cost us six KIAs and ten WIAs. It was my meeting engagement. In the after-action report, the cadre told me that I halfway fell apart on that hill. In a real combat situation, if I had run back down the hill, I would have been relieved from command. So I ended up doing the right thing, but too late for the lives of six soldiers. Even though this was just an exercise, it really got to me. The truth knocked me flat: I was no Alexander the Great. All in all, OCS was a sobering experience.

It was during OCS that I developed a parallel strategy to Nixon's secret plan to end the war; namely, I showed my faith in his plan by volunteering for enough training to let him finish the war before it was necessary to send me over.[8] Volunteering for the language school fit my plans well because it was a yearlong assignment. The only language available, however, was Vietnamese. This was a choice that narrowed my escape routes. To learn Vietnamese, I was sent to the Defense Language Institute in Monterey, California: yes, "Monterey by the sea," a scant 100 miles south of San Francisco, and even less to Palo Alto, where my cousin Tom was enrolled at Stanford. Even if the future on my horizon had been channeled into a clear path to Vietnam, I was in for a pleasant interlude in this California Garden of Eden. Though I am not terribly gifted in languages, I at least do better with them than math; and, despite the six hours a day, five days a week in class learning nothing but Vietnamese, it was not an overly taxing assignment. I hardly felt I was in the military. I had my weekends to myself. There was gorgeous scenery all around, and my cousin at Stanford set me up with a few gorgeous and intellectual young coeds. Like Frank Sinatra's song: I was twenty-four, and "it was a very good year."

But I also knew that a very different future awaited me after this year, and I needed to continue to do something about this plan. Classes let out early in the afternoon, and I joined a tennis club both for fitness and enjoyment. Soon I was playing two or three hours every afternoon, and entering tournaments on the weekends. I was getting serious about this. Without really trying, the quality of my tennis had risen above the level I had played in college on the tennis team. Dimly, I became aware that there were athletes in the Army who were excused from their military duties to go on athletic tours. In particular, I was aware that the tennis star Stan Smith was playing for the Army on the global tennis circuit. Maybe I should try for this as another way—a Plan B—to get out of going to Vietnam.

From just playing tournaments at the club, I started playing against other clubs. Then I started playing in army tournaments. I won the championship at the language school. Then I did well in a match at the larger post at Ford Ord. From this I qualified to play in a match that would go on to the Sixth Army tournament in Seattle. From these various "armies," there was a "global" army tournament—and the winners would go on the tour. I now saw the path in front of me, a path that was actually a real possibility. In the match at Fort Ord, I had only to win two rounds to qualify for the Sixth Army tournament. It might actually happen. As I warmed up with my first round opponent, I felt I would have no problem with the match. When we started to play, however, I got so nervous realizing that I might just win that I could not even hold my racket steady. As I tossed up the balls to serve, too many of them fell on my head. I lost in two humiliating straight sets. There went my vision of becoming another Stan Smith.

So, my life returned to Plan A. I finished the forty-seven-week course in Vietnamese in September 1971—and the war was still not finished. The longest subsequent training I could find was for that of an "Area Studies" course in Intelligence, which lasted six months. I just wanted to give Nixon more time. Upon arriving at Fort Huachuca, Arizona—the new army intelligence post[9]—it became clear that this was not an academic seminar but a professional training course on how to both conduct espionage and recruit agents to spy for you. This was not for me, and I took what was known as "the ethical drop."

There were two features of the training that provoked this action. As a military officer, I had just been trained in OCS to take responsibility for my actions. It had been made crystal clear to all of us that whenever any troopers were killed or wounded in our command, it was our responsibility to write the letters home to the parents and loved ones. This I understood. In the spy business, however, we were told that every operation had to be predicated on a "writ of plausible denial"; that is, if the operation were compromised in some way, there had to be a credible denial of any U.S. government involvement in the operation. In army talk this meant, "Mr. Nguyen, we never knew you. Sorry 'bout that!" Though I could see the policy side to this, personally I found it hard to think of walking away from the responsibility for "Mr. Nguyen's" life.

The requirement of living a double life was driven home to the class early on, when the instructor went to the board and drew two boxes. One was for the qualities of an officer and a gentleman, and the other was for a recruiter of spies. The officer, of course, was honest, trustworthy, and loyal, but the successful spy-handler was a master of deceit, skilled in double-dealing, and coldly capable of treachery. He went on to say that this training required us to live in both boxes at once: to be honorable and aboveboard in our personal conduct and in our dealings with brother soldiers, but to rely on these other qualities in the pursuit of our profession. In brief, we had to compartmentalize our lives between our individual and collective responsibilities. If any of us couldn't handle this, we should take the "ethical drop" right now, we were told. This would not be the last time I would face this issue.

As I surveyed my classmates, they were among the brightest folks I had ever been associated with; but, for all their brilliance, they seemed to be missing an ethical gene. I mean, none of this seemed to faze them. My ethical gene was already pretty oversized, and it was about to pop on this one. I took the drop. In taking it, I made the first clear break with, and limit to, my military commitment. I would let the Army take my life, but not my soul.

Since five other students took the same drop the day after I did, I was accused of mutiny. It took an Article 34 Investigation (equivalent to a Grand Jury) to clear me. What aroused the suspicion of the board of three infantry colonels assigned to conduct this investigation was that all six of us (out of a class of fifteen, so the Army had reason to be concerned about such a mass defection) had come from California, where, of course, we had become "infected by hippie ideas." Since I jumped off the wagon first, I was seen as the ringleader. I was acquitted when I was able to show the colonels that even though we had all been in California, I did not know any of the other five gentlemen. In fact, the two friends that I had made in California had passed through this very training ahead of me, and were now serving in Vietnam; and, I told the good colonels, I was looking forward to joining them soon. This won them over, although, in truth, I was having some misgivings.

In the course of this "discussion," one of the three colonels—not the one who made the accusations—pressed me out of what seemed to be a genuine curiosity. He professed to having a hard time understanding my moral qualms about this dual standard, since the military life of the officer corps was also predicated on living a dual standard: one that answered to the democratic rights we enjoyed as citizens and the other to the hierarchical ethos of military discipline. So, how was this dual life of the agent handler and military officer any different, he wondered?

The difference to me, I replied, was that the distinction between "an officer and a gentleman" was between separate but parallel principles of social order, whereas the difference between a spy and a lieutenant went to the heart of individual ethical values, between disreputable behavior and honorable conduct. Unlike principles of social order, this distinction with the spy business involved an intervention into my individual soul. As a Christian soldier, I was willing to give Caesar his due, but my soul was not mine to hand over to Caesar like this. I made the further point that the Army, officially at least, relied on this individual sovereignty over values by granting soldiers the right—nay, duty—to disobey an unlawful order. Ever since the My Lai massacre, the Army was forced by Congress to make a point of this ultimate right of the individual soldier in all of its training—a point about which the Army was supremely uncomfortable. (What I did not say—because I was a long way away from being a political scientist then—was that this individual sovereignty over conscience went to the heart of why our constitutional system of government is built on a limited view of government from John Locke, among others. He insisted that the social contract of a constitution reserved certain "inalienable" rights to remain outside the reach of government for the citizens making this contract.) Apparently satisfied, the more gentle colonel relented, and I was free to leave.

What left me uncomfortable from this incident was that the gentle colonel had rubbed me on a sore spot. Beyond these ethical qualms, I just did not like the hierarchy of military life. I had volunteered for OCS to get out from under the hierarchical "tyranny" of sergeants. But now, even in this victory, I had hit a hierarchical wall with colonels. I seethed under the petty slights of rank that were a normal part of military life. The most personal this ever became happened in Vietnam when I returned from a leave, and told my colleagues about my good fortune of sitting next to a very pretty "round-eyed" woman on the returning plane. I actually got her phone number and took her out on an unheard of event in Saigon, a date! Clearly, I overplayed my hand with this story because a captain demanded her phone number. My immediate civilian response was, of course, "No way!" His military response was to finger the two silver bars on his collar and command, "Hand it over!" I never saw the young lady again.

More philosophically, this little discussion evoked what I really disliked about military life: it reminded me too much of India's caste system. My most graphic brush with this system happened when I was six years old. My mother, in a little experiment with my independence, sent me across Chirala in a cycle rickshaw all by my-self to the other missionary compound. Getting through the central bazaar brought us into such a swirl of human flesh that the driver had to get off the rickshaw and pull me through on foot. Most of this sea of humanity was skin and bones, but there was one very large Brahmin (of the highest priestly caste in this system) with a very fat belly, around which my erstwhile rickshaw *wallah* (driver) could not negotiate. Only wanting to help, I gave this belly a good whack with my six-year-old fist. At this moment, the planet Earth stopped dead in its orbit. The Brahmin reeled around and berated the poor rickshaw *wallah* for letting this foreign brat touch him, thereby endangering his soul with karmic dust from the pollution I had caused him. He then lifted his cane and beat this poor man mer-cilessly until blood was streaming from his face. Then the Brahmin stomped off into the crowd. Stoically and without a word, my driver got back up on the rickshaw and pedaled me to my destination, say-ing nothing. He was, after all, an Untouchable (the lowest caste), and to even raise a finger against a Brahmin was unthinkable. At this destination, I also said nothing to the unsuspecting missionary lady who met us. Whenever I had these "rank" moments in the military, I would cringe with the eruption of this childhood memory.

After leaving "spy school" class, I completed another intelligence training program in short order, the military intelligence staff offi-cer course. This focused on analytical skills involved in interpreting intelligence and drew on the critical thinking skills I had developed in college. I had no moral problems with any of this, and I consid-ered myself to be back "with the program." In fact, I picked up a new skill; namely, that of summarizing complex information into single-page "briefs," or two- to four-page "talking points." It's a skill I subsequently lost as an academic.

After completing this course, I arrived in Vietnam on a "Jail Bird" flight (the return flights were called "Freedom Birds") on March 12, 1972. Three months later, on June 28, President Richard Nixon went on television to announce to America that, from then on, only vol-unteers would be sent to Vietnam.[10] My strategy had come up a little short. If I could have found just one more school to sign up for, I would have made it. I tried to volunteer for airborne school, but I was turned down because I couldn't justify the need for an intelligence officer to know how to jump out of an airplane. I also

38   applied for photo interpreter training, but I was again denied because I could not display any credible passion for photography. Basically, I think the Army was finally on to me. Speaking of "secret plans," now that I was in Vietnam, I was secretly glad my strategy had failed. Caught up in the middle of the war and in the drama of a major enemy invasion was an adrenaline rush, even for a REMF. Honestly, I did not want to be pushed into the awkward position of taking advantage of an option I no longer wanted.

Nixon's plan unraveled more disastrously than mine. His pillars and instruments were successful in forging a peace agreement in January 1973, but no one appeared to mean anything they said or signed, and the agreement unraveled into the inevitable collapse of South Vietnam in two short years. For the United States, what made this doubly tragic was that the abandonment of South Vietnam amounted to a betrayal of itself. This, at least, is what I felt—but I am getting ahead of my story.

Part II

Over There

My Arrival In-Country

On March 12, 1972, after all these bumps, agonies, investigations, second thoughts—and even training—I was finally in "The Nam." Our plane landed at Bien Hoa Air Base, about 20 miles from Saigon, and I disembarked, hopefully, with my tennis racket over my shoulder in what amounted to a hopeless rearguard action of Plan B. All of us in the Army were shunted over to nearby Long Binh, the sprawling army base that was the largest U.S. army installation in the world outside of CONUS (the continental United States). There were no tennis courts that I could find at Long Binh, but I did catch sight of a massive prison. I made a mental note of not wanting to ever see that place again. After only a day or two at Long Binh, becoming aware of how hot and humid the climate was, I was put on another bus, this time for Saigon. I was getting the feeling that the war was ignoring me as I landed in a dilapidated barracks at a Holding Company that seemed to be in a time warp. Fittingly, they called it MACV (Military Assistance Command, Vietnam) Annex, a lost satellite to the main MACV Compound. There we languished for about a week, not knowing what was happening next, or what wartime assignment would be our destiny. Since there was a convenient swimming pool nearby, I swam in it every day.

As I sat around the pool, I couldn't believe where I was. It was like my first day in OCS when a Tac came into our barracks, braced us all against a wall, and started shouting at us. I became so addled that soon I didn't even know my own name. Indeed, right next to me, my bunky buddy Neil Jaquet (the Augustana fraternity brother who had entered the Army with me) was asked by the Tac what name he saw on his (the Tac's) name tag. He couldn't say. When you have no idea of the future, not even of the next five minutes, your sense of the present collapses. Reality dissolves.

No one was yelling at me now, but my sense of the present had completely collapsed. Here I was in "The Nam," going to some pool every day that might have been anywhere—like Sheboygan, Wisconsin—and slinking back to a bunk in a barracks with a tennis racket waiting for me. Yet, somewhere out there, all around me, a war was going on. In fact, I had been sent to fight in it, and yet this damned war was nowhere to be seen. Was any of this even real? Was I real? I was losing my grip.

Surprisingly, one day I met a buddy from OCS at the pool, Mike Ruble. This chance meeting was a lifeline out of this purgatory because he was someone I knew in the real world, and he served as a reconnection back to it. He was a briefer in the Tank and wanted to know if I wanted his job, since he was DEROSing (Date of Estimated Return from Over Seas—that is, going home) in a few days. At the time, it sounded like paradise. I interviewed and got the job. My reality in Vietnam was now fixed. It was REMF Land.

The Tank was in the headquarters building of MACV, just outside of Saigon and conveniently right next to the airport, called Tan Son Nhut. The Tank was a secure area where the commander, General Creighton Abrams, and his very large staff made the central decisions of the war on the ground. Everybody in it had top security clearances and was very "rank," so lieutenants like me made the coffee. The atmosphere was stifling, but I did get to play tennis with a colonel. Occasionally, a guy with four stars on his collar would watch, and he would invariably snarl (I hoped playfully) about how lieutenants should be out in the Boonies earning their Combat Infantry Badges, not playing tennis with rear-echelon colonels. I soon learned this was Creighton Abrams himself, COMUS MACV (Commander of U.S. forces of the Military Assistance Command, Vietnam). He became my hero.

The MACV Headquarters stood at the apex of the largest U.S. war machine put in place overseas since World War II. At its peak in 1969, there were a half million men in-country; but with all the naval vessels offshore and air force bases in Thailand, the Philippines, Taiwan, Japan, and Guam, the total U.S. military presence in the "Vietnam theater of operations" was closer to 700,000. At this continental level, this presence consisted of the Seventh Fleet operating out of Subic Bay in the Philippines and its several bases in Japan; the Seventh Air Force (of tactical fighters and bombers) with bases in the Philippines, Taiwan, Thailand, and, of course, Vietnam; the Eighth Air Force (the strategic B-52 bombers configured for conventional bombing missions in Indochina) with its in-theater bases in

Guam and Utapao in Thailand; and MACV (mainly an army command) in Vietnam.

Offshore, the Navy bombed North Vietnam from its aircraft carriers, ran coastal bombardment missions with its cruisers and destroyers along the South Vietnamese coast, operated the successful Market Time and Farm Gate campaigns that blocked supplies from reaching Communist forces from the sea, and in-country conducted riverine patrols in Swift Boats that sped up and down the rivers and canals of the Mekong Delta. The Air Force launched their own bombing missions over North Vietnam; conducted massive search-and-rescue missions; dropped bombs, sensors, and "other things" along the Ho Chi Minh Trail; and supported U.S. troops in the field with a network of fighter-bomber bases. Finally, of course, there were the B-52s that lumbered unseen through the skies with their massive payloads from bases on Guam and Thailand. Six thousand aircraft of all types plied the skies of Indochina.[1]

In theory, coordinating all this was the CINCPAC (Commander-in-Chief, U.S. Pacific Command) in Hawaii. The COMUS MACV only commanded U.S. forces in South Vietnam "proper." And, in Vietnam itself, the only forces over which this authority was unchallenged was over its own Army. At the height of the war in 1969, there were eleven Army division "equivalents" in Vietnam. Obviously, these arrangements were not without their problems, particularly with the III Marine Amphibious Force in I Corps that had its own air corps and fighting philosophy.[2] One thing for sure, and perhaps by design, there would be no field marshal playing independent war lord in Vietnam, as General MacArthur had attempted to do in Korea.

Within Vietnam, MACV presided over two separate commands. One was literally the Military Assistance Command, Vietnam that was in charge of the network of U.S. military advisers who were assigned to South Vietnamese military units throughout the country and to the various headquarters of the South Vietnamese military. At the peak in 1969, nearly 10,000 U.S. military advisers worked with the slightly over one million personnel total in the RVNAF (Republic of Vietnam Armed Forces). About half of these forces were in the national military forces, and the other half were in the Regional Forces/Popular Forces (referred to as "Ruff Puffs" by American

44   advisers).[3] This thin American line performed a myriad of duties such as ensuring that American military equipment went to the right places, helping their counterparts fix logistical snarls (usually with American largesse), seeing to the training and feeding of Vietnamese soldiers, and delicately offering tactical planning and combat advice. By far their most important function, however, was calling in U.S. air strikes in support of combat operations.

MACV's far larger command was over all the American units stationed in Vietnam. If you were in the Army as I was, you were assigned to a unit in the United States Army in the Republic of Vietnam (USARV). In my case, I was assigned to the 525 M.I. (Military Intelligence) Group, homeported in Hawaii. If you were in the Marines, you were assigned to a unit in the III Marine Amphibious Force (III MAF), headquartered in Danang. If you were in the Navy, some activity of the Seventh Fleet claimed you. The boys in blue in the Air Force were assigned either to the Seventh Air Force (all tactical air force units—TACAIR) or to the Eighth Air Force (all units somehow involved in supporting the huge B-52s, the strategic bombers). Servicemen and -women were paid by these specific units, which also cut their orders (in other words performed all the paperwork in their military lives). However, everyone worked for MACV. It was messy.

In-country, MACV was divided into four Military Regions. They were first called Corps Tactical Zones: I Corps, II Corps, III Corps, and IV Corps. In 1970, they were renamed as the four Military Regions. Then in 1973, they were changed again to Regional Assistance Commands (or sometimes Groups). But each region remained unchanged, as the same territory on the map. During the war, each region was typically commanded by a U.S. two-star general in the four regional headquarters, north to south, in Danang, Pleiku, Long Binh, and Can Tho.

Each regional commander faced very different wars. In I Corps south of the Demilitarized Zone (DMZ), conventional North Vietnamese army units squared off with a host of U.S. Army and Marine artillery batteries in a string of interlocking fire support bases. Conventional American units patrolled in the hills surrounding the coastal cities of Hue and Danang, blocking North Vietnamese attempts to attack them. Veterans of the Korean War would find much that was familiar in I Corps.

The region of II Corps, across the middle of South Vietnam, was the largest geographically. It covered an area of rolling hills inland and a thin but populous strip of communities along the coast. In peacetime, these communities could boast some fabulous beaches. The huge naval port and logistical hub of Cam Ranh Bay was in II Corps. At the height of the war, it was the world's busiest port. Inland, the vast distances called for Air Cavalry helicopters to launch surprise assaults and rapid extractions. The war in this region was a chopper war, and these aerial formations etched the unique signature of the Vietnam War.

The III Corps included the area in and around Saigon. In addition to the teeming millions of the capital city, Saigon was ringed by settlements of progovernment Catholic refugees. These settlements were often called the "rocket belt" because of the frequent rocket attacks launched at them by Viet Cong mortar crews. Further out from these settlements were the rubber plantations, many of them still in French hands. Beyond that were the triple-canopy tropical jungles of War Zones C and D and the Iron Triangle. The United States launched repeated sweeps to clear them out in bitter jungle fighting reminiscent of Guadalcanal or New Guinea in the Pacific War of World War II.

Half the population of South Vietnam lived in the Mekong Delta, the site of IV Corps. By Vietnamese request, there were few U.S. forces in the Delta, just the Ninth Infantry Division and the Swift Boat patrols of the U.S. Navy.[4] The North Vietnamese presence in the Delta was light as well. The war in the Delta was a guerrilla one, and this is where most of the activities of the "other war" of pacification were concentrated, including the highly successful land reform program that was implemented late in the war.

There was also a secret war lurking in the shadows of this clearly visible war machine. The MACV SOG (Studies and Observation Group) was an amalgam of Special Forces troops, CIA operatives, and South Vietnamese recruits that conducted reconnaissance and sabotage missions along the Ho Chi Minh Trail and launched mostly fruitless attempts at clandestine disruptions inside North Vietnam. Without apparent success, they also sought to pinpoint the locations of POW camps in Laos and North Vietnam.[5]

There were other agencies of the U.S. government in Vietnam besides the military. All told, these employed about 2,000 American civil servants and another 5,000 private contractors.[6] Though smothered by the vast military complex, this was still a considerable presence. At the time, Saigon had the largest-staffed U.S. embassy anywhere in the world. In addition to the massive official $140 billion total spent on the military war effort, U.S. economic assistance from 1950 to 1976 came to a hardly insignificant $9.4 billion.[7] This financed the so-called other war or what also fell under the term "pacification." A host of activities fell under this rubric.

The Chief of Mission was the ambassador. The career diplomat Ellsworth Bunker served in this role from 1967 to 1972, which overlapped with General Abrams's service as COMUS MACV from 1968 to 1972. The two men got along well. In 1972, Bunker was succeeded by the more flamboyant Graham Martin, who presided over the gradual collapse of Vietnam all the way until the frenzied helicopter evacuations off the embassy roof in April 1975. In addition to the embassy's diplomatic duties of relating to the various ministries of the Government of Vietnam and the other diplomatic missions in town, the scale of the war called for some other very visible functions. The traditional USIA (United States Information Agency) ran a series of Vietnamese-American friendship associations in the cities as well as libraries in most of the consulates. It was USIA's central mission to acquaint foreign societies with American culture, and all sorts of events, tours, and celebrities were brought in to "bring America" to Vietnam. The most popular of these activities was the large program of English-language classes.[8]

As a big war, Vietnam was often the dominant media event of the Baby Boom generation, and the embassy established the Joint United States Public Affairs Office (JUSPAO) to relate the war to the media. In addition to press conferences and briefings, JUSPAO published innumerable studies on the war, many of which were based on sophisticated analytical research. It also stored important archival information for scholarly study.[9] Though JUSPAO was accurately perceived as a propaganda mill for the war, its employees saw themselves as educators. My friend Bill Gausmann worked there, and the colleagues of his whom I met formed a pretty impressive stable of intellectuals.

The largest civilian operation in Vietnam, however, was CORDS, Civil Operations and Revolutionary Development Support. It attempted to coordinate a host of U.S. and GVN programs that sought to build a government presence in the 12,000 towns and villages of Vietnam. The largest civilian contingent came from AID, the U.S. Agency for International Development. It funded infrastructure projects of roads, bridges, and schools as well as offering low-interest loan programs for farmers and small town entrepreneurs. Despite this heavy civilian presence, MACV, in fact, ran CORDS, and its heaviest footprint here lay in advising the Regional Forces and Popular Forces. And the CIA participated in several ways, most notably in the Phoenix Program. At its peak in 1969, there were 6,500 military advisers and 1,100 U.S. civilians assigned to CORDS.[10] To put this in a larger perspective, at this same bureaucratic level, the South Vietnamese government employed nearly half a million civilians, and all agencies of the U.S. government in Vietnam employed another 150,000 Vietnamese.[11]

Having just mentioned the CIA, it is worth acknowledging that "the company" was heavily involved in Vietnam, and much of what its operatives did that was visible was controversial. They worked with MACV SOG. They also worked with the Special Forces in recruiting a Civilian Irregular Defense Group (CIDG), originally Montagnards (mountain tribals), to serve as a trip-wire border defense force in the Central Highlands. They provided invariably pessimistic intelligence estimates that clashed especially with the optimistic estimates coming out of MACV.[12] They even ran their own companies, like Air America. Indeed, this little "company" boasted (quietly) a force of a few hundred airplanes, 200 American pilots, and 10,000 other employees.[13]

But the program the CIA was most known for was Phoenix. Phoenix, or *Phung Hoang* in its Vietnamese equivalent, was the GVN and American counterterror program. It was designed to root out the entrenched Viet Cong infrastructure in the countryside. Most of the personnel involved were Vietnamese drawn either from Ruff Puff forces or national police and province officials who would identify suspects. On the American side, Phoenix was a part of CORDS, and a few hundred CIA types and an equal amount of military folks were involved. Unfortunately, not always the right people were picked up, and civil liberties did not receive much priority. Such abuses erupted into media scandals. How successful it was is a matter of debate, but it clearly made a dent in the Viet Cong infrastructure. This is evident in just the aggregate results. Viet Cong losses to the Phoenix

Program were 74,000, 34,000 of whom "rallied" (or came over to the GVN side).[14]

On the economic front, one of the most successful counterinsurgency efforts of the U.S. Mission was the Commodity Imports Program (CIP). A central part of any insurgent strategy is to sow potentially explosive discontent among urban populations by disrupting the food supply through crop seizures and roadblocks that prevent food grain from getting to their markets. These interferences, of course, create bottlenecks in the supply chain that can set off inflationary spirals that trigger that pièce de résistance of civil discord, the food riot. The resultant chaos has proven, time and again, to be the precipitant of a regime downfall. To avoid this scenario, the United States, from its agricultural bounty, brought in huge stocks of food grains (rice, corn, millet, and wheat) to warehouse a huge grain reserve. From this, the U.S. Mission could make judicious infusions into the markets to ensure there were no disruptions of supply, thus enabling prices to remain stable. Of all the many misadventures of the Vietnam War, food riots were not one of them.

The Nam, in brief, was a massive and complex war machine. Academic treatises about the "asymmetry" of this conflict notwithstanding, there was nothing small about this war. As I worked my way into the Tank and MACV (Pentagon East), this was the maze in which I was trying to find my place. As I struggled to get my bearings, two people came into my life—both outside the Green Machine—that set my course in Vietnam: Carol Dahl and Bill Gausmann. I do not doubt for a minute that they were two new angels sent to me from the Great Upstairs.

Carol Dahl is my cousin. Actually, she is my mother's cousin. So she is my first cousin, once removed, but she is only a few years older than I. Carol grew up in North Dakota, a depopulated state full of Norwegians. Her dad was president or presiding bishop (I forget the precise title) of the Norwegian Lutheran Church in America. She was in Vietnam with her husband, Leif Dahl, who was working in Saigon as the chief accountant for Lutheran World Relief (LWR) that was part of a larger effort called Viet Nam Christian Service (VNCS). The dislocations of the war had tossed up nearly a million refugees, and LWR was one of the NGOs (nongovernmental organizations) engaged in supporting the people in the refugee camps, many of which ringed Saigon.

I remember playing with Carol in her backyard in North Dakota when I was four and she was about ten. We were playing school, and she was the schoolteacher. I loved to pretend to be in school. (When I finally got to real school, I didn't like it very much. These grown-up teachers were not as nice as Miss Carol.) I did not meet her again until Saigon, so I missed seeing her when she was Homecoming Queen at Pacific Lutheran University.

She was still a beauty-to-behold, particularly in Saigon where American women were so rare. As soon as I was more or less settled at work, I got a call from Leif inviting me over to their house on a Sunday afternoon, the only time I had off. Theirs was a modest villa in a tidy, middle-class neighborhood consisting mostly of Vietnamese, but with some foreigners sprinkled in. One of the few Confucian temples in Saigon was nearby. They had a daughter, Kristen, about two years old, who was as blond and blue-eyed as her mother.

They were a lovely family. Carol was a charming conversationalist and Leif was just a supremely nice guy. It was nice for me to make this connection with what amounted to a second ring to our family. I was flattered that they wanted to know me, and they knew better than to ask too many questions about my work. I suppose it was just a normal wholesome home, but for me in Saigon it stood out like a Garden of Eden. Their home—right there in the middle of Sodom and Gomorrah—was everything that I wanted in life, and it was a riveting reminder of what was worthwhile to hold out for. Literally, from the inspiration of their home, I could "put on the full armor of God."

And I needed it. I lived in the Newport BOQ (Bachelor Officer Quarters), which was in walking distance from MACV Headquarters. It was also right next to the Third Army Field Hospital and the large BOQ for the doctors and nurses.[15] I got to ogle a lot of nurses, but only from afar. The doctors had a lock on them. I also got to see the medevacs whirling in the daily casualties from the field. Mostly, they were Americans, but I did see some Vietnamese, and even some men wearing North Vietnamese and Viet Cong uniforms. I couldn't keep my eyes off all the blood on these stretchers that kept coming off the helicopters. In my bureaucratic world, it was a vivid reminder of the grim business we were in.

On my walks to work, there were women all around—and they *were* beautiful whirling by in traditional silk *ao dais*. These were full-length, full-sleeved dresses that were form-fitting from the neck to the waist and then billowed into a front and back flap slit to the waist on each side. Covering their legs were various styles of pajamas. They presented entrancing ensembles that were modestly provocative.

At work, my immediate boss was a bright, but shy, major from Wisconsin. I was detailed to pick up the phone, and a female Vietnamese voice kept asking for a "Major Mu." This was not remotely close to his name, so I kept telling her that there was no Major Mu here. These were secure phones, and locals were not supposed to be using them. She persisted, and in exasperation I finally bellowed, "Is there a Major Mu here?"

To my shock, my boss, who was right next to me, grabbed the phone. Despite the photo on his desk of a very Wisconsin-looking wife and three beaming kids, I soon discovered that this telephonic woman was his "wife for a year." As I found out, this was a pretty common arrangement, even though all intelligence officers were forbidden such "fraternization." In truth, I was not overly shocked because I had met some of these "Wisconsin wives" in Monterey, California.

The Naval Postgraduate School (NPS) in Monterey was designated a "waiting wives" installation for the dependents of officers deployed to the "unaccompanied tour" that was Vietnam. Every Friday afternoon when I was in language school, there was a happy hour at the NPS Officers Club—and these women were on the prowl. I came to these gatherings thinking that the gals were all single. Though some of them seemed a little old, I didn't see any wedding rings. One particular evening I hit it off with one of these women, and she invited me home for a drink. We came to an apartment, and once inside there were two screaming kids. I noticed a picture of a uniformed man with these kids. She noticed that I had noticed, and just casually acknowledged, "Oh. That's my husband. He's in Nam and won't be back for six months. Just let me get these kids down, and you and I can have some drinks." With this guy's picture looking over us: not on your life. As soon as she left the room, I bolted. That's when I was shocked.

It would be easy to say that Vietnam caused all this, but I think there were some highly developed degenerative tendencies in the culture already that Vietnam, on both sides of the Pacific, just brought to fuller expression. Unlike in Monterey, in Vietnam these easy morals could turn dangerous. One morning when I was walking to work from Newport, a captain whom I had seen in the MACV building was just ahead of me. I caught up with him, and struck up a conversation. He was a nice enough fellow, even though he was a captain. Suddenly, one of these billowy *ao dai*–clad women leaped out at us. She had a big rock in her hands and smashed him in the face, knocking him to the ground. He was nearly unconscious and bleeding profusely. The whole time she was screaming, "You number ten! You no butterfly around, or you one dead G.I.!" She pounced on him fully intending to hit him again. This fireball could not have been more than 100 pounds or five feet tall, but it was all I could do to pull her off him.

This was not going to be the path for me. Carol and Leif Dahl were proof of a better future. Almost to reinforce the point, the Dahls invited me to join them for church on Sunday evenings, since I told them I was not too enthusiastic about the generic Protestant services at the MACV post chapel. There was a small French Huguenot chapel sandwiched between the French and American embassies in downtown Saigon. A group of Lutheran expatriates had formed a small congregation that met in this church on Sunday evenings. The pastor was a civilian cleric from the Wisconsin Lutheran Synod. This is a brand of Lutheranism that is so conservative they do not believe in any church ties to the state, including providing chaplains to the military. However, they willingly provide church services to government personnel outside of military installations.

One of the members of this little parish group, clearly the lay leader, was a distinguished gentleman with slicked-back silvery hair and very thick black-rimmed glasses. Carol introduced him to me as Bill Gausmann, the embassy's Hanoi watcher. Since the Dahls returned home to the States in May, they were handing off the custody of my soul to Bill. On the way home, they stopped in India to visit my folks with the reassuring report that I was in good hands.

Bill Gausmann was a Lutheran and a socialist—and prominent in both circles. Beyond his role as the informal lay leader of our little Lutheran congregation in Saigon, "he was closely associated with the Lutheran Seminary in Gettysburg, Pennsylvania." After he returned from Vietnam, he became a member of the bicentennial commission of the Lutheran church in America. Politically, he was a committed socialist. In the 1930s, he traveled with Norman Thomas, the party's head, who appointed Bill to the party's national executive committee. Bill served in Europe in World War II in the army, and while there found time to serve as the representative of the American Socialist Party to the Socialist International in London.[16] Norman Thomas, in fact, was the subject of some of Bill's longest and dearest stories. One thing I learned ideologically from these stories was that as a true socialist, Bill was a vitriolic anti-Communist.

While different, Bill's world was closer to mine than that of the Dahls. His expertise on Hanoi filled a deep need of mine to understand the war. His willing help in this regard sustained a friendship that lasted the rest of his life, and I dedicated my first book to him, and to my wife, Ana Maria.[17] In fulfilling this yearning for knowledge, Bill was my second angel in Vietnam—though, compared to the Dahls, he was a bit of a fallen angel. After the Dahls left Saigon, he proposed that we continue our "conversations" (his soliloquies, really) in his flat. There was always a generous wet bar of alcohol awaiting us, and these libations were the nearest I would come to Plato's symposium.

Though often I would come alone, there were several times when there were others of his companions whom I would meet. There was Jim Haley, married to the daughter of a Cambodian general, and an expert on both Hanoi and the Cambodian military. There was a foreign service officer named Jones who had the most extensive private library I had ever seen. There was an Australian general who was an attaché and a counterinsurgency expert. And there were often representatives of the media. These were lively gatherings.

Beyond just superintending my enlightenment, Bill began to use me as a shield for his own virtue. He always spoke adoringly of his wife Doreen, and of his two children, Deborah and Paul. But Bill had been in Vietnam since 1969, and that was a long time to be alone. There was a classy Vietnamese woman whom he called Madame Nho. He met her somehow in his work at JUSPAO. He would have her over to visit, as long as I was there. She was a very sophisticated lady of about forty or forty-five. Her smile was radiant, and she had an aristocratic giggle. I was glad to help out.

I also told Bill about my travails at work. He was someone who could understand. As much as I liked working in the Tank, I was expecting to be working with Vietnamese, since I spent a full year learning the language. Bill agreed that this was a crime. How he did it, I'll never know, but he wrangled me an assignment as an English language instructor at the Vietnamese Military Academy (its West Point) in the mountain resort of Dalat. Just when I was about to leave, the colonel in charge of the intelligence analysts of the four military regions found out, and blew a gasket. Two things outraged him. First, no State Department "Commie" was going to interfere with military assignments. Second, lieutenants were in Vietnam to do what they were told, and not to lobby around for dream jobs in the middle of a war.

Since, however, I was so enterprising, he gave me a choice. I could stay where I was—and make the coffee, not meet any Vietnamese, and be happy. Or I could meet all the Vietnamese I wanted by leading "lurrp" patrols into War Zone C from Tay Ninh City.

"Lurrp" was Nam Speak for Long-Range Reconnaissance Patrols. War Zone C was a region of impenetrable jungle outside of Tay Ninh full of notorious Viet Cong tunnels and bunker complexes. These patrols were conducted in support of combat divisions that needed actionable intelligence on enemy troop movements and supply networks. Helicopters would drop off these teams (ranging from three or four to a dozen troopers) somewhere in the night, then pick them up somewhere else from seventy-two hours to a week later. As this option became vivid in my mind, I recalled with horror my OCS experiences. I remembered first how often I became utterly lost on compass and map-reading exercises, and these were all in broad daylight. Second, my hesitant attack on the mythical village at Camp A. P. Hill enshrined within me my battlefield command limitations. If I were to take this honorable option, not me or any of my men would survive. The colonel was not unaware of this.

Up until this point, I had navigated military life with my integrity intact. Now this colonel had slammed me up against an impossible wall. It was a moment of truth. Though it does not have to happen in a war, it often does: the moment when you assume responsibility

54 for your own life, and become a man. There was no one who could help me out of this one: not my parents, not Leif and Carol Dahl, not even Bill. This was the moment that I owned. I chose survival over honor. I stayed in the Tank. I was now a man. But a very diminished one. There was no glory for me in this war. ⋎

As a man, I felt very alone in this strange place, and strange war. My Wisconsin Synod minister clearly sensed my pain (and probably similar pain in others), and preached on Psalm 139's message that God is with us everywhere. Alone as I was, I felt the comfort of God's presence, even in Vietnam, as I listened to verses 7–10:

> Whither shall I go from thy Spirit?
> Or whither shall I flee from thy presence?
> If I ascend to heaven, thou art there!
> If I make my bed in Sheol, thou art there!
> If I take the wings of the morning
> and dwell in the uttermost parts of the sea,
> even there thy hand shall lead me,
> and thy right hand shall hold me.

I was set. On the job. In the Tank. And not a moment too soon: the war was about to break over us in crashing waves.

How the War Was Run: The Easter Invasion

March 30, 1972, was Good Friday. In the States, the date marked a brief recess from a heated presidential campaign. In Vietnam, it was the day when fourteen North Vietnamese divisions launched the three-pronged Easter Invasion against the South: one across the Demilitarized Zone (DMZ) at the seventeenth parallel, aiming ultimately at Vietnam's traditional capital city of Hue; the other across the Central Highlands from Laos trying to cut the country in two; and a third toward Saigon from Cambodia. Huge battles arose on all three fronts.[1] These were all conventional conflagrations, not guerrilla-led hit-and-run attacks with rockets and mortars. The decision to launch this invasion was made in Hanoi in the summer of 1971. The Armed Forces High Command mobilized a force of 127,000 men, and supplies had been pouring south along the Ho Chi Minh Trail ever since. The prizes of this flotilla were hundreds of T-54 main Soviet battle tanks and 130 mm long-range artillery pieces. When Communist forces struck, they had more armor and artillery than ARVN. It was conventional war.[2]

The Communists put their weight of effort into MR 1, ultimately committing six divisions to the desperate battles that unfolded there. In response to the first PAVN (People's Army of Vietnam) blows across the DMZ by three divisions—the 304th, 308th, and 320B— ARVN forces reeled south into Cam Lo and the provincial capital of Quang Tri where they held off follow-on assaults on April 9. Communist forces then paused for three weeks, reportedly because they feared amphibious landings by U.S. Marines across the vulnerable North Vietnamese panhandle just north of the DMZ.[3] Meanwhile, the PAVN 324B Division launched a separate offensive from the Ashau Valley leading into the western approaches to Hue. A string of artillery fire support bases fell one by one.[4]

On April 27, North Vietnamese forces resumed their offensive by launching a second assault on Quang Tri. Miscommunication

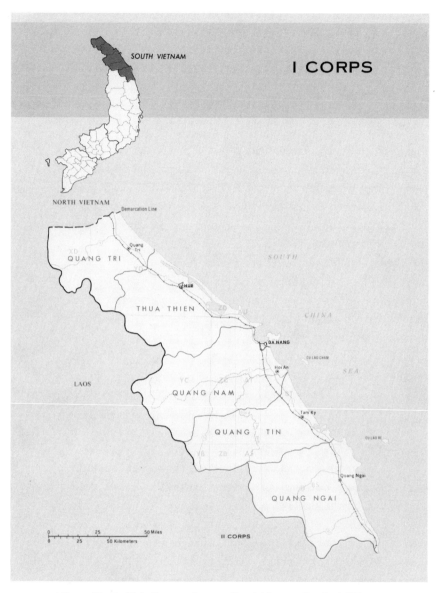

I Corps (Central Intelligence Agency, *South Vietnam Provincial Maps*,
September 1967; in the author's possession)

between the ARVN MR 1 Commander, General Hoang Xuan Lam, and the ARVN Third Division leader, General Vu Van Giai, and with one of his subordinates—involving an order of withdrawal, which was then countermanded—led to exploitable gaps in the ARVN position and to the complete battlefield disintegration of this division. Quang Tri City fell on April 28 and the entire province on May 2. Troops from this division streamed into Hue, triggering a breakdown of law and order in the Imperial Capital. To make matters worse, in the west, Fire Support Base Bastogne fell on April 29 and nearby Fire Support Base Checkmate was evacuated. These were the last of Hue's westerly defense positions still in the mountains. General Creighton Abrams began to report doubts that Hue could be held.[5]

Realizing the gravity of the situation, Abrams and the U.S. ambassador Ellsworth Bunker requested an emergency meeting with President Thieu. They stressed that competent leadership was essential in this crisis and provided Thieu with a list of deficient commanders and competent replacements. Thieu did take some of this advice. General Ngo Quang Truong, the commander of MR 4, took command of MR 1 the next day. To help him in this critical assignment, Thieu dispatched a brigade of the Airborne Division and put the full 15,000 troop complement of the ARVN Marine Division at Truong's disposal. In wartime, it is always amazing what a single well-placed leader can do, and General Truong was one such amazing leader. He immediately put a stop to the looting in Hue by reconstituting the Third Division with a new general and leadership cadre, and then he set about stiffening the resolve of the other three divisions under his command.[6]

Under Truong's leadership, the ARVN First Division pushed the PAVN 324B division back into the hills toward the Ashau Valley. On May 15 these ARVN forces recaptured Bastogne, and Checkmate on May 20, thereby ending any immediate threat to Hue. South of Quang Tri, under relentless pressure from U.S. air strikes and coastal barrages from U.S. naval vessels, North Vietnamese forces failed to gain any ground throughout May and June. On June 28, General Truong launched the arduous counteroffensive, Lam Son 72, to retake Quang Tri with ARVN's elite Airborne and Marine divisions.[7]

Meanwhile, MR 2 had always been ARVN's weakest link. Its vast space and thinly spread forces made it vulnerable to being sliced

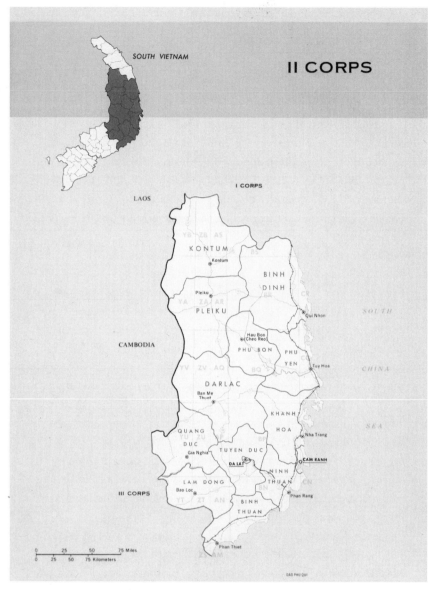

II Corps (Central Intelligence Agency, *South Vietnam Provincial Maps*,
September 1967; in the author's possession)

in two. And that, precisely, was Hanoi's plan. Effecting such a division would isolate the raging battles around Hue and Quang Tri by blocking southern reinforcements, while permitting the North Vietnamese panhandle to furnish indefinite resupply to Communist forces. Succeed here, and half the country would be theirs. With half the national territory and only 20 percent of the population, MR 2 was defended by just two ARVN divisions, the Twenty-second and the Twenty-third, widely considered to be the worst in ARVN. On top of this, the MR commander, General Ngo Dzu, was not up to the job. Even more serious was the fact, unknown at the time, that both the deputy commander of MR 2 and the commander of the Twenty-second Division were Communist sympathizers. Seemingly, an epic disaster loomed.[8]

But the three Communist divisions assigned to this assault—the 320th, Second, and Third NVA Divisions, plus the 203rd Armored Regiment—had not counted on John Paul Vann, the flamboyant civilian senior military adviser to MR 2, or the B-52s, or some basic ARVN pluckiness. The Twenty-second ARVN Division was generally deployed in the north of the military region and the Twenty-third in the south. Naturally, Communist forces struck in what they expected to be the more compliant northern sector. The "northern" highland town of Kontum was shelled on March 30, the same day Communist columns thrust across the DMZ in MR 1. On April 3, ground assaults by the Second NVA Division hit Dak To, just north of Kontum. The Third NVA Division followed with attacks along the coast. By April 11, the fighting by the two divisions became a general front athwart the country's middle. Not surprisingly, on April 22, the Twenty-second Division Headquarters surrendered, with one of its regiments defecting to the Communist side. Two days later the small towns of Dak To and Tam Canh fell. Effectively, the coastal province of Binh Dinh, adjoining Kontum in the Central Highlands, had passed to enemy control. The danger of the fulfillment of Hanoi's plan had become real.[9]

As in the case of MR 1, however, Communist forces then hesitated and did not march the 25 miles south to Kontum. The delay permitted President Thieu to send a brigade of the Airborne Division to Kontum, and for the Twenty-third Division to redeploy under its charismatic commander, Colonel Ly Tong Ba. Fighting soon concentrated on Kontum, and ground attacks by Communist soldiers commenced on May 1. On May 10, Thieu replaced the MR 2 Commander, General Dzu, with an offensively minded armor officer, General Nguyen Van Toan. It was John Paul Vann, however, who took personal control over developing targets and calling in air strikes. He succeeded in getting a full day's worth of B-52 strikes on May 12, just when Communist columns unleashed their heaviest ground assaults on the town. Hundreds of Communist soldiers were killed in a few hours.[10] Though these North Vietnamese forces launched further attacks on Kontum, by the end of May they withdrew from this mountain battlefield. Similarly, while the Third PAVN Division continued its fight along the coast, by the end of July enemy forces had withdrawn from the entire military region. One of his subordinates called John Paul Vann "the heart and soul" of the defense.[11]

In the third prong of its invasion, Hanoi's objective for MR 3 was simple: it was to plunge south from its Base Areas in eastern Cambodia, overrun shielding ARVN forces, and storm Saigon. While MACV and ARVN understood this, they weren't sure whether the torrent would come straight south down Highway 13 through Binh Long Province or angle from the northwest through Tay Ninh Province. The MACV analysts favored Tay Ninh because it had 300,000 people to potentially conquer, while Binh Long had only 60,000. Furthermore, Tay Ninh City beckoned as an attractive compromise prize for an alternative revolutionary capital, in case the attack on Saigon itself faltered. But Hanoi chose the straight path down Highway 13, probably because it was closer to the Communist supply network, and the route had much more protective, surrounding triple-canopy jungle than Tay Ninh.[12]

To aid the VC Ninth Division, Hanoi sent the VC Fifth Division (despite the "Viet Cong" designation, both divisions were completely northern in composition by 1972) and the NVA Seventh Division south into Cambodia to launch this offensive. The campaign opened with a diversionary thrust near Tay Ninh on April 2, followed by its main blow down Highway 13 on April 5. The first obstacle south of the border was Loc Ninh, a sleepy village of just 3,000 mostly Montagnard (mountain tribal) residents. It succumbed on April 7, and all the fighting soon centered on the provincial capital of An Loc, an unfortunate town of 15,000 souls just 50 miles north of Saigon. It was held by the Fifth ARVN Division.[13]

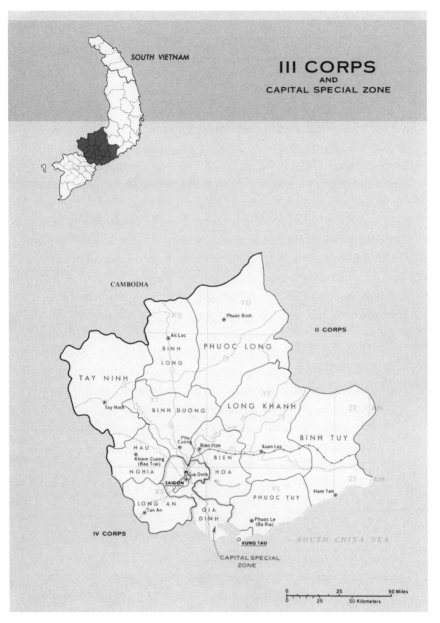

III Corps and Capital Special Zone (Central Intelligence Agency, *South Vietnam Provincial Maps*, September 1967; in the author's possession)

Following the pattern of the other two offensives, after seizing Loc Ninh the Communist formations halted. This enabled Thieu to send the First Airborne Brigade[14] just south of the town and to dispatch the Twenty-first ARVN Division from the Delta as a blocking force against an attack on Saigon. The first ground attack against An Loc came on April 12 and 13, and the shock of T-54 tanks yielded the northern half of the town to the Communists. A follow-on assault on April 18 was repulsed; and, though the Airborne forces were dislodged from their fortified hill, they were able to join the defenders in the town. From April 22 to May 10, a lull in ground assaults turned An Loc into a "hell in a very insignificant place," as Communist units could not overwhelm the town, just as ARVN columns inside could not break-out, nor could relieving formations from the outside break-in. Both sides hunkered down under American air strikes and Communist artillery barrages.[15]

The three Communist divisions, however, were preparing for a massive all-out ground assault on the town. The TRAC (Third Regional Assistance Command) Commander, Lieutenant General James Hollingsworth, got wind of this and persuaded his old friend, General Abrams, to give him the first of a full day's B-52 strikes that Abrams had promised to each of the three regions. Hollingsworth got his on May 11, and the bombs rained down on a three-waved general attack in which Communist forces were decimated. On May 15, Hanoi conceded that "our troops ended the attack."[16] By the middle of June, An Loc was under complete ARVN control, and by July 20 the road to An Loc was declared open. The third front had collapsed.[17]

What is noteworthy about the Mekong Delta is that nothing noteworthy happened in MR 4. With three ARVN divisions—the Seventh, Ninth, and the Twenty-first—protecting half the country's population and three-fourths of its rice production, Hanoi's objectives in the Delta were modest. It was simply to tie down the rich number of ARVN soldiers so they could not be used to reinforce the other military regions. In this, the Communists utterly failed. In 1970, the First NVA Division, which had been infiltrated into the Delta, withdrew to Cambodia to deal with President Nixon's Cambodian Incursion. A battle in March 1972, just before the Easter Invasion, blocked the division from reentering South Vietnam. Communist forces in the Delta then suffered a series of defeats,

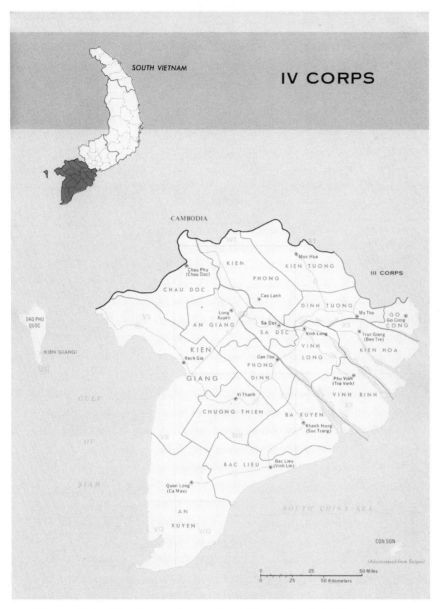

IV Corps (Central Intelligence Agency, *South Vietnam Provincial Maps*,
September 1967; in the author's possession)

culminating in the annihilation of an NVA battalion in November. In the Delta, ARVN fought without any U.S. air support.[18] On the other side, Communist units in this region were crippled by the loss of the supply port of Sihanoukville in Cambodia in 1970 due to the pro-American coup by Marshal Lon Nol that overthrew the more compliant King Norodom Sihanouk. The main Ho Chi Minh Trail supply network ended at the Mekong River. This wide river and the open country of its tributaries formed an effective barrier against further supply traffic south. Thanks to all these Communist misadventures, ARVN was able to send half its forces from the Delta to the battles in MR 1, MR 2, and MR 3.

This was the war fought by MACV and ARVN against the invasion of South Vietnam. On May 8, 1972, President Nixon announced his own war, almost separate from MACV's. Pushing the "China flashpoint" to the edge of its envelope, he unleashed Operation Linebacker as a punishment of North Vietnam for its invasion and intransigence at the conference table. (The "flashpoint" was the feared trigger of a Chinese military intervention such as occurred in the Korean War when U.S. troops advanced toward the Yalu River bordering China.) Like the Easter Invasion itself, this campaign had been built up for a long time. Even as he pulled out U.S. ground troops from South Vietnam, in a huge riptide, he swamped the Indochina theater with a tsunami of American air and naval power. From a peak of 543,000 U.S. forces in-country in 1969, President Nixon drew down U.S. troops at a rapid rate. In January 1972, there were still 104,500 U.S. ground forces in Vietnam, but this figure fell to 31,900 in May 1972 and to 15,000 by year's end. In fact, at the height of the Easter Invasion, the only American combat units left were the First Aviation Brigade (of helicopters) and the Third Brigade of the First Cavalry Division around Saigon (in 1969, there were four American army divisions in MR 3), and elements of the 196th Infantry Brigade in MR 1.[19]

In the wake of these ground force withdrawals, Nixon sent in a crashing wave of U.S. air and naval forces that doubled these forces in the theater. He doubled the tactical air squadrons from 35 to 74, and dispatched an additional 161 B-52 bombers to Guam and Thailand. This made for a total of 210 B-52s dedicated to the fight, which, at the time, was over half the total U.S. B-52 force. On the high seas, he surged an additional 50 naval vessels to the Pacific's

Seventh Fleet. This included a new total of 6 aircraft carriers (with 4 on station at all times) supported by the coastal gunfire from 3 cruisers and 38 destroyers.[20] All of the planning and marshalling of operations for Linebacker were done at CINCPAC Headquarters in Hawaii in coordination with the White House, significantly bypassing MACV. This was Nixon's war.[21]

The naval forces mined all the ports and waterways of North Vietnam with the sowing and reseeding of over 11,000 mines from May to November that successfully shut down nearly all maritime traffic. Accompanying aerial bombardments were massive with over 34,000 tactical sorties (that is, attacks by a single aircraft) over North Vietnam and nearly 5,000 by B-52s over the whole theater. As a result, rail traffic south of Hanoi came to a virtual halt, and imports from China, Hanoi's main supplier of basic manufactured goods and military supplies, dropped from 160,000 tons per month to 30,000.[22] Although Hanoi was able to keep some supplies traveling down the Ho Chi Minh Trail by trucks, it was unable to replenish the devastating losses incurred by PAVN forces. In October, Nixon scaled back and then halted Linebacker as Communist negotiators became more forthcoming at the Paris Peace Talks, mainly by dropping their demand that Thieu resign the South Vietnamese presidency as a precondition.[23]

The Easter Invasion was a devastating war all by itself. With their numbers killed as high as 100,000, Communist losses were heavy. They also lost half their conventional inventory of tanks and artillery.[24] The ARVN losses, while considerably less, were nevertheless the highest rate they had yet sustained in the larger war with an estimated 30,000 killed, 18,000 wounded, and 14,000 missing. Civilian casualties in the South included 25,000 killed and 600,000 rendered homeless. The relatively lower level of civilian casualties reflects the fact that there was no fighting in any major urban centers. Finally, in all this carnage and firepower, only 198 Americans died.[25] In these shifting balances of death, Vietnamization was a huge success.

In reading over the accounts cited for this synopsis of the Easter Invasion, and from my own experience of it, several points stand out. First, most obviously, U.S. air power, in all its components, but particularly the B-52s, was the central ingredient in turning the tide. Second, the American military advisers were the implementing arm in these successful aerial campaigns, both in developing the targets and in calling in the strikes during fluid battle conditions. Third, more than just waving this aerial wand, these advisers often exercised tactical leadership on the ground and shored up the morale of ARVN troops at critical combat moments. Fourth, for all this American support, and despite some combat disintegration, ARVN troops did fight, go on the attack, and regain almost all their lost ground in very heavy fighting. In this regard, it is noteworthy that in this invasion, unlike the offensives of 1965 and 1968, U.S. ground forces—since they were mostly withdrawn—were not engaged.

Fifth, all battlefield accounts make clear that the North Vietnamese attackers fought with relentless determination and courage. In the battles of MR 1, 2, and 3, Communist forces launched attack after attack until their manpower was depleted and their supplies exhausted. Even so, these forces made mistakes at both the tactical and strategic levels. Their pauses in all three Military Regions allowed ARVN forces to regroup and bring in reinforcements. They never figured out how to use their tanks and ended up losing almost all of them. Also, in all three regions, they kept their massed offensives going for far too long, and needlessly lost almost their entire expeditionary force. In MR 1, they sent in two more divisions in a desperate but futile attempt to hold on to Quang Tri. In this battle, PAVN lost four divisions. Further, they lost two more divisions each in MRs 2 and 3. Indeed, the legendary North Vietnamese commander of the invasion, General Vo Nguyen Giap, the hero of Dienbienphu, was eventually demoted after the fighting was over.[26]

Sixth, in the Easter Invasion the character of the Vietnam War changed fundamentally. A war that previously fit into Andrew Mack's definition of asymmetric warfare had now become virtually symmetrical. The guerrilla forces that had been nearly wiped out in the Tet Offensive of 1968 were never really replenished. Instead, main force PAVN units were shipped south as replacements. They came as conventionally equipped divisions. The reason I have called this an "invasion," rather than just an "offensive," is that in this campaign the divisions came with tanks, which they handled poorly, and deadly 130 mm artillery, which they employed with devastating effect. Unfortunately, as a tragic harbinger, the effect of this escalation was to put a higher premium on offsetting American air power.

Finally, the critical ingredient of leadership again proved to be key. General Abrams demonstrated his leadership in three pivotal ways. Strategically, he was single-minded in his four-year tenure as COMUS MACV for his devotion to Vietnamization at all levels. He called this "the one war." Politically, he was able to persuade President Thieu to make essential changes in his military commanders. And militarily, as shall be discussed momentarily, he was deft in his use of B-52s. I would be remiss if I were not to acknowledge that President Thieu as well displayed political fortitude in making these leadership changes, and he allocated his military resources among the three military regions with some prescience.

Basically, the deal discussed in chapter 1 held and it was validated. It was best expressed by the South Vietnamese hero-of-the-day, General Ngo Quang Truong: "The American response during the enemy offensive was timely, forceful and decisive. . . . This staunch resolve of the U.S. to stand behind its ally stunned the enemy. Additionally, it brought about a strong feeling of self-assurance among the armed forces and population of South Vietnam."[27]

★   ★   ★

In the middle of this epic historical event, I was privileged to see how the war was run at MACV Headquarters in Saigon. With the onslaught of multiple Communist attacks in three Military Regions, intelligence poured into MACV in indigestible amounts. Instead of leisurely early morning briefings, there were now two densely packed briefings a day. I had been assigned as an analyst on the Military Region 3 Desk (the jungles, rubber plantations, and Communist guerrilla zones astride the Cambodian border radiating away from Saigon), but these extra briefings demanded more people involved in setting up meetings and reading the briefings. As the new man on the totem pole, who knew the least, I was expendable and so attended to other duties: making sure all the generals were seated in rank order protocols and that each had the beverage and type of smoking pleasure of their choice at their table places. I was also often dragooned by a major to read the briefing in place of someone else who at the last minute could not make it. Despite these trivial duties, it was an unforgettable experience because I witnessed the key decisions that turned back this invasion.

The man responsible for these decisions was General Creighton Abrams, who clearly relished the crisis atmosphere. Abrams, the man, was a soldier's soldier. He chomped a cigar (touching off a cigar fad at MACV that made the air foul) and swore freely, to the delight of this very male society. He was often a little frumpy in appearance, and did not have the "strack" spit-polish carriage of General Westmoreland, his predecessor. A big part of this was because, after these morning briefings, he would take off on a helicopter and observe the fighting in some particular theater of the day, as well as consult with the senior American regional advisers. The next morning, he would always open the briefing with an inspiring story of derring-do by some captain or corporal at a bridge or bunker somewhere. Every so often, after these briefings were breaking up, he would look at me and say, "Lieutenant, one of these days I am going to take you with me, and leave you off somewhere so you can earn your spurs." This always got a big laugh in the room, and I would try to recover by saying, insincerely, "I would love that, Sir."

"Nah, Lieutenant, you stay here and play tennis. I like watching you play." I began to think of my tennis as a knightly mission. It wasn't just that I now felt redeemed for the implausible addition of my tennis racket to my Jail Bird flight duffel bag, but that I realized I had landed in the middle of a modern Camelot beset by a historic invasion. The generals that gathered every morning in the Tank at MACV Headquarters formed into a literal Council of War. This was far from an academic seminar with students acclaiming the stunning insights of their bespectacled professors. There was a veritable King Arthur here who was discussing the progress of the campaign with his knight-errant generals as he barked out the orders that would unleash lethal bolts of destruction from the air and move lumbering columns of military muscle on the ground. As a modern King Arthur, General Creighton Abrams was a bit disheveled and foul-tongued, but he commanded these forces with a mastery that radiated throughout the Tank. He was loyally served, including by me on the tennis courts. In my serve-and-volley, I was doing my bit to win the war. He was watching.

As I said, I was initially assigned to the Military Region (MR) 3 desk, and I found the intelligence very confusing. Fortunately for my addled wits, I was pulled into working on the briefing meetings themselves. Then, as the air war heated up, I was moved over to the Air Intelligence Division. As a little mouse in the room of these briefings, however, I listened to all the briefings and read most of the reports that went into them.

There were three levels of intelligence briefings and reports at MACV: DISUMs, WIEUs, and MIEUs (pronounced "dyesums," "woos," and "moos"). The DISUMs, or "daily intelligence summaries," were literally twenty-four-hour reports on enemy activity and movement in the four military regions, along the Ho Chi Minh Trail, and on troops and supplies coming into, and going out of, North Vietnam. This was tactical level intelligence. The WIEUs, or "weekly intelligence estimate updates," looked at enemy capabilities and intentions focused on given operations—in the case of the Easter Invasion, the status of the battles in the three military regions and likely courses of enemy action. These were always held on Saturdays and would often involve presentations on specific issues from field commanders or their staffs. This was operational level intelligence.

The MIEUs, or "monthly intelligence estimate updates," were big-picture briefings held once a month. These were "dog and pony" shows with "bells and whistles." The ambassador and his senior staff would attend, including the CIA station chief. Occasionally, high-ranking dignitaries from the State Department or Pentagon, and even the occasional delegation from Congress, would also be present. In addition to these high-level personages, there were always fancy audiovisuals with a film clip or two at MIEUs. At this level, in addition to all the military briefings, there were also welcome summaries from the Intelligence and Research (INR) Bureau of the State Department in Saigon, as well as something from the local CIA station. The MIEUs consisted of overall diagnoses of the war-to-date and prognoses on the future course of events. General Abrams and Ambassador Ellsworth Bunker would often offer their own take on these events. I never heard them disagree, so there must have been a lot of private consultations ahead of time. This was intelligence at the strategic level.[28]

At the analytical desks, for all these reports the business was the same. Intelligence information bits, or data ("factoids" we sometimes called them), streamed into the inboxes of all these desks day and night. This was "raw intelligence." What made it into the DISUMs, WIEUs, and MIEUs was "finished intelligence." Writing up these reports was similar to writing a college term paper. The big difference was that all the information that went into one of these reports was evaluated for the reliability of the source and the validity of the information. Sources, as I recall, were evaluated on an A to E scale, and the information itself from 1 to 6, with A and 1 being the highest and E and 6 the lowest. Instead of footnotes, each paragraph had to have a source reliability and information validity code: A-1, A-3, E-6, whatever. The code E-6 meant that neither the source nor the information could be assessed or verified. It was rare that anything E-6 made it into a report.

In Vietnam, sources that we relied on were open sources (media and library materials), imagery, SIGINT, HUMINT, TIC, and POW reports. I have listed these in rough order of their reliability. Open source information was critical in developing an analyst's basic stock of knowledge on his military region or other responsibility. When other sources of intelligence turned up blank, open sources might be all that an analysis had to go on. The most reliable intelligence source of information was imagery. Imagery refers to all forms of imaging, whether from actual photographs, radar, satellites, and even more exotic forms. The phrase "pictures don't lie" gave imagery its top-flight reputation. But even pictures could be manipulated. I remember a set of photographs coming to the MR 3 Desk of a concentration of T-54 tanks just across the border from Tay Ninh in Cambodia. It turned out these tanks were literally made of cardboard, and were designed to deceive us into thinking that the major line of Communist attack would be directed at Tay Ninh, rather than Loc Ninh.

Signal and communication intelligence, or SIGINT, was considered the next most reliable. This intelligence came from communication intercepts of all kinds, including phone taps, sensors, and even satellites. As scientific as SIGINT sounds, it could be a tricky source of information. Unfortunately, it is amenable to innocent distortions or more deceptive manipulations. Sensors along the Ho Chi Minh Trail could detect heat-moving objects. This could mean formations of southbound troops or very confused buffaloes. More manipulatively, Communist units would change their radio call signs frequently, thereby confusing us both as to their location and as to just how many units we were really dealing with.

Human intelligence, or HUMINT, was the most problematic source. There are a variety of HUMINT sources, but the most common come from spies recruited by agent handlers, what I was initially trained for at Fort Huachuca. These sources typically take a long time to develop, at least for sources that reach into inner circles of the enemy. It is also difficult to receive reports from these spies because each "drop" can risk exposure. Further, these sources cannot always be trusted because they may be either playing with us for money or doubling for the enemy. Constant cross-checking of these sources is critical. But there is no better source for the motivations of your adversary. Parenthetically, I should note that liaison officers are another source of HUMINT, which is what I did in my second tour as a civilian. In these Intel reports, HUMINT sources were rarely rated at better than C-3. MACV did have a highly placed source at COSVN Headquarters (discussed in chapter 8), and that person proved invaluable in alerting us to North Vietnamese movements in Cambodia.

The TIC is "troops in contact," and reports from combat troops are most valuable for DISUMs. Their chief advantage is that they come from direct observation and detail, and their chief disadvantage is that they come from direct observation and detail. The difficulty here is in the standardization problem typical of multiple eyewitnesses to a traffic accident. The same incident is described differently by different observers, and observers of different incidents do not have objective selection criteria for their characterizations of events. For example, an enemy unit seen lounging in a field could be described as demoralized or just taking a break. The primary advantages of information from TIC are enemy locations, unit identities, and lines of march. The disadvantage is that this is a very perishable source of information. After a few days, TIC is no longer of much use.

The POW reports share many of the advantages and disadvantages of TIC. Since, however, a POW report can offer an inside view of what TIC only sees from the outside, POW reports can often be priceless gems. In the Tet Offensive of 1968, a POW caught just outside of Nha Trang twelve hours before the offensive began had on his person a document with the game plan for the entire offensive. This permitted an armored force under General Fred Weyand to hastily reposition its tanks in front of one of the major arteries into Saigon, thereby blocking a major advance into the city. Fighting in Saigon, though spectacular, was localized and could be contained in a piecemeal fashion. Similarly, in the Easter Invasion of 1972, prisoner interrogations revealed the basic North Vietnamese battle plan for the Central Highlands, which proved invaluable in deploying ARVN troops and plotting U.S. air strikes.[29] The problem with this source, more generally, was that different interrogations needed to be cross-checked, and the use of torture only made truthful reports more difficult to come by.[30]

Assessing the second part of the equation, the validity of the information itself, is where the desk officers and analysts earned their spurs. How well a particular desk could sift out misinformation from solid intelligence, and differentiate enemy feints from true objectives, depended on senior analysts with deep knowledge of the underlying forces responsible for patterns of enemy behavior. It also depended on an intuitive understanding of the basic assumptions motivating this behavior.[31] An example of the pitfalls to which even senior analysts can succumb was the misreading MACV made on Communist objectives in MR 3. Analysts thought that Tay Ninh offered the more lucrative target to PAVN divisions than the sleepy village of Loc Ninh. Heretofore Communist strategy had been driven by the People's War with its emphasis on winning the war by winning over the people. Since Tay Ninh was a province of 300,000 and the capital city was the strategic stronghold of the Cao Dai sect, while Loc Ninh, and even the provincial capital of An Loc, were little more than jungle clearings, Tay Ninh seemed the obvious route-of-march to these analysts. But the three PAVN divisions assigned this mission were conventional forces, not popular guerrilla formations, and they were interested in terrain access to Saigon, not people. The analysts had failed to change their assumptions to match these differently motivated Communist forces.[32]

The central concern of each desk was to keep track of its Order-of-Battle (OB). Order-of-Battle consisted of the basic enemy units in the region, the type of units, their location, a constant updating of the numbers in each unit, their equipment, and their training and morale. Attempts were made to compile leadership profiles of all unit commanders. From the data in the OB files, analysts would track enemy movements to discern patterns of behavior that led to the ultimate analytical prize of what the enemy would do: where, when, and how.

There were plusses and minuses to this process. On the plus side, there was caution and precision. The caution rested on both the practice of the code of reliability and validity in intelligence reporting and on the fact that all information that made it into a finished report had to come from at least two sources. The precision lay in the scrutinized language of the reports. I remember that for each of these reports—whether DISUM, WIEU, or MIEU—the colonel in charge of all four MR desks (and each of these were headed by a major) would carefully edit the reports for flamboyant language. If an enemy launched "a massive onslaught" in the newspaper, the DISUM called this "an attack by fire" followed by "a ground attack," and then provided estimates of the number of rounds fired and the size of the attacking units. Rather than "slashed through the outer suburbs," the DISUM would give the precise distances and geographic coordinates of the location of enemy forces.

This once-in-a-lifetime perspective on the contrast between intelligence reporting and media sensationalism was illuminating. In Vietnam, our major news sources were the *Stars and Stripes* newspaper and Armed Forces Radio, outlets of the Department of Defense. They both were a compendium of wire service and other media accounts that comprised a basic summary of the conventional news reporting of the day, albeit with some deliberate inattention to the antiwar movement. During the Easter Invasion, just reading *Stars and Stripes* put you at the edge of your chair as you felt sure that the sky itself was about to fall around you. It made you all the more susceptible to the vicious rumors that whirled around Saigon under what seemed like an imminent and crushing assault. In sharp contrast, the determined, low-key accuracy of these Intel reports was comforting. I felt sorry for those who weren't able to read them.

There were two drawbacks to this process, however. The first arose from the principle of compartmentalization. In order to safeguard intelligence reports from penetration from the outside, and to contain the damage if it occurred, people in the intelligence community, whatever their level of security clearance, only had access to information they "needed to know" to do their jobs. Hence, if you worked at MACV in military intelligence, you did not need to know political intelligence about Hanoi or the political strategy of COSVN (Committee of South Vietnam), Hanoi's military-political wing in the south. On the other hand, if you worked in the embassy for the State Department's Bureau of Intelligence and Research, you did not need to know the holdings of military OB at MACV. In truth, both groups of analysts needed to know both sets of intelligence to really do their jobs, but this information was not shared between and among the working echelons of the different analytical shops.[33]

The second drawback had to do with the politics, or bureaucratic structure, of the military staffing system. When I was in the Army, the staffing at military headquarters was divided into five functional areas of responsibility. The first, J-1, dealt with personnel and administration. At MACV briefings, J-1 reports dealt with U.S. and ARVN troop levels, unit rotations and drawdowns, and resultant redeployment of forces. The J-2 area was intelligence. The third, J-3, was operations; J-3 was responsible for reporting on the progress of ongoing "friendly" operations, and then for proposing, planning, and scheduling further "friendly" operations. The heart of these J-3 briefings was all about whether the commander would accept these recommendations, what modifications needed to be made, or whether they should be delayed or shelved. This was usually the keystone to the arch of these meetings. It was the moment at which key decisions were likely to be made, or more accurately, pronounced. Private discussions among the generals clearly preceded these public declarations. Down the bottom of the slope, J-4 was logistics and covered nuts-and-bolts matters like the status of inventories of U.S. supplies, equipment, maintenance readiness, and especially of all forms of transportation. The J-5 area was responsible for plans, but usually at pretty grand and ethereal levels. If these plans got too far down to earth, there would be inevitable clashes with J-3. Not surprisingly, at most headquarters, J-5 was always perilously undermanned. At MACV, there was considerable J-5 air time at MIEUs. Also, J-5 had recently come to own civil affairs, and thanks to the rise of CORDS in Vietnam (with its considerable military component), J-5 became something of an inadvertent, but valuable, link to the embassy.

The point to be noted here is that J-3 was always the premier staff function in any military headquarters, and the J-3 "chief" typically outranked the other J "chiefs" in seniority.[34] The J-3 operational proposals were always designed to defeat threats depicted by J-2 reports. This put a huge cautionary cast to intelligence reporting. In military bureaucratese, CYA ("cover your ass") Intel reporting was ritual. The more daring the J-3 planning, the thicker this Intel tortoise shell became. This difference in styles could become exasperating to J-3 staffers and chiefs. If the COMUS was of the daring type, and they often were, he would quickly share in the exasperation of J-3. There was also a cultural issue that hardened the lines of this tension. The personnel of J-2 were pretty solidly from the Military Intelligence Branch of the Army. The J-3 staffers and chiefs were all from the combat arms: the Infantry, Armor, or Artillery Branches. Theater commanders invariably came from the combat arms, not the staff branches. Hence, the commander's innate sympathies lay with J-3.

On top of all this, whatever the demands of J-3 for the "best Intel," intelligence was never going to be perfect, and J-2 wanted to be sure that some huge operational disaster could not be blamed on faulty intelligence. The J-2 reports on enemy intentions came down to a continuum of four predictors: unlikely, possible, probable, and likely. All of these terms came with appropriate caveats. The difference between probable and likely lay in the density of these caveats, but they were never absent, even for likely. There were no "slam dunks" coming out of intelligence in Vietnam.

When I was in high school in India, I played goalie for our soccer team. Serving in intelligence was like playing goalie. Whenever the opponents scored, it was always the goalie's fault. In the Tet Offensive of 1968, the surprise of the offensive resulted in the brief Communist penetration of Saigon and three-week occupation of Hue. One could say that the enemy scored at least two goals before being turned back. In the Easter Invasion, there really were no enemy goals. The Communists pushed us into the back field three times, but they were not able to score.

One final note is that the military staffing system operated like a truncated seminar. The military is a hierarchical bureaucratic structure, and ideas and proposals were folded into a vertical circulation of "discussion." No-holds-barred debates would often occur among analysts at the desks, and consultations between the senior desk officers and the colonel division chief could be intense as well, but the colonel's word was final as to what went into the reports. Occasionally, the J-2 chief himself (Major General William Potts, when I served) might intervene in the content of these reports. At the briefings, the reports were read ("briefed") to the generals by the desk officers, and sometimes by the analysts. The generals could stop the briefer and ask questions—and they often did. This was the only opportunity for a lowly desk officer or analyst to say anything on his own. Occasionally, General Abrams would throw out a general question: "Can anyone tell me . . . ." This was the only time that anyone in the room could speak up. Usually, the response was silence. If there were a response, there was a clear, if unspoken, military etiquette of hierarchy whereby analysts and desk officers could comment on facts, but only field grade officers were supposed to offer analysis and interpretation. Further, the generals would often talk among themselves, but briefers (often referred to as "talking dogs") could never initiate a comment. The value of the whole staffing process, then, depended on the quality of the reports themselves, on the acuity of the generals in their questioning, and on rare acts of vocal courage on the part of analysts.

Making sense of this huge flood of information overflow that gushed into these briefings from the five staffing tributaries was the business of the general officers. Generals built their careers climbing up the three company grade ranks (Second and First Lieutenants, and Captains) and three field grade ranks (Major, Lieutenant-Colonel, and Colonel) through the separate ladders of their branch of service—whether the combat arms of infantry, armor, or artillery, or the staff branches of intelligence, quartermaster, transportation, engineers, signal corps, military police, finance, and the like. After putting in their time as colonels, those selected for the general grades (Brigadier General [one star], Major General [two star], Lieutenant General [three star], and General [four star]) were sent to the National Defense University at Fort McNair in Washington, D.C., or to the Army War College, or the Naval War College, and so forth, where they shed the snakeskins of their individual branches and took on the new skins of the general officer corps of the Army, Air Force, Navy, and Marines. In a course of postgraduate study, they learned to view their responsibilities from the perspective of the uniformed services as a whole, and how their duties served the larger geostrategic interests of American foreign policy. This was a good theoretical intention, but in practice the overwhelming majority of general officers, in all services, came from the combat arms. From my parochial perspective as an intelligence officer, this gave the whole military decision-making system a huge J-3, or operational, bias.

Biased or not, in my view General Creighton Abrams was a superb general officer, and a true embodiment of this ideal. I soon learned that these "dog and pony show" briefings that I have just described were a little bit "for show," or to communicate actions already decided. Although there did appear to be some genuine discussions at the briefings where ideas were amended and plans were tweaked, there were more intense discussions "offstage" day and night. The generals would consult among themselves in their MACV offices and conference rooms. Abrams would frequently visit with his senior MR advisers in their headquarters, or they would come in from the field and meet with him. He would have meetings with Ambassador Bunker and his senior staff. Abrams was a commander who met frequently with his ARVN counterparts, and even with President Thieu. Most importantly, there were "back channel" communications to Washington with Secretary of Defense Melvin Laird as well as with Secretary of State Henry Kissinger and Deputy National Security Adviser Alexander Haig in the White House.[35] Abrams would sometimes make cryptic and passing references in the Tank to some of these meetings and conversations.

At least in wartime, commanding generals have considerable leeway in marshaling the forces at their command. In Vietnam in 1972, the principal force remaining under American military command was the B-52 bomber, and Abrams deployed this weapon with devastating effect. As the Easter Invasion reached its climax almost simultaneously in the three military regions, he decided to give a full day's worth of B-52 strikes to each military region, one-by-one, in a decisive shock to turn the tide of the invasion. I remember an atypical wide-open debate during the briefings on the order of these strikes. The intelligence was so confusing on the relative importance of these three battles that I thought that resorting to a coin toss could do no harm. Having listened long enough, Abrams interjected, "Listen, I don't give a damn any more about the intelligence, here is how we are going to do it: MR-3 around An Loc is going to get the B-52s on May 11, MR-2 around Kontum on May 12, and the western approaches to Hue on May 13." He quickly continued with a brilliant lecture on hitting waves at their crests, and how he had a feeling that the crests of these Communist waves would hit at just these moments. As noted in the account of the invasion above, the B-52s hit An Loc and Kontum at just these cresting moments, and in Hue they set the stage for the First ARVN Division's recapturing of the westerly mountain fire-support bases. I think there is no question among any of us who worked in the Tank at MACV that this stroke of military intuition saved South Vietnam—at least from *this* invasion. As the TRAC Commander, Lieutenant General Jim Hollingsworth, simply said, "By God, it just saved us, that's all."[36]

Perhaps a little detail can shed light on the salvation claims of these Big Ugly Fat "Fellows." A single, conventionally armed B-52 bomber typically carried 108 bombs, which translated into 60,000 pounds of explosives (or 30 tons). During the Vietnam War, B-52 bombers flew in three-plane formations that dropped their ordnance into target cell rectangles of one mile long by a half mile wide (or two kilometers by one). Into these geographical coordinates fell 324 individual bombs, in a different mix of 500- and 750-pound bombs that detonated 180,000 pounds (90 tons) of explosives.[37]

Truong Nhu Tang, a high-ranking Viet Cong leader and defector, who survived a few B-52 strikes, gave this eloquent testimony:

> The first few times I experienced a B-52 attack it seemed . . . that I had been caught in the Apocalypse. The terror was complete. One lost control of bodily functions as the mind screamed incomprehensible orders to get out. . . . even the most philosophical of fatalists were worn to the breaking point after several years of dodging and burrowing away from the rain of high explosives. . . . Pursued relentlessly by such demons, some of the guerrillas suffered nervous breakdowns and were packed off for hospital stays; others had to be sent home. . . . Times came when nobody was able to manage, and units would seek a hopeful refuge across the border in Cambodia.[38]

During the Easter Invasion, 90 to 100 B-52 bombers struck 30 such target cells every day![39] They were, indeed, game changers.

With the fighting on the ground largely in ARVN hands, the sole remaining weapon under U.S. command was this airpower. And over this, command authority was split. This split, and the scissors play between "Abrams's War" and "Nixon's War," erupted into a donnybrook from a seething internecine bureaucratic battle. On all aerial operations over the skies of South Vietnam, control of American air assets had been turned over to COMUS MACV, an army general. This did not sit well with the Seventh Air Force, which had "possession" of U.S. tactical aircraft.[40] Its principal headquarters was in Thailand, but it had a field headquarters at Tan Son Nhut Airport that just happened to be next door to MACV Headquarters. The Navy also chafed at having its carrier planes, and the air service of the Marines, under MACV control. Consequently, these two services jealously guarded the direct control they enjoyed over their operations in North Vietnam.

But the Air Force overplayed its hand. Officially, it had been caught undertaking "protective reaction raids" into the North Vietnamese panhandle without securing President Nixon's approval ahead of time. The reality was more Byzantine. In November and December of 1971, the Air Force was conducting bombing missions along the Ho Chi Minh Trail in Laos (Steel Tiger, as it was called). General Abrams, with President Nixon's approval, authorized Air Force fighters to fire on North Vietnamese anti-aircraft positions in "protective reaction," if the radar from these sites had "locked on" to the American planes for a firing sequence. The Seventh Air Force Commander, General John Lavelle, took the liberty of launching twenty-eight of these raids without any such "lock ons" because he thought he had been encouraged to do so. Whether or not he was correct in this assumption, his command submitted false reports on these "lock ons." An enlisted-rank airman blew the whistle to his congressional representative, and Lavelle was fired in late March 1972, days before the start of the Easter Invasion.[41]

The donnybrook for the Air Force (and the Navy) fell on June 26, 1972, just days before General Abrams left Vietnam. Despite the official denial of any connection to the "Lavelle scandal," its impact was unmistakable in the terse public announcement that: "the operations and intelligence components of the Seventh Air Force have been removed from its headquarters at Tansonnhut [sic] air base outside Saigon and incorporated into the headquarters of . . . MACV." At the same time, the U.S. Navy publicly acknowledged that the Navy Liaison Office for the Seventh Fleet, and its carrier-based air arm, had also been moved to MACV.[42] On the ground, this meant that every Seventh Air Force intelligence and operations agency at Tan Son Nhut was physically moved across the street to MACV where two agencies would merge, an Air Force one and a MACV one. In virtually every case, the ranking officer was an Army officer over an Air Force one. The Army had taken command of the air in South Vietnam.

The notable exception to this coup was the Arc Light Panel, the board that selected the daily targets for the B-52s. This was one pride of the Air Force that the Air Force kept under its charge, primarily because the B-52s were part of the Eighth Air Force on Guam, and not from the offending Seventh Air Force. The Panel was commanded by a two-star Air Force general with a one-star Army general who looked on, along with a few Army and Air Force colonels. At the bottom of this totem pole were two Army lieutenants, Harold Lesser and myself, and an African American Specialist Four who were brought over from MACV to evaluate the intelligence of the nightly target nominations for the morning Arc Light Briefing. Actually, we had been transferred to Air Intelligence some time earlier. At our level, the impact of the Lavelle scandal came on the momentous day when we Army lieutenants became formal briefing officers to the Panel.

We evaluated the target nominations on the basis of a system of numerical values that were to be assigned to each target nomination. This scheme had been developed some time shortly after the Fall of Troy, well, probably around 1965 when the B-52 bombings of Southeast Asia began. In any case, the ancient vintage of this system meant that the rationale for these assigned values had long been lost. At least some of it did make sense. The two basic criteria, each of which had its own subsets of categories, were the reliability of the intelligence and the value of the target.

The reliability of the intelligence was the defensible criterion, and was evaluated similarly to the ground analysis in the MR Desk "shops." Photo reconnaissance was the top-drawer Intel source. Pictures don't lie. But secret agents do. Sometimes they outright lied for just another case of Jack Daniels whiskey. More often, their memories lost precision: "I thought for sure that that bunker complex was to the north of the truck park. Well, maybe it was to the south." Communication Intel was far more reliable than agents, but less reliable than pictures. There were tricks that could be played with this source, as well as numerous obvious and more subtle mistakes. In addition, the Intel in these target nominations had to be timely, and the point value to a nomination degraded as the time of an Intel report lost currency. A photo of a truck park with fifty vehicles in the past twenty-four hours was pretty "moochy" (of high value). But if the picture were a week old, it wouldn't be worth "sh-t," in the quaint parlance of the business. The Intel numbers for

these nominations did make sense, and I felt I could defend them 81
before the Panel.

The values assigned to the targets themselves was a completely different story. Here there was a range of opinions. This haggling over target values really turned on an almost philosophic difference between the Army and the Air Force over the very purpose of B-52 strikes and, hence, what constituted valuable targets. The Air Force had "loaned" the B-52s (BUFFs—Big Ugly Fat "Fellows") to the Vietnam War with extreme reluctance. After all, they were configured as strategic nuclear bombers to serve as a sure second-strike retaliatory force in the country's strategic nuclear deterrent triad (the other two being the first strike intercontinental ballistic missiles [ICBMs] and the second strike missiles aboard submarines [SLBMs]). To the Air Force, even in a conventional war, it was still a strategic weapon whose purpose was to destroy the enemy's war-making capacity. The Vietnam War with its truck parks and bunker complexes was really beneath the dignity of these BUFFs. Since, however, these were the largest targets along the Ho Chi Minh Trail, these were the preferred target values to the Air Force.

The Army, on the other hand, saw the BUFFs as the ultimate battlefield weapon. There was nothing like a B-52 strike to raise the morale of ARVN troops, or to devastate that of North Vietnamese forces. The Army liked battle staging areas, troop concentrations, and even very temporary headquarters locations, despite their fluidity. As one ARVN Division Commander put it, "I say that the best strategic targets for the B-52s is right in front of my position."[43] On the other side of the coin, our previously quoted Truong Nhu Tang called the B-52s the "invisible predators" that created "an experience of undiluted psychological terror into which we were plunged, day in, day out, for years on end."[44] But the numbers system was an Air Force design so the total numbers of a target nomination ended up supporting Air Force–favored logistical targets rather than Army cells built on enemy troop formations.

This could lead to some absurdities. I remember one day when there was a major battle in progress in the Central Highlands threatening the provincial capital of Kontum. There were some targets proposed around troop-staging areas designed to break up the attack. The Intel supporting the nominations was not too good, just the commander's assessment that this particular valley had been a historic staging area for previous battles for Kontum. As an Intel source, the commander rated slightly above an agent, and the "mere" history counted for nothing. The winners on the Arc Light Panel that day went to a truck park along the Cambodian border and a bunker complex in the Delta. These nominations had been developed from recent photography, and their point totals were off the charts—even though there had been no enemy activity in either location for weeks, and no indications of anything imminent.

What drove the Air Force generals crazy at the Arc Light Panels were "Godley Grams." The U.S. ambassador to Laos was G. McMurtrie Godley. The Hmong tribal leader, General Vang Pao, commanded a CIA-trained and -equipped irregular army that was keeping two North Vietnamese Army divisions at bay on the strategic Plain of Jars (a mountain plateau looking down on Luang Prabang and Vientiane, the two major cities of Laos). To do this, however, Vang Pao depended on a generous supply of U.S. air strikes, including, by some prior arrangement well above MACV, a daily quota of B-52 strikes. Nominations for these targets would come from personal messages from the ambassador consisting of long narratives tying the strikes to at least a rhetorically coherent battle plan. Despite repeated remonstrance from MACV, he often failed to say what precisely was in these target boxes or to reveal just how he knew what he said was in them. His constant justification was their potential impact on the battlefield morale of Vang Pao's worthy guerrillas, or even on Vang Pao himself. I remember that one day's Godley Gram Preamble talked about how Vang Pao had had a very bad night last night, and a B-52 strike would do wonders for his spirits. Not surprisingly, these targets did not receive very high scores, but the good ambassador got his targets anyway.

Evidently, these Godley Grams irritated General Abrams as well. His biographer related Abram's insistence that Godley use the MACV *system* (this process I have just outlined) in submitting his nominations, which was to no avail.[45] Given the tremendous destructive power of these BUFFs, and the fact that they were the sole remaining weapon in the war zone in exclusive American hands, their use became a highly sensitive political and military football. In fact, the Arc Light Panel's target selections were only recommendations to COMUS MACV. Thus, despite the Air Force's operational control over the B-52s, their use was under Abrams's command. And he was not bashful about occasionally stepping in and issuing his own orders for the daily strikes. Such indeed was the case on the day mentioned above when Abrams diverted the high-numbered targets in Cambodia and the Delta to the combat exigencies of Kontum. But President Nixon got into the act as well and became embroiled in a dispute with Abrams over the president's insistence on diverting a number of B-52 strikes from the MACV system for Linebacker strikes in North Vietnam.[46]

Returning to this much-vaunted system, the job of my compatriot First Lieutenant Harold Lesser and myself was to score the nominations that came into our office each evening. We would read the intelligence supporting each nomination from the Intel branch of the four Military Region Headquarters. We would put an overall score on each nomination based on a weighted formula based on the Intel itself, its timeliness, and the target value. Numbers ranged from 500 to 2,000, as I recall. At the end of the evening, we would put the nominations on a chart in the order of their point scores, which we would brief (present) to the Arc Light Panel. The locations of the nominations would also be plotted on a map that would be hauled in for each of the Panels. There was no numerical category for the proximate tactical situation to the grid coordinates of the target cell or for a more general relevance to the current battlefield in the country—though I noticed that the generals spent as much time poring over the map as they did over the chart. Harold Lesser and I were Army officers who, of course, felt the battlefield situation to be a "critical variable," and the temptation to cheat was extreme. Our immediate boss was an Air Force lieutenant colonel from Louisiana for whom I had a great affection. He would come into the office every morning before we all marched off to the Arc Light Panel and briefly check our charts. But his "auditing" was perfunctory; he trusted us.

Neither one of us cheated, but I resolved this crisis of belief by not defending the numbers in the briefing. It was my fond hope that one of the generals might ultimately get fed up with the system. After the Air Force "scandal" discussed above, the Arc Light Panel got a new boss, Major General Hudson of the U.S. Air Force. He was immediately skeptical about this pointing system, and he fired a lot of questions at us. We could tell him how we scored a nomination, but really not why—especially on the value of the target itself.

After my deliberate failure to defend some egregiously high point total for a nomination, he caustically asked me questions and I had to come up with some answers:

"Lieutenant, tell me something: what do you think of this point system?"

"Not much, sir," I replied.

"What do you know about math, Lieutenant?"

"Not much, sir."

"I figured. You're in the Army, after all! So, what confidence should I have in this system if you're in the Army and you can't do math?" he thundered.

"My partner, Lieutenant Lesser, is very good at math, sir, and he checks my figures," I replied in weak defense.

"Shut up, Lieutenant (he loved calling me this, and it sounded like a curse). I am not going to scrap these numbers, but we'll add in a new category for battlefield situation. And don't you and Lesser put any numbers on this category. Just tell us what the situation is around the nomination, and we'll decide right here whether battle-field relevance should override your stupid numbers," he declared.

Despite what he did to me at a subsequent briefing, I liked this man. In fact, I thought something akin to a bureaucratic revolution had just happened in favor of some sanity to the Arc Light target se-lection process. For a person in REMF Land, it is moments like these that are the equivalent of combat victories in the Boonies.

As a result of the "scandal" and resultant Army control of even the B-52s as well as all the stratospheric actors lusting (in a bureaucratic way) after the BUFFs, the Arc Light Panel briefings in the morn-ing became extremely tense. Whatever he may have come to think of us personally, General Hudson, who chaired the Panel, did not like being briefed by two Army lieutenants. In his briefings, Lesser was pretty matter-of-fact in sticking to the bare-bones intelligence in each nomination. When my turn came, I occasionally tried to link the target nominations to larger patterns of war strategy. In other words, I loved to insert a little bullsh-t, the mark of a future college professor. More generally, as I have said, the Air Force did not like their prized B-52s brought into this guerrilla war as a conventional weapon. This distaste boiled over one morning when a cluster of target nominations came in around the Central Highlands town of Kontum (again). General Hudson demanded to know why all these

nominations were lumped together like this. I quickly responded
that this series of targets would serve as aerial artillery for an ARVN
operation to retake the surrounding area around the town. The
word "artillery" was a lightning rod because the Air Force was going
to be damned if their nuclear B-52s would be dragged down to the
ignominious role of providing ground support for the Army. "A B-52
nuclear bomber is not an artillery piece," he shouted, as he threw
his briefing pointer at me.

At this point, the Army brigadier general, John McGiffert,
stepped up and tersely stated, "If you do that again, I will make sure
this lieutenant gets a Purple Heart!" General McGiffert, a former senior military adviser to MR 3, was now serving as General Weyand's
representative on the Arc Light Panel. He was also in the loop on
the activities of SOG (Studies and Observations Group), the secret
forces operating along the Ho Chi Minh Trail, and he officially attended the Panel to ensure that none of these clandestine troopers
inadvertently ended up in a B-52 target box.[47] I considered him my
personal protector. For awhile, General Fred Weyand, the four-star
Army general who later became General Abrams's replacement as
COMUS MACV, stepped in and personally presided over the Arc
Light Panels. I kept my job, but did not get my Purple Heart. Despite my failure to get the medal, I treasure this moment as one of
my fondest "war memories."[48]

With Mom and Dad. Studio portrait in Guntur, India, in 1949. I was two.

Happy Augustana Days. The tennis team on a road trip in the spring of 1967, my sophomore year. I am on the far left.

Leaving Fort Leonard Wood after training in April 1970. I am on the far left along my '64 Chevy.

Gateway to Officer's Candidate School Regiment at Fort Belvoir, Va. I am with a fellow cadet from the same province (Andhra Pradesh) and language area (Telegu) where I grew up in India. We are in the traditional greeting pose in India of *Namaste*.

Our Officer's Candidate School unit forming up to go on parade. I am second from the left with my typical smile problem. We were supposed to look grim in all formations. Smiles were punishable by push-ups. These punishments contributed to my success in physical training tests.

I was sworn in as a second lieutenant by Richard Dishno, a schoolmate of mine from Augustana.

With Mom at my Officer's Candidate School graduation, September 25, 1970. I have my Honor Physical Training Graduate trophy in hand.

Language School tennis champion, July 1971. Runner-up played on the tennis team from Luther College in Decorah, Iowa.

My Vietnam passport photo, February 1972.

Night on the town at the Dragon, 1972. I am third from the left with my Benedictine & Brandy.

Returning from Bien Hoa on my "secret mission" in April 1973. The famous heel of Saigon with its central downtown District One is in the center of the picture.

With Lt. Col. Vu Van Nho at the entrance to the Combined Intelligence Center, Vietnam (CICV), March–April 1972.

With my two secretaries at the CICV: Co Suong (*left*) and Nguyen Thi Huong (*right*), March–April 1972.

Nho with his family on the front porch of his Saigon home, March–April 1972.

With one of Nho's daughters in the living room of his home, March–April 1972.

At the Army of the Republic of Vietnam (ARVN) Military Intelligence Headquarters in the Joint General Staff Compound with my assigned driver (*far left*), my translator (*second from left*), and secretary Co Cho (*on the right*), March–April 1972.

William C. Gausmann lecturing at the Order-of-Battle Conference held at the CICV in early June 1973.

With Nguyen Phu at a roadside Cao Dai Shrine on our trip to Tay Ninh, Summer 1973.

At a Defense Attaché Office party with a friend wearing one of the new civilian hairstyles, Summer 1973.

Brig. Gen. Maglione (*foreground*) visiting the CICV accompanied by Lt. Col. Nho (*left*) and Col. William E. Le Gro (*right*), June 6, 1973.

Gen. Maglione at the CICV viewing photographs of the North Vietnamese pipeline along the Ho Chi Minh Trail. Also viewing these photographs from left to right are Col. Le Gro, Lt. Col. Nho, and Col. Hoang Ngoc Lung (commander of ARVN Military Intelligence).

Maj. Gen. Murray, head of the Defense Attaché Office, visiting the CICV, welcomed by Lt. Col. Nho with Col. Le Gro looking on, June 14, 1973.

Gen. Murray at the CICV being shown a map of the North Vietnamese pipeline along the Ho Chi Minh Trail. Looking on are Col. Le Gro (*first on the left*), Tony Suarez, my boss (*third on the left*), and myself (*fourth on the left*). Two CICV analysts are also at the table.

Gen. Murray leaving CICV accompanied by Col. Lung (*on the left*) and Col. Le Gro (*on the right*). The CICV building is in the background.

Col. Lung pinning me with the Vietnamese Army Staff Medal, First Class, at an awards ceremony at the Military Intelligence Headquarters at the Joint General Staff compound, late July 1973.

On the same day I received the Vietnamese Army Staff Medal, Lt. Col. Nho presented me a plaque of appreciation from the CICV.

In my office at Saint Louis University with a sign from the post in Saigon. It was taken from my office door at the Military Intelligence Headquarters on the compound of the Joint General Staff.

Life in Saigon and a Trip to Tuy Hoa

The U.S. military prided itself on sending a fully integrated force to war in Vietnam. Like American society itself, however, it was a very racially stratified force. In the early stages of the war, the infantry units became heavily black. In order to avoid high black casualty rates, President Nixon directed that combat units become racially proportionate to the American population, even as he speeded up the general withdrawal of these units. Still, blacks remained concentrated in the enlisted ranks, while the officer corps was predominantly white. Around Saigon in 1972, blacks were to be found in logistical support activities such as installation maintenance, transportation activities, and repairing vehicles in the motor pools. There were only a handful of blacks in a headquarters complex like MACV.

The African American "Spec 4" who worked with us was Remus Lamb. Like all the rest of us, he was a REMF. We all did our REMFing in Saigon, a teeming tropical Sodom and Gomorrah. In our office, no one reveled in this more than Remus. He felt right at home in Saigon, and constantly talked of his discoveries "downtown." Remus knew where the best food was, the cheapest deals on anything that you cared to name, and, of course, where to find the finest women. He worked during the day, while Harold Lesser and I worked at night. After the daily Arc Light Panels were over, Harry and I would be putting our briefing stuff away to go home just when Remus would walk in. He always had a story. "Hey, L. T. [pronounced "el tee"], I gotta tell you about this one. Hang on a minute." And I always would hang on. Remus had a flashy gold tooth that would sparkle in the light when he laughed—which was a lot. He always sucked us in. Informally, he was a one-man morale booster who ruined our productivity with his stories of this city—and its life—that he had figured out how to relish.

Before the war, or in between wars, maps called Saigon "the pearl of the Orient." With its spacious boulevards, French colonial buildings, and cool breezes from the Saigon River, Saigon was evocative, to French colons anyway, of Marseilles. That was in 1960, when there were only 2.3 million residents. For comparison, the city limits

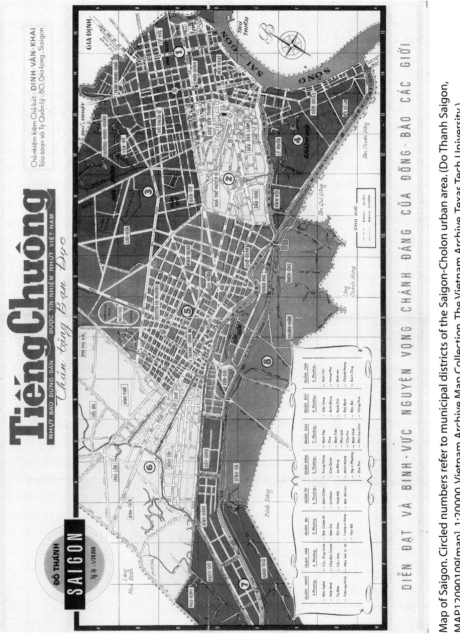

Map of Saigon. Circled numbers refer to municipal districts of the Saigon-Cholon urban area. (Do Thanh Saigon, MAP12090109[map]. 1:20000. Vietnam Archive Map Collection, The Vietnam Archive, Texas Tech University.)

of Saigon encompassed an area equivalent to Washington, D.C., and its 500,000 residents. Pearls get swallowed by squalor and sleaze when wars bloat "alabaster cities" with refugees seeking safety and fortune in any war-profiteering guise they can find. In a decade, by 1970, Saigon had swollen to 3.2 million.[1] Some reports put the population at over four million in 1972, which was about a quarter of the total population of South Vietnam.[2] With eight times the population of Washington, D.C., the spacious boulevards had turned into torrents of traffic, a cacophonous din of multicultural modes of transport that did not get along, accompanied by sea breezes turned rancid by too much human habitation.

Saigon is shaped like a human foot, and if you add the 10-mile vertical stretch to Tan Son Nhut and MACV, the foot has a bit of a leg, cut off at the calf. It is angled like a foot and leg just stepping off on its daily walk with the heel off the ground and the toes lifting off it. The top of the cut-off leg to the ankle runs from the northwest to the southeast, and the ankle to the toes flows from an upper southeast to a lower southwest.

If you were driving into town from Tan Son Nhut, you would come down a highway called Duong Cach Mang, or Revolution Road, with a conspicuous sign thanking allied soldiers for their sacrifices. At the city limits, the highway becomes Cong Ly Road and would take you to the ankle, or axis of the city, the Presidential Palace. Radiating to the east to the heel was what was left of the Marseilles-like glory—the central downtown of District One. The Saigon River, with its harbor for the 40-mile journey to the sea, marked the heel's border. Flowing into this river were two tributaries: the Tin Nghe Canal (really creek) slithered along the northern border and the Ben Nghe Canal along the southern limits. In the words of the novelist Donald McQuinn, these canals "glistened like rancid chocolate."[3] The image of chocolate did not cross my mind so much as that of a sludge of motor oil mixed with mud, which erupted in such a stink that your nostrils would turn into prunes just to survive driving over the bridges.

The city, in fact, was a labyrinth of several cities, each living its own life, connected at least in the daytime by the many boulevards where these many Saigons colorfully mingled without knowing each other. Of course, there were the Vietnamese, the one people that were mostly everywhere, who made up three-fourths of the population. But there were different groups of Vietnamese. There were the high-class Vietnamese, who lived away from Europeans and around the few Confucian temples in town. They lived in the north on top of Cholon, radiating northwest from the Presidential Palace. Closer in was the next rung that made its living interacting with the American and French enterprises. They had their villas and servants, just like the French. Then there were the government officials, police, and military men, who lived in all the middle-class neighborhoods of the city. Again, these areas were still to the north, but many bureaucrats lived in the northeast in an arc that extended to the National Zoo at the top of Saigon's heel in the east.

Surrounding this relatively prosperous central downtown, and threatening to swamp it, was the bulging semicircle of slum dwellers and impoverished refugees who lived along the northern canal, bee-hived across the Saigon River in the mosquito-infested swamps, and bulged under the southern foot of Cholon along the Ben Nghe Canal. These districts in the south of Districts Seven and Eight teemed with nearly a million people. It was here where no foreigners dared venture. These slum dwellers dominated the fish market south of Cholon. Most of the riverine commerce of Saigon was actually in and around the fish market, though the official Saigon Port and some of the Fish Market was along the Saigon River in District One. Unfortunately, in this market and in many of the smaller markets around southern traffic circles, petty crime thrived, along with people out to even old scores; and it was in these markets that the occasional terrorist grenades detonated. Only the latter activity caught anyone's attention.

All of the Saigons mingled in the main Ben Than Market on the western edge of the prosperous District One. It, in turn, was just west of the famed Tu Do Street (Rue Cantinat under the French) with its restaurants, bars, Indian tailor shops, disgruntled intellectuals, and hopeful prostitutes. Just west of the Market was about a five-block square area of open markets, which served as a huge intersection of the traditional and modern economies. Vietnamese foodstuffs of all kinds were for sale as well as bolts of textiles. Traditional craft wares of lacquer-polished pictures and ceramic elephants (called "buffies") were out on the sidewalks as well as contraband of everything available in the American base exchange system. The hottest-selling item was American cigarettes, especially Marlboros.

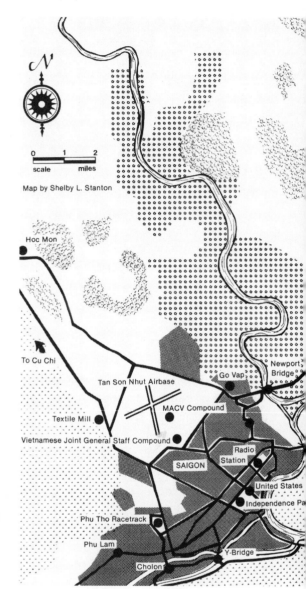

Saigon–Bien Hoa–Long
Binh (Map from Shelby L.
Stanton, *The Rise and Fall of an
American Army: U.S. Ground
Forces in Vietnam, 1965–1973*
[Novato, CA: Presidio Press,
1985], pp. 380–381.)

Along all of these boulevards were the many denizens of the
flesh trade that plied among the 25,000 American servicemen, who
lived in scattered installations clustered near these boulevards and in
the central downtown. If the enlisted ranks did not live right on post
at MACV Annex or at the Seventh Air Force at Tan Son Nhut, they
lived in a string of BEQs (Bachelor Enlisted Quarters) along Plantation Road that formed an umbrella over Saigon. Donald McQuinn
referred to it as "the white man's ghetto."[4] Officers lived in BOQs

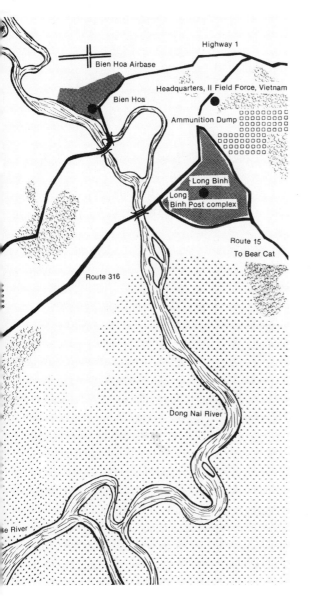

(Bachelor Officer Quarters) dotted along the boulevards going to the central downtown that served as the stem to this umbrella.

This central downtown was highlighted by the National Parliament building, the Presidential Palace, the American embassy, the Rex movie theater, the Brinks BOQ (in this case, high-ranking officers), and the Continental Hotel. It was on the famous verandah of this hotel where the people living the glitzy life of war profiteering hung out, of course including the journalists who reported on all this activity. In short, this was where Saigon was on display; where insolent expatriates and important Vietnamese paraded their prominence as they were beset by stampeding street urchins, salespeople of all types, and prostitutes. Here Westerners came to experience the Orient. There was a lot of drinking and swapping of stories, and savoring the food—and other delights, as they chose. Mostly, as a war capital, Saigon was a Las Vegas of rumor.

Indeed, it was all the rumors that made Vietnam so surreal. In the alcoholic haze of the central downtown, rumors swirled throughout the city eddying with the heat to spread mists building into ominous clouds that obscured reality in episodic storms. When the storms cleared, and reality returned, the sunlight was often too bright, and all the squinting made you lose sight of what you were really seeing—at least, in my case, until I got back to my office. The difficulty in sorting them out was that they slid along a hazy and elusive slope of rising wartime fears from the quite likely, to at least the possible, to the implausible but scary, and finally to the utterly fanciful that nevertheless breathed life into ill-concealed paranoias.

The quite likely were all the coup rumors that circulated around the restaurants, bars, and cafes, since, politically, coups were the main business of laconic Saigon generals and colonels who fed the stories to idle intellectuals and pliant journalists. Hence, any one of them might well happen, but what made them rumors was that most of them were just talk. The possible were all the tales of dramatic deaths of important personages, whose passing promised dramatic shifts to the course of the war. The North Vietnamese General Vo Nguyen Giap died at least four times when I was in Vietnam. In fact, at this writing (2011), he is still alive at age ninety-nine. But one of his colleagues, General Nguyen Chi Thanh, did die in a B-52 strike (maybe). Hence, what gave life to the rumors was that a few of them (a very few) were true. The implausible were the thunderbolt reports of catastrophic collapses on the battlefield. One prominent one I remember in the summer of 1972 was that ARVN defenses in An Loc had collapsed, and that Communist forces were shelling nearby Bien Hoa in support of a massive attack on Saigon itself that was going to happen the following afternoon. Traffic-jam panics were the terrified outbursts of such fear-mongering, which were probably deliberately planted to achieve just these effects.

The rumors that Saigon relished, however, were the utterly

fanciful ones. These were the ones you could linger on over several drinks and spin into creative yarns of subterfuge and conspiracy. These were the rumors that were pulled from thin air and spawned back into an ether of rumbling, ominous clouds. Behind the North Vietnamese onslaughts in the Central Highlands were hordes of Chinese infantry converging on the jungles of neighboring Laos poised to spring into Vietnam, armed with atomic hand grenades. The "madman" President Nixon was pulling off a secret deal with Russia to bomb Hanoi with Moscow's tacit permission as an elaborate smokescreen for an American withdrawal from Saigon. Somehow the ever-secretive Chinese community in Cholon was mixed up in some bizarre venture to paralyze the economy, thereby enabling a Communist takeover in the resultant food riots, in exchange for their continued dominance over this same economy. Naturally, there were always the French who were plotting fiendish schemes—with the Viet Cong, with the Russians, and even with the Americans—to engineer a return of Saigon to the French imperial fold.

Speaking of the French, there were still about 10,000 of them in-country, and, by far, most of them lived in Saigon.[5] There were, indeed, enough of them around, along with all their colonial buildings, to still give Saigon something of a Marseilles atmosphere. Though disdainfully and purposively aloof from this nouveau riche Americana, the French deliberately parked themselves in the central downtown to ensure that the French language would be heard at every street corner. They had their restaurants tucked away by the river (there was always an air of exotic danger around these restaurants, where one could still imagine the shadowy death of "Alden Pyle" in The Quiet American), their neighborhood of walled-in villas behind the American embassy, and, of course, their Cercle Sportif, a compound of tennis courts that defiantly pretended that the French imperium reigned on. Later, one of these aloof French families became a particular interest of mine.

When I came downtown, which was as often as I could, I came for the escape of Chinese movies and for immersion into the food. At that stage in my life, food, and lots of it, was the central quest of my daily existence. To me anyway, one remnant of the Garden of Eden, in this otherwise God-forsaken war, was the delicious, and very cheap, food that could be had anywhere in town. In these urban forays, I would head straight to a movie theater and make a beeline for a restaurant right afterward. I avoided going to the bars in the downtown hotels or the famous verandah of the Continental. In these perches, journalists lurked like vampires ready to pounce and sink their teeth into the necks of lieutenants like me, or other junior minions of REMF Land, who might be coaxed into an indiscreet revelation about the war. In fact, I had been warned that if I were ever caught just speaking to a journalist, I would be put on the next chopper to Tay Ninh to join the "lurrp" patrol to which I had declined an earlier invitation. In any case, the folks who hung around these hotels were pretty sophisticated civilians and high-ranking officers, and I felt out of my league. Really, no one was under forty. Further, most of them had come to the country to prove some cherished negative belief about the war, so anyone actually serving in the military was a target for their contempt. This condescension and hostility I cheerfully dodged in favor of the higher priority of delighting my palate.

It did not take me long to settle on French cuisine as my favorite. Two restaurants in particular vied for my stomach's affection: the Givral and the Guillaume Tell. Both were equally formidable, but the Givral was too stuffy and too expensive. The Guillaume Tell was incredibly reasonable for its exotic menu, and the owner was incredibly friendly. She was a buxom woman in her fifties who looked more Scandinavian than French. She had flowing blond hair with the kind of black horn-rimmed glasses that were chic in Alfred Hitchcock movies. It was a discordant image, but she made up for it with a pleasing laugh and earnest enquiries of every customer as to how they liked the food. She either liked my answers in my very bad French, or my money, because my friends and I became favorite customers. It was at the Guillaume Tell that I gradually came to love frog legs and, much too quickly, Mateus Rosé. Someone else who was a favorite customer was the flamboyant Air Force General Nguyen Cao Ky, who had been President Thieu's predecessor in 1965–1966. Every time I saw him, I got the impression that he and his entourage were plotting yet another coup d'état.[6]

Most mysterious of all was Cholon, where 500,000 of the 800,000 Chinese in South Vietnam crammed into what geographically was the foot of Saigon.[7] More precisely, Cholon was the top of the foot. The Ben Nghe Canal flowed along the bottom of this foot (the direction of the flow was from the toes to the heel, as its sludge churned into the Saigon River at the heel). South of this canal was the huge Vietnamese slum. To the north of the Canal was District 5 and the southern half of District 10, the informal boundaries of this China Town. Cholon itself divided into an East and a West side. The East was the commercial district, where everyone worked. It had wide boulevards, spacious traffic circles, and large buildings for businesses and warehouses for these businesses. After the hours of the business day, the center of life in Cholon shifted to the West with its incoherent web of pencil-thin streets interrupted by tiny blocks that housed multiple families piled on top of each other in ramshackle tenements. The smell of food and the noise of people held the night at bay until exhaustion settled over the neighborhoods and put the town to sleep—except, of course, for the dogs that barked pointlessly through the night.

Like many cities of Southeast Asia, these Chinese citadels were beehives of many different layers of activity, so that one had the sense that somehow the very secrets of the universe were wrapped up in this global cobweb of Chinatowns. Every establishment that you visited was like the tip of an iceberg. You, as an outsider, would do your business in the front of the shop, but behind all these glass bead curtains in the back were layers of activities and networks of people that you were never allowed to see. If you ate in a restaurant, you never really knew where the food came from. If you bought anything from a store, it was seldom from the shelves, which were always incredibly bare. Rather, your host would tell you to wait. He would bark something to a minion lurking behind the beads who would scurry off somewhere and return with a suitcase full of the category of items you had asked for. Under these circumstances, it was more than mere courtesy that propelled the purchase. Any thoughts of refusal would conjure fears for one's life.

I would go to Cholon with Bill Gausmann. I felt safe with him as my very sophisticated guide. His interest was in cheap leather-bound volumes of classic books. Seeing all of the obscure works he was constantly able to procure from these stores, one day, as a dare to myself, I asked for the *Jewish Wars* by Josephus. With a glare of contempt, the proprietor clapped his hands, and half an hour later the volume appeared. It was not cheap, but I felt that I had purchased my own life with this sale. It has a proud place on my bookshelf to this day.

It was in Cholon where the wheels of Vietnam's agricultural economy were set in motion. The rice millers were all Chinese. Most of the trucking concerns were Chinese-owned, as was most of the riverine and sea commerce. The buying and selling of agricultural commodities was all done in Cholon. In the midst of this war, it was Cholon that enabled the somewhat normal functioning of agricultural production, marketing, and distribution. Because of this, into these behind-the-screens backrooms in Cholon came agents of French plantations and businesses, Viet Cong "tribute" collectors, and government agents of all stripes and a little off-purity, to do business with these Chinese concerns that were running a country behind the backs of the Americans and those Vietnamese officials who were clueless because they did not understand this multipartisan economy.

But the place Remus spent most every night was Soul City. I never quite knew where it was—Remus never invited me—but it was reported to be in the Kanh Hoi section of the waterfront by the fish markets south of Central Cholon. It was an area that had hosted Senegalese soldiers during the French Indochina War (1946–1954) and had many people of mixed African blood.[8] Remus was always happy when he came to work in the morning. He loved the food and the women from the night before. In this rear-echelon world, whites still counted the days to DEROS when they could return to the "world," a country they understood, where could quickly pick up their previous positions of place—and advantage. But Soul City was a special place where blacks ruled, and no one was going to bother them—as long as they stood by their day jobs in this white-appointed war. Those that didn't ended up in Long Binh Jail.[9] But for those who played along by day, the night was theirs.

Fascinated by all his stories and adventures, I began to pester Remus to take me to Soul City. He would laugh and always reply, "Man, L. T., I can't take you there. You got to be a brother. I mean you cats in the office is OK, but this place, this MACV, is no place to live, know what I'm saying. I mean we live downtown. I live downtown with the brothers." For some reason, I wouldn't quit. I was more than curious. I was envious. Finally, Remus put it to me, "Listen, L. T., if you want to go to Soul City, you gotta do the 'dap.'" The "dap" was an elaborate greeting ritual performed by black soldiers toward the end of the war. It consisted of multiple handshakes punctuated

by the smacking of fists, high fives, and improvised body-shaking
resembling a dance that could go on for minutes. It was an exclusive
"black thing" that not too subtly was a poke in the eye at hierarchical military courtesy—namely, the salute. It was a practice that grew
in REMF Land, but was rare among combat units in the Boonies.

"OK. Let's try," I said. I had never seen a white do the "dap,"
but I wanted to prove that I had "soul." So Remus and I started the
handshaking and the slapping. I even started rolling my hips, but
the effort was too deliberate, and I forgot about my hands—until
an unblocked swipe by Remus slapped my forehead. He burst out
laughing again, "L. T., see, you just too white!" I never made it to
Soul City, but later I did get to the coastal cities of Nha Trang and
Tuy Hoa. I had an escort.

As Remus got closer and closer to his DEROS, his chattering sub-
sided and sighs started to heave out of his chest. On one of his last
days, Remus came up to me and said, "L. T., I know this is a war and
all that, and we're supposed to want to go back to the world, but
Saigon is really a better world for me. Understand?" I understand
that wars are strange.

In this city of war, there was still a city of God much in evidence—
in all "His" manifestations. There was the An Quang Pagoda where
militant Buddhists withdrew from a world and war they disdained.
They wanted no part of foreign occupiers from the past nor to be
part of an atheistic future. They had their moment in the Buddhist
Crisis from 1963 to 1965, but that had turned sour. They were done
with politics. Other more everyday Buddhists trickled into the temples to pray. There also were Confucian shrines, but people visited
them more as museums than for prayer. The Roman Catholic presence was prominent in Saigon. President Thieu was a convert to
Catholicism. The tall Notre Dame Cathedral in John F. Kennedy
Square was just two blocks east of the Presidential Palace. Its lofty
spires glowered over the Babylon of Tu Do Street that ran straight
south from the church doors.

There were churches for the expatriate community as well. Near
the American embassy was the International Church, which was
quietly affiliated with the Southern Baptist Convention. Here, and
at the nearby Episcopal Church, American civilians put in a showy
Sunday morning presence. Somehow in this far-flung war, the Lord
used his servants to serve as beacons of His kingdom to me. There

had been my cousin Carol Dahl, and, as always, Bill Gausmann. Now in the spring of 1972, along came Alice. Of all things, Alice came to Saigon to get married.

Alice Tegenfeldt was a big sister of my best friend in India, John Tegenfeldt. Their parents were Baptist missionaries to Burma (Myanmar today), but they sent four of their children to Kodai School. When we were in boarding school, John and Alice were very close. Since John and I were roommates, Alice and I were related by osmosis. Alice came to Saigon to marry Norm Mundhenk, a missionary kid from India who went to that other unmentionable American missionary boarding school in India, Woodstock. Woodstock was in Mussoorie in far North India in the foothills of the Himalaya Mountains. Those of us from Kodai pretended that Woodstock did not exist; but, in truth, it was bigger than Kodai.

Norm was a linguist who worked for the United Bible Societies, while Alice worked for the Summer Institute of Linguistics, otherwise known as the Wycliffe Bible Translators. It was affiliated with the nondenominational, but fundamentalist, Christian Missionary Alliance. The mission of both organizations was to translate the Bible into every tongue on Earth. Mostly, this meant working with the dialects of remote tribal and mountain peoples. Few of these dialects had written scripts, so they would develop one so that a biblical manuscript could be translated into it. In these projects, they worked through native "informants" who would help catalog the words and ensure that the words used had meanings appropriate to local, tribal contexts.

The wedding was at the International Church, and I was thrilled to be invited and be a part of church society—at least for a moment. The wedding was a delicate cultural blend of American Protestantism and Vietnamese dress, food, and music. There was no alcohol served, and I had a fleeting thought of Jesus turning water into wine at the wedding at Cana, but this is not an appropriate Baptist thought. It was good to have someone from "home" as another anchor in this strange war wrapped up in this morally convoluted and enticing city.

Alice and Norm promptly took me under their wings, and I served as a reference for them as they set about adopting two girls from different orphanages. To Alice, I was still just "Lumpy," John's friend, so she had no question about including me in their world.

Theirs was the world of the Church Universal that went about the Lord's business of extending His kingdom to the uttermost parts of the Earth—in their case to the Montagnard tribespeople of the Central Highlands whose scores of dialects formed a last-ditch barrier to the light of the Gospel. They stayed in Saigon to keep their links to their world headquarters and its resources, even as they hired "informants" to move their operation into the Central Highlands. In all their planning, they never even mentioned there was a major war going on. The Lord's work would march on come famine, pestilence, or this little matter of an Easter Invasion. It blew my mind.

I soon learned that not everyone was so inclusive. After their wedding, they spent a lot of time in Nha Trang, a beautiful town along the central coast in MR 2, to be closer to their work. Some time after they had settled "up north," I received a call asking me to accompany them on a trip to Tuy Hoa, another coastal town about a two-hour drive up shore. It seems there was a Catholic orphanage there that had a Cambodian girl available for adoption. For this to happen quickly, they asked me to come along to serve as an official reference, and sign the papers as a sign of U.S. government approval. Since this passed as official business, my superiors gave me their blessing for the trip, as long as it was done in the day, and involved no night driving. This was my first trip out of Saigon. On it, I gained some perspective I had not intended.

Alice and Norm met me at the Nha Trang Airport in a blue minivan, and we started out on the famous Highway One (what Bernard Fall called *la rue sans joie,* the street without joy, in honor of all the fighting that took place along its Saigon to Hanoi length in the French Indochina War [1946–1954]) for the two-hour drive up the coast. There was a mountain range that interrupted the coastal plain in between the two towns, and we snaked up a steep grade to a high ridge. Once on this ridge, we looked down on waves of elephant grass chasing the breezes into the sea. The wind wrapped around us and made us hungry. What a picnic it was! As we were munching on some fruit, a woman in a very colorful *ao dai* emerged from a stand of trees to the side of the road—followed by two disheveled ARVN soldiers. There was not much mystery as to what had taken place; and, given the company I was with, it was an awkward moment.

Once at the bottom of the hill, Highway One stayed pretty close to the beach all the way to Tuy Hoa. The ocean along this coast was incredibly placid; the effect of turbulence instead came from the tumbling of the mountains into the sea. This tumbling produced a lot of streams squirting into the ocean, and the highway needed a lot of bridges and culverts to stay above all this rushing water. All of these little bridges struck me as tempting targets for saboteurs. Sure enough, at one of them we were slapped by the sight of two corpses lying to the side of the road. The ARVN soldiers hanging around told us they were VC shot the night before while planting explosives under the bridge. They were letting them lie there as a warning to anyone contemplating similar attacks. Despite the hundreds of deaths I had plotted in all the B-52 target cells, these were the only corpses I saw in my two tours of duty: these two dead guerrillas on a picnic to Tuy Hoa with a missionary couple on an idyllic journey to begin their family with the adoption of this little baby girl, who was of mixed Cambodian-GI descent. The shock of this discovery stunned us into an awkward silence as each one of us privately struggled to process this sudden encounter with death.

The image of this dead duo burned an indelible memory in my "mental album" of the war. Years later, I was reminded of these very dead guerrillas when I came across Philip Caputo's *Rumor of War*. He was a marine combat veteran who began his memoir with a quote from the Gospel of Matthew about the hope of salvation, even through a time of war. Midway through his combat tour, his faith was shattered by encountering mutilated bodies along the trail, just like I did:

> And the mutilation caused by modern weapons came as a shock. We were accustomed to seeing the human body intact; to us, a corpse was an elderly uncle lying in a coffin, his face powdered and his tie in place. Death admits to no degrees: the elderly uncle who dies decently in bed is no less dead than the enemy soldier whose head has been blown apart by a forty-five-caliber bullet. Nevertheless, we were sickened by the torn flesh, the viscera and splattered brains. The horror lay in the recognition that the body, which is supposed to be the earthly home of an immortal soul, which people spend so much time feeding, conditioning, and beautifying, is in fact only a fragile case stuffed full of disgusting matter. Even the brain, the wondrous, complex organ that generates the power of thought and speech, is nothing more than a lump of slick, gray tissue. The sight of mutilation did more than cause me physical revulsion;

it burst the religious myths of my Catholic childhood. I could not look at those men and still believe their souls had "passed on" to another existence, or that they had souls in the first place. I could not believe those bloody messes would be capable of resurrection on the Last Day. They did, in fact, seem "more" dead. *Massacred* or *annihilated* might better describe what had happened to them. Whatever, they were gone for good, body, mind, and spirit. They had seen their last day, and not much of it either. They died well before noon.[10]

Maybe, because the bodies of my two guerrillas were intact, my faith was not shattered, but I was deeply unsettled by what I saw. Their bodies were bloated and their skin had turned ashen, the same color of the dusty ground: "ashes to ashes, dust to dust," I thought. But the eyes spooked me. In all the movies with dying scenes that I had seen, dying people had the courtesy to close their eyes so that you were sure the curtain on this moment had fallen. These gentlemen still had their eyes open, and they were long since dead. They were like obsidian coals of brown rock: there was nothing living in their eyes. Like Caputo, I saw empty chaff, and these windows to the soul had turned into frozen stones.

Symbolically, standing with my "brother" Philip Caputo, we both had encountered death, the currency of war. In this currency, these corpses (intact and mutilated), as well as Philip and I as individual soldiers potentially, were its mere pennies. My mind quickly spun a crescendo to this currency. The value spiraled to dead platoons as its quarters; dead companies maybe a buck; dead battalions a fiver; dead brigades a twenty; and a dead division a golden fifty. And how much of this currency did my lumbering BUFFs carry in their bomb bays? However you wanted to measure this currency of death, its hierarchical values in war were not a good theology of the soul. With all the hierarchical relativity to this currency, for these two young men on the bridge the end of the universe to them that day was absolute. Indeed, with the planting of these corpses in my mind, bloody bayonets as death's more personal "medium of exchange" slithered back to haunt me. Even in the mind, War is Hell.

Back in the blue van on Highway One, we all tried to shake this off as we continued on our journey. We all agreed that what was unfolding all around us was simply incredible scenery. It reminded me of another Highway One, the one along the California coast—only the sea was calmer here and the beaches wider. When we got to Tuy Hoa itself, the beach was as spectacular as any beach I have ever seen. The sharp yellow of the sand contrasted sharply with the water, which was an incredible azure blue. The horizon across this deep blue was studded with islands near and far and in all sizes and shapes, each beckoning with its own exotic mysteries. If peace could just settle over this land, I was convinced Nha Trang and Tuy Hoa could outdraw the Riviera.

For now, however, we had this little reminder that there *was* a war going on. When we reached the humble dwelling of Alice's German co-worker, the woman became upset. And she was upset about me. She would not even let me in the house. To her, I was no missionary kid "Lumpy." I was an American soldier whose very presence was endangering her life. (Though I had just become a civilian, I still looked like a soldier.) She wanted us to move the van out of the neighborhood, and for me to stay in it. I knew this woman was right, and that I had allowed myself to live in a dream world. I felt like I had been returned to that coffeehouse in Philadelphia and was thrown out once again. I did, however, sign the papers that I needed to help move along the adoption process. I had served my purpose, and Norm and Alice thanked me.

The drive back, though, was strained. The fears of this woman had worked into our skins as the realities of the war settled uneasily between us. I began to realize that I had put them all at risk. Despite the unquestioned acceptance I received from Alice, I was on a military mission here in Vietnam, whomever else I might be, or had been, somewhere else. I could still be a Christian as a soldier, but I was not a neutral noncombatant. Whether I was a REMF or not, according to Just War Theory, and all conventions of war—just like the guerrillas, I was a legitimate military target. At any time, I could be a cipher of death. They needed to keep their distance. Indeed, shortly after our little picnic, Norm and Alice were transferred to Thailand after they had adopted two wonderful girls—and these two angels passed out of my life.

Back "home" in Saigon, I began to take more personal stock of the military situation. By midsummer of 1972, the Easter Invasion had quieted on all three fronts. Well afterward in Saigon, however, the siege of An Loc had spooked us with the specter of a breakout. Though there were two full ARVN divisions blocking this path, there was only a single U.S. battalion and a contingent of American helicopters protecting us in Saigon. The memory of the buckling of the ARVN Third Division in MR 1 was very fresh in our minds.

With the growing antiwar movement back home, those of us still in country in the fall felt vulnerable and expendable. With all the clamoring for "Peace Now" back home, if these defense lines were to break, none of us felt that any reinforcements would be sent to rescue us. The hippies, and their minions in Congress, wouldn't let them. We would be goners. It was a time well before "support the troops" slogans had even begun to dawn in the American imagination. In 1972, we were baby-killers and Fascist pigs—or so I was told in Philadelphia. I was coming to believe that we would become sacrifices on a geopolitical altar of American public indifference—and even outright hostility.

I became very serious about my running. If there were a Communist breakout, my life might depend on it. Quick feet might make all the difference as to who would make it to the fleeing helicopters. Memories of Philadelphia again flooded in with the ominous warning that no one from these coffeehouses would be throwing us any lifelines. These were the memories anyway that played through my mind when I was out on an abandoned horse-racing track, just outside my BOQ, running and running to get ready to jump on one of those helicopters.

It was also during these runs, contrarily enough, that I became committed to staying and really helping save the Vietnamese people from Communism. Like it was for Remus Lamb, the "world" had become a hostile place for me in my mind, overrun as it was by hippies. Secretly, like Remus, I didn't want to go back either. Maybe I would just miss those helicopters. I might not be fast enough anyway! This was no longer just a "tour of duty." In the terms of Thomas Fowler from Graham Greene's novel *The Quiet American,* I had become *engagé.*

In truth, it might have been more than this. Maybe I had gone over the edge and was succumbing to the fear of the foreign legionnaire, "a fear that we all had, that we would stop wanting to come home, that we would get really messed up in the head, and we couldn't go home anymore."[11]

Peace Talks, Christmas Bombing—and an Indian Interlude

By the end of the summer of 1972, the Communist invasion had lost its steam. Massive U.S. air strikes had finally dislodged the Communists from An Loc, but the Viet Cong made something of a capital of Loc Ninh, a district town further north along the Cambodian border. The Central Highlands around Kontum returned to government hands, as Communist forces throughout the region had pretty much collapsed. But the glory went to the front in MR 1, and to its charismatic general, Ngo Quang Truong.[1] The only provincial capital to fall in the invasion was Quang Tri, a town just south of the DMZ. As mentioned in chapter 4, on June 28, General Truong launched the arduous counteroffensive, Lam Son 72, to retake Quang Tri with ARVN's elite Airborne and Marine divisions. The "best of the best" of both Vietnams would face off in this showdown.

First honors on the Saigon side went to the Airborne's Second Brigade (the Fourth was defending Hue, and the other was in An Loc), though some marines and rangers supported the Airborne's advance along Highway One. At the same time, the Marines carried out an amphibious assault on the coast as an elaborate deception. Since the PAVN force had obtained advance warning of the plans for this assault, it was slow going. It took the Airborne a full week to traverse the 18 miles from its starting point at Cam Lo to the outskirts of Quang Tri. On July 4, however, the Airborne captured "the four forts," PAVN's outer defense perimeter. On July 8, the Airborne launched a two-week-long urban, house-to-house campaign that carried it to within 50 yards of the ancient citadel, PAVN's last redoubt.[2]

At this point, the Armed Forces High Command in Hanoi decided to make an all-out stand to hold onto this lone provincial trophy of the invasion. It reinforced the citadel with two more divisions: the 325C Division from the North Vietnamese panhandle and the 312th Division from Laos. With just one division left in Laos and a training division in the Red River Delta in North Vietnam itself, Hanoi,

literally, had nothing left. But the Airborne as well had reached its
limit, and could not breach the citadel. On July 27, General Truong
ordered the Marines to take over from the exhausted Airborne. The
month of August was a stalemate as Communist forces dug in and
ARVN Airborne and Marine units engaged in some unhelpful turf-
squabbling. As in the other two battlefronts, troops on both sides
hunkered down while ARVN forces were hit by barrages of 130 mm
artillery and PAVN troops were bombed by round-the-clock U.S. air
strikes.[3]

At this juncture, an American technological innovation tipped the
battlefield stalemate into an ARVN triumph. To the aerial armada
of Operation Linebacker, the U.S. Air Force introduced SMART
bombs, ordnance that was directed to their targets with pinpoint accuracy either by laser beams or TV signals. In early September, such
ordnance blasted a set of holes in the citadel walls. On September 9,
ARVN Marines poured through these holes, and on September 15,
after ferocious PAVN resistance, they ran up the GVN flag on the
central flagpole. In this ultimately futile stand, Hanoi sacrificed four
divisions, half of its unit losses in the entire invasion.[4] As Dale Andrade concluded, "With the recapture of Quang Tri City, the heart
went out of the North Vietnamese offensive."[5] In the decisive defeat
of PAVN forces at Quang Tri, the ARVN/MACV war handed President Nixon the ace he needed to finish his war.

With the invasion over, Henry Kissinger and his North Vietnamese counterpart Le Duc Tho could get down to the serious business
of negotiating an end to the war. In his war, it was Nixon's central
goal, in Operation Linebacker, to finally settle the war after three
years of inconclusive secret talks between these two principals. To
get Hanoi off the dime, in addition to these forceful battlefield measures, he realized he would need to make some concessions. The
one that came to mind was to back off from his earlier insistence
of a mutual withdrawal of external forces from South Vietnam
to accepting the PAVN troop presence in the South as an off-the-
negotiating-table fait accompli.[6] The North Vietnamese were steadfast in insisting that their forces were not "external." Leaving this
"semantic quibble" aside, Nixon reasoned that these forces had been
beaten anyway and could now be contained by ARVN. As an offset
for this concession, Nixon thought in terms of some residual U.S.
force in South Vietnam; and, as a further deterrent, a guarantee to

120 the South Vietnamese of U.S. military retaliation to any major military moves on the part of the North Vietnamese.

On the other side of the coin, Hanoi also made its key concession. Hanoi clearly needed a breather after the devastating losses it had suffered in the invasion and the symbolic loss of Quang Tri. Throughout these intractable three years, Le Duc Tho was insistent that President Thieu would have to be removed from power, whatever the other modalities of a political agreement. In exchange for getting the Americans out, Hanoi now agreed to drop the condition of Thieu's departure. In the merging of these two wars, a negotiated settlement nearly came to fruition. On October 26, less than a week from the presidential election, Henry Kissinger called a press conference to declare, "Peace is at hand."

The essentials of the deal were as follows. On the military side, PAVN forces and equipment could remain in the South at the same levels as when a ceasefire in place occurred at the signing of the agreement. These forces and equipment could be replenished only at six designated replacement points that would be monitored by an International Commission of Control and Supervision (ICCS) consisting of a small military force drawn from Hungary, Poland, Indonesia, and Thailand.[7] For the United States, all but fifty U.S. military personnel would be withdrawn from South Vietnam in a sixty-day period following the signing of the agreement in return for a complete listing—and exchange—of prisoners from all sides. A Joint Military Commission (JMC), composed of military representatives from the United States, South Vietnam, North Vietnam, and the Provisional Revolutionary Government (the political title of the Viet Cong from South Vietnam), would oversee these withdrawals and exchanges. Hanoi also agreed to work with the United States in accounting for all MIAs in a Joint Casualty Resolution Center under this new JMC. Finally, the shadow of an American residual force would be preserved in the creation of a civilian Defense Attaché Office.[8]

Politically, despite the concession of leaving Thieu in office, the agreement called for the creation of a National Council of Reconciliation and Concord (NCRC) within a year of the signing of the agreement to form a national unity government. It was to be composed of one-third of the delegates selected by the Thieu regime, another third named by the Provisional Revolutionary Government, and the final list jointly chosen by the two sides.[9] As a deal sweetener, Nixon offered Hanoi $2 billion in reconstruction assistance, as long as the provisions of the agreement were honored. Nixon thought of this as a magnanimous mini–Marshall Plan. After it became public, Hanoi insisted that this measure constituted reparations for all of Washington's "war crimes."

But demons lurked in the shadows of Kissinger's pronouncement, and the deal soon unraveled. The first demon was South Vietnamese President Nguyen Van Thieu. He had not been a party to these negotiations; and, when briefed shortly after Kissinger's announcement, he balked at the provisions, loudly. Nixon quickly deployed a lavish carrot and a very blunt stick. Throughout the month of November, the Pentagon rushed $2 billion worth of military equipment to Saigon in an operation called Enhance Plus, an addition to an ongoing Enhance program lasting from May to October that had been underway to replace ARVN losses from the Easter Invasion.[10] To all appearances, Saigon gained a powerful inventory. Enhance Plus included 266 combat aircraft, 277 helicopters, 197 armored vehicles, 1,726 trucks, and 66 artillery pieces.[11]

By the end of 1972, the South Vietnamese Air Force (VNAF) had over 2,000 airframes, making it, on paper, the fourth largest air force in the world. The problem was VNAF lacked trained pilots to fly their planes or a system of maintenance to keep them in the air.[12] Indeed, earlier in the summer, in order to accommodate the huge influx of equipment in Enhance, and later Enhance Plus, a Department of Defense study proposed a U.S. military advisory presence of 2,500 advisers after any peace agreement in order to ensure an adequate level of training and maintenance for the military deployment of the equipment. The proposal called for 20 advisers per ARVN division and 50 each for the Navy and Air Force (for a total of 380 tactical advisers), 500 staff advisers for each of the Military Region Headquarters, 220 advisers for the South Vietnamese Joint General Staff, and 1,600 advisers for nation-building/rural security activities performed by CORDS.[13] Essentially, this proposal would have allowed for some continuation of the ARVN/MACV war by enabling the real use of this equipment. In jettisoning this proposal, Nixon, in effect, abandoned the idea of a residual force. The civilian Defense Attaché Office of bureaucrats that eventually became the institutional expression of this idea was no substitute. As a result, the vast majority of this equipment remained in storage, unused. In this supposed largesse, the president in reality decoupled his war from the Vietnamization "one war" of ARVN/MACV.

For Nixon in his war, the purpose of Enhance Plus was to serve as the diplomatic leverage to get Thieu to go along with the agreement. Despite these waves of supplies coming in, Thieu remained annoyingly recalcitrant. On December 17, Nixon sent his personal emissary Alexander Haig to deliver a letter conveying to President Thieu his blunt stick, which was rendered starkly clear in the last paragraph:

> I have asked General Haig to obtain your answer to this absolutely final offer on my part for us to work together in seeking a settlement along the lines I have approved or to go our separate ways. Let me emphasize in conclusion that General Haig is not coming to Saigon for the purpose of negotiating with you. The time has come for us to present a united front in negotiating with our enemies, and you must decide now whether you desire to continue to work together or whether you want me to seek a settlement with the enemy which serves U.S. interests alone.[14]

At this eleventh hour, Thieu fell in line.

The second demon was time. Despite Nixon's landslide victory at the polls in his presidential election in November—he defeated George McGovern by 61 percent to 38 percent of the popular vote—the Democrats made gains in the congressional elections. Thus, even in this victory, both Nixon and Kissinger felt constrained by a deadline of antiwar congressional votes that were sure to come when the new Congress convened in January.[15] This "press of time" factor pushed such an urgency to the negotiations that even Kissinger's staff felt that their concerns, as well as critical details, were just being brushed aside.[16]

Kissinger compounded this by an almost outright refusal to involve local American officials in Vietnam in working out the implementing details on the ground. This led to such glaring mistakes as the failure to include withdrawal dates in the agreement for North Vietnamese forces in Cambodia and Laos.[17] What troubled both Kissinger's staff and these local American officials was the lack of such "details" as clear provisions for inspection and enforcement of the agreement. For example, though the proposed agreement called for six designated "replacement sites" so that Communist troop and supply movements could be monitored, Hanoi refused to agree to any specific sites, or else proposed locations so remote that they were inaccessible to any transport. Further, regarding enforcement, Hanoi insisted that both the ICCS and the JMC operate under a unanimity principle, essentially ensuring their inability to act.[18] As a result, in Frank Snepp's words, "the peace of Paris was no peace at all."[19] Indeed, the American mission in Saigon felt just as imposed upon in this agreement as did President Thieu.

The final demon to this unraveling was Hanoi, whose recalcitrance surfaced at the appearance of these other demons. When Thieu publicly opposed the agreement in late October, and when Washington tried to placate him with Enhance Plus, Hanoi called foul. Once again, it balked at Thieu's continuance in office. In addition, it quibbled at length with the inspection and compliance provisions. Privately, it demanded that Nixon's offer of reconstruction assistance be called "reparations."

On December 15, Nixon lost his patience and gave Hanoi seventy-two hours to return to the negotiations or face the consequences. With Hanoi's stony silence as a response, Nixon unleashed the pièce de résistance of his war, the twelve-day bombing campaign that he called Linebacker II. Because it occurred over Christmas—from December 18 to 29 (with a single-day halt for Christmas itself)—it quickly earned the title "the Christmas Bombing." Over these eleven days, nearly 2,000 sorties (over 700 by B-52s) were flown over North Vietnam dropping 20,000 tons of ordnance.[20] Although 500,000 tons of bombs were dropped in Linebacker I over five months, this latter campaign was much more concentrated in time and space with the majority of targets hitting the previously unstruck Hanoi and Haiphong areas, the nerve centers of North Vietnam.[21] Rather than hitting the vast logistical supply network to the South as in the first campaign, the Christmas Bombing lashed out at the vitals of the Hanoi government, the Armed Forces High Command in Hanoi, and a systematic devastation of the electrical power grid that brought what industry there was to a standstill. Indeed, Hanoi secretly admitted these losses were crippling.[22] Civilian casualties, however, were remarkably light. Hanoi itself acknowledged only 2,000 killed.[23]

Against these aerial invaders, the North Vietnamese launched 1,242 SAM-II missiles.[24] American losses were fifteen B-52s and thirteen other aircraft shot down or otherwise destroyed. A shortage of missiles, however, plagued the DRV after the very first night. By the third day, the batteries protecting Hanoi City were out of missiles. After Christmas Day, the game was up: the DRV could no longer assemble any more missiles for deployment, and the skies over North Vietnam emptied out of missiles two days later.[25] On December 26, Hanoi agreed to resume "technical talks" with Washington. Nixon, in return, ended the bombing on December 29. The final "full talks" preceding the agreement were held in Paris from January 8 to January 13. When the dust had settled, the two sides essentially returned to the terms agreed upon the previous October.[26] All this led the British counterinsurgency expert Kenneth Thompson to exclaim to Nixon, "You had won the war. It was over!"[27]

When sheer destruction, however, is not the goal in a war, but some political result instead, the question of winning depends on achieving it. In terms of destruction, Hanoi was nearly as helpless in January 1973 as Berlin and Tokyo were in 1945. The differences were that the allies demanded unconditional surrender, and neither capital had anywhere to turn for further support. Their economies, in fact, were shattered. Although Hanoi's capacity to defend itself had nearly vanished and most of its economy was in ruins, in 1973 the goal of the United States was not the destruction or unconditional surrender of Hanoi, just that it let South Vietnam alone. This gave the DRV ample room to equivocate. In the meantime, it had two international patrons in Moscow and Beijing, who remained steadfast and quickly made good on Hanoi's losses. Not so Saigon. Enhance Plus proved to be a parting shot. American will, even before Watergate, was spent.

This was something that Nixon and Kissinger understood better in their war than the American mandarins in Saigon who had been running the ARVN/MACV war of Vietnamization: men such as General Abrams, Ambassador Bunker, and CIA Station Chief William Colby.[28] Indeed, as a harbinger of this collapse, Nixon's job approval ratings plummeted eleven points after the Christmas Bombing.[29] The tragedy, of course, was that the will of South Vietnam depended on the will of its American patrons, and this umbilical cord, decoupled in the tensions leading up to the Paris Peace Agreement, was subsequently sawed off with each decreasing aid appropriation from Washington. Thus, the MACV Camelot fell not to the internal divisions of a Lancelot, Guinevere, or Mordred of the Table Round itself, but to the very ground on which the Table Round of the Tank stood—crumbling under the collapsing will of the American people.

On January 27, 1973, delegates from the United States, the Government of Vietnam, the Democratic Republic of Vietnam, and the Provisional Revolutionary Government gathered in Paris to sign the Peace Agreement that called for a ceasefire in place and a signed commitment to resolve their political differences peacefully. It was signed with unanimous insincerity. With the Americans gone, Hanoi had no intention of honoring the ceasefire. Saigon would do nothing to implement the political provisions. Washington, President Nixon anyway, really wanted to extricate itself from Vietnam so it could move on to larger Cold War pursuits. And the PRG would not survive as a political entity any longer than Saigon did.

In fairness, it should be noted that President Nixon had written several letters of assurance to President Thieu of a decisive U.S. military response in the event of major violations of the agreement by Hanoi. For example, on January 5, 1973, he wrote: "But far more important than what we say in the agreement on this issue is what we do in the event the enemy renews its aggression. You have my absolute assurance that if Hanoi fails to abide by any terms of this agreement it is my intention to take swift and severe retaliatory action."[30] Nixon was not bashful about reiterating these assurances in public. In a press conference in January, he made the same commitment to South Vietnam that he wrote in the above letter.[31] Thus, both the U.S. Congress and the American public were fully aware of these promises.

For us in REMF Land, all of this had taken place way over our heads. Like Linebacker I, the Christmas Bombing was entirely orchestrated from CINCPAC, SAC Headquarters, and Washington. Indeed, after the November elections, day-to-day work at MACV Headquarters slowed to a turtle's crawl as everyone was just marking time waiting for all these stratospheric machinations to trickle down to us bureaucratic mortals below. After working twelve hours a day, and nearly seven days a week, suddenly we had time on our hands: time to think and take stock of our situations.

In my case, I took this time to go to India. Except for the first few days, I missed the entire Christmas Bombing episode. As luck would have it, I had applied for a two-week home leave over Christmas to visit my parents. What had caused my bosses consternation was that my request was to go to India of all places—which was not an approved R and R site. Who knows what compromising "Third World messes" I might get caught up in, they said to me, worriedly. But I got my green light before all the bombs started raining down, and off I flew. My trip to India, away from the swirling bureaucratic chaos of a MACV whose future was disintegrating, was a journey to never-never land.

I was met by my Dad at the airport of Madras (now Chennai) with a gift of Glaxo Biscuits (something like graham crackers), a luxury I had forgotten to miss. We boarded the train for an overnight trip north to Guntur in my native Andhra Pradesh. This was a trip I had taken many times as a boy, and the rhythm of the clickety-clacking tracks kindled memories of my experiences of "home." Mom was waiting in the bungalow in Guntur the next morning with a delightful Scandinavian/Indian breakfast of poached eggs and *idlees* (rice cakes) served by the cook, while the gardener watered all the plants on the verandah. This was the "normal" life I had grown up in, but now I felt out of place.

We spent a lot of time catching up on family news amid endless cups of tea and all of Mom's cookies, date bars, and assortments of her other exotic treats. But I also thought about, and talked through, my options in Saigon. My parents could not believe that a pending Peace Agreement would bring all of us home. That reality began to sink in for me as well. But to my parents' surprise, and even horror, I began to express an ever-increasing reluctance to leave Saigon. Several reasons bubbled up whenever I came too close to anticipating a return to the States and to graduate school.

Whatever may have been going on in domestic politics in the United States, I was still under the spell of my hero, General Abrams, and his vision of "one war" enabling the South Vietnamese to hold back the North Vietnamese tide. It would just take a core of American knights to act as a reassuring American presence to steady the Southern will. Added to this political commitment was the frustrating fact that I still had not had any direct, professional contact with the Vietnamese, despite my language training. If I stayed on, I could complete my tour with fulfilling Vietnamese experience.

Furthermore, over the last several months, a sense of alienation

grew in me over the antiwar direction of American politics. The
stridency of the war protests unnerved me, and I seriously began to think of the antiwar movement as treasonous, as giving
"aid and comfort" to our enemies, which Article III, Section 3 of
the Constitution defines as treason. In my more sober moments, I
did understand that war protesters were also exercising their First
Amendment rights to their freedom of speech and assembly. What
the protesters did not fully realize, I felt, was that their acts of free
expression played to two audiences. The first was the immediate one
at home where the histrionics of protest were readily amplified by
a sensation-abetting media. This amplification, however, resonated
loudly in the second audience of the war theater itself; and to those
of us who were trying to make a go of this war, this message did
seem treasonous. In any case, if this is what had become normal in
America, it was not a home to which I wished to return.

Finally, having all these thoughts and conversations "offstage" in
India reminded me of my own reality. I was an expatriate American, not a homegrown one, and I really was more comfortable as an
American living on the outside—even in Saigon. This expatriate reality was fine with Mom and Dad, but not the craziness of returning
to Saigon. They both felt I had more than done my duty. Sometimes
I thought they were looking at me as if I were a walking corpse.
Because of this undercurrent, even though we relished every moment of our time together, tears welled beneath the surface. When
you know you have to go back, taking time out from a war, even a
REMF war, makes it hard to keep a grip on who you are and what
you have become.

But their expatriate world in India was unraveling as well. From
the "white missionaries with black heart" days of the early 1960s,
the Indianization of the Andhra Evangelical Lutheran Church was
proceeding apace with the Vietnamization of the war in Vietnam.
(In this process, the church in India survived, and thrived, as the pull-
out of missionaries extended to 1984, while financial support from
New York continued.) Just before I returned to Saigon, I was invited
to join my parents for the annual missionary retreat at Vodarevu, a
small beach "resort" of four scattered cinderblock buildings nestled
in a grove of casuarina trees. As a boy, I remembered these retreats
as resplendent knightly tourneys. Over a hundred missionaries with
scampering kids and dutiful servants in tow would set up camp,

pitching their touring tents into a bustling campopolis to welcome in the new year. These tents were issued to the evangelical missionaries for their circuit tours of the villages surrounding their mission stations to proclaim the Gospel with flannel graph-puppet shows and 16 mm movies.

Pitched together at Vodarevu, this tent city made for a dazzling display to the local fishermen of Westerners at play. During the day, in fact, the grownups would retire to quiet glens with podiums and lawn chairs for thought-provoking seminars on "Karl Barth and the Evangelical Movement" or "The God Is Dead Movement in India," interspersed with raucous business meetings. For us kids, thus neglected, retreats were utter mayhem. We would chase through the camp, charge up sand dunes, and unsuccessfully try to climb up palm trees—all to the ineffectual protests of the servants. More daring yet was to hide behind pine-leaved sand dunes in the woods and spy on these adult conclaves. At night, after grand suppers, when we weren't listening to thrilling stories about the nearby "Marco Polo place," we were catching hell from our parents for something we had done during the day.[32] Invariably, one of us would either break something or get hurt. One year, I ran through a thinly submerged pile of hot coals in the sand, and that was the end of that retreat for me.

This year, there were no tents, and no kids—just me. Instead, there was a small huddle of missionaries who just gathered to support each other. They hardly bothered to have much of a program. As a result, I became much more the object of attention than I wanted. These missionaries had all been my "aunts" and "uncles" growing up, so it was heartwarming to be back in their company, but not when they were feeling so sorry for me, and so publicly praying for me and for my poor suffering parents. I was not overjoyed by my life in Saigon, but I was not wallowing in any misery worthy of such plaintive pleas for divine mercy.

I had to return to Saigon from Hyderabad, one of India's largest cities, which was about a half-day's drive to the west from Guntur. In January 1973, Andhra Pradesh was in the throes of the Telengana Crisis. The Telengana Movement was an attempt by the more rural, interior half of the province to separate from the more prosperous coastal half against the determined wishes of the Central Government in New Delhi. Hyderabad was in this interior, and all roads

leading into this capital city had been taken over by "students." They
set up checkpoints about every ten miles, and demanded money for
their cause before they let any vehicles through. Dad was armored
by the centuries-long Western domination of the Orient, and the
automatic confidence that came with it, that our white skins alone
would get us through without having to pay anything. What I saw
in the eyes of these "students" were flickers of a desire to visit all the
sins of the British Empire on our white skins. I convinced my Dad
to just pay the money. At each stop, the amount of money escalated,
and these little flickers of hate turned into glares that seemed on the
verge of explosive action. The highway had turned into a crescendo
of anarchy.

Once we got to the Hyderabad airport (very much impoverished), I told my parents to leave the car behind and go home by
train, since there were paramilitary police guarding the lines. Once
on the plane, I looked forward to the safety of Saigon. At least in a
war, where and when there isn't any fighting, someone is in charge
of these middle places and in-between moments. People count on
this. Under anarchy, no one can count on anything, and that truly is
Hell. War is only Hell part-time.

In this already surreal war that now was turning into ethereal
mists, I had one last job in my military career when I returned to
Saigon in early January. On Tan Son Nhut Air Base, there was an
Army installation called Camp Davis. It was called upon to house
the North Vietnamese and Viet Cong delegation for the Joint Military Commission that was to carry out discussions for the military
implementation of the agreement in Saigon. Still in uniform, I interviewed for the position of an interpreter for these talks. My Vietnamese was not deemed good enough, but I was given the duty of
an escort officer for these local enemy officials at Camp Davis.

I arrived on the scene to find an extremely tense situation. The
other Americans working there were enlisted ranks, whose command of Vietnamese was much better than mine. The North Vietnamese officials, all officers of at least major and lieutenant colonel
rank, were insulted by such a low level in rank of host support. But
more than insulted, they were clearly scared out of their wits by an
ARVN MP detachment, whom I overheard loudly talking of plans
to hose the place down as soon as the Americans weren't looking.
The American enlisted personnel, who had also heard this, made a

point to me of being sympathetic with these ARVN intentions. I decided I needed to park myself there for a good while as a barrier.

There was a North Vietnamese major who had been keenly taking all this in. He made a point of befriending me. In civilian life, he told me, he was a history professor; and, as an officer, he knew I was an intellectual. In spite of myself, I was flattered, and he proceeded to deliver quite a seminar on Vietnamese history—which I actually found fascinating. I was particularly impressed that I could mostly understand him. Also, there was a warm, empathetic quality to him that threw a wrench into my image of the enemy. I found myself liking him. When I later delved into the famous Vietnamese literary classic, *The Story of Kieu*, he came to mind as a symbol of what the Vietnamese like to call "a man with heart." It was a bizarre couple of days. In a war, every once in awhile, it is nice to report that nothing happened.[33]

Strange to say, in my encounter with this good major, I made my decision: I was staying. MACV might be crumbling all around me, but this lonely Sir Galahad was going to truck on. There was a real "world" here; and, like Remus Lamb, I felt more at home in the tawdry Camelot of Saigon than I did in any contemplated return to the land of Philadelphia.

I Spy 1: My Time as an Intelligence Liaison Officer

When the Paris Peace Agreement was signed on January 27, 1973, all American uniformed personnel (save for a skeleton staff of fifty supervising officers at a newly created Defense Attaché Office [DAO] in the U.S. embassy) had sixty days to leave the country. As the remaining few thousand troops boarded their flights out of the country, a new wave of Department of Defense civilians—1,200 of them—streamed into Saigon to flesh out this new office. In fact, it was just the same MACV Headquarters building. There were another 5,000 Americans in-country working as contactors for the DAO, half of them in Saigon. All told, there were 9,000 official Americans left in Vietnam after the sixty-day withdrawal period of remaining American military personnel. The MACV itself officially stood down on March 28, but many of its activities were just displaced to a remote air base in Northeast Thailand, Nakhon Phanom, which housed a U.S. Support Activities Group (USSAG). It was, in the words of Lewis Sorley, a "MACV in exile."[1]

The Defense Attaché Office was activated on January 28, 1973. It was headed by Major General John E. Murray, a logistician. Though officially an entity of the U.S. embassy, it reported to USSAG in Nakhon Phanom, Thailand. It was always called NKP. There were five divisions to the DAO. Three of them managed the military assistance programs to the RVNAF (Republic of Vietnam Armed Forces); one was for Communications and Electronics. By far the largest division was Operations and Plans, which included the Intelligence Branch on one side and a branch that ran the training programs for maintaining the American military equipment on the other. Most of the contractors worked in this program.[2]

One function that was absolutely verboten for the DAO was the provision of military advisers. It was not to be a substitute for the network of military advisers proposed by the Department of Defense the previous fall. In fact, the DAO could not even keep up with the maintenance part. One indicator remains stuck in my mind, partly because helicopters were the linchpin of the American way of war in which the Vietnamese were trained. The helicopter, in truth, was a mechanical nightmare. American units considered themselves lucky if three-fourths of them were operational at any one time. After the ceasefire, under this new arrangement, this figure of operationally ready helicopters plummeted to 20 percent.

The Intelligence Branch was headed by Colonel William E. Le Gro, an infantry officer. Most of the people who came into this branch were from the Defense Intelligence Agency (DIA), often called the CIA of the Department of Defense. This branch was further divided into a traditional Office of Analysis and Estimates (continuing what was done in the Tank) and an Office of Intelligence Liaison. I viewed the signing of the Paris Peace Agreement with skepticism, as did many of my colleagues. Nevertheless, since we were already in-country and established in the bureaucratic ways of this American "imperium," we were easy targets for those managers and recruiters trying to fashion an organization that had to effect a handover of the MACV war to the Vietnamese Armed Forces. Two of my brother MACV first lieutenants were willingly pulled in with me. John Berwind had come to the Tank about the same time that I had, and he was my longtime dinner and drinking buddy. He was an excellent analyst, and enjoyed what he was doing. Bill Laurie had been in the Delta but had been transferred to the Tank as an analyst a few months earlier. He was absolutely fluent in Vietnamese, had a serious Vietnamese girlfriend, and was too committed to leave. They wanted to stay working in whatever remained of the Tank. I wanted out of the Tank, and in with the Vietnamese. I was recruited by a Colonel Walker on February 6 to be an intelligence liaison officer. Finally, I was given a chance to work with the Vietnamese—and help them with their cause. My two friends got hired by this reconstituted analytical shop, and our friendship continued into this new phase.

While most of this civilian traffic was to and from Washington, D.C., there were other waves of U.S. government employees from Thailand, Japan, Taiwan, and even Europe. My two immediate bosses in the Liaison Office were longtime government civilians: Lee Washer came in from the U.S. embassy in Thailand and Tony Suarez, after serving in the Army in Vietnam, had been working for years with the National Police in Saigon. He had just married the daughter of one of the senior police commanders. Included in this wave of DIA civilians from Washington, D.C., were a goodly number of women, most of them young. For the first time, there were a lot of American women in Saigon. It changed the city in a lot of ways. Whether favorable or not, all Vietnamese gained a more complete view of American society; and, for Vietnamese men, these women provided a welcome deflection of American males away from their own women.

The new intelligence system desperately tried to keep the same flow of information that the full-scale U.S. military had generated so that contingency plans could still be honed and updated in case any of them became necessary. As an intelligence liaison officer, I found myself doing a circuit of "liaising" with three different Vietnamese intelligence organizations. I was supposed to have an office and a Vietnamese staff in each installation. At either the beginning or the end of each day, I was supposed to report in to my American Branch Office and get directions from my superiors. Here I theoretically also had an office and a secretary. Since I was rarely around my American surroundings for very long, I found that no one ever did much about an alleged office for me, and the secretary assigned to me always seemed to be "otherwise engaged." In terms of the new demographics to our office culture, and all the "politics" that swirled around, it was just as well that I spent 90 percent of my day in the "field" with Vietnamese counterparts.

During the war, each of these Vietnamese offices had its own individual U.S. liaison officer, all with field rank (major, lieutenant-colonel, or colonel). I had "retired" in-country as a first lieutenant in early February, but when I was introduced to my offices the following week, my Vietnamese counterparts were told that I had been a major. The main office to which I was assigned was the Intelligence Headquarters of the ARVN Joint General Staff. Colonel Hoang Ngoc Lung commanded all of Vietnamese military intelligence, and he was an extremely competent officer, who clearly had the respect of everyone in his command. The second place I related to was CICV (the Combined Intelligence Center, Vietnam). This was an entity created by the Americans primarily for sharing intelligence with the Vietnamese. Its commander was a Vietnamese Army lieutenant colonel named Vu Van Nho. He was probably the most intelligent man I met in Vietnam, and we had very lengthy, and sometimes surprisingly intimate, talks. I was a guest in the homes of both these senior officers, and such invitations to foreigners were very rare. The third office to which I was assigned was the CDEC (Combined Document Exploitation Center). This center was a huge repository for captured enemy documents.

At the General Staff Headquarters, I had an extremely spacious office with a Vietnamese secretary and an elderly gentleman who served as a translator of official documents. I was also assigned a jeep and a Vietnamese driver. The official part of this responsibility was to convey intelligence requests between the two commands: from my American bosses to the Vietnamese, and from Col. Lung to the Americans. Unofficially, I found myself fending off repeated requests from Vietnamese officers for goods from the American PX. In exasperation, I began to minimize my time at this headquarters.

It was at CICV where I came to spend most of my day. I had a nice office right next to the commander, Lt. Col. Nho, and the two of us were in each other's offices constantly. I had two secretaries in a reception area who were in a permanent feud that I studiously ignored. This center was producing a lot of intelligence reports, something the Americans were no longer doing, and the bulk of the American intelligence requests ended up coming to CICV. As a result, I found myself in the constant business of chasing away from my building CIA people, who were attempting to buy intelligence documents that I was still trying to get for free. This got so nasty that one CIA type actually threatened me with a gun. My Vietnamese counterpart was so incensed at this incident that from then on, all Americans entering the building had to be personally cleared by me. I liked this.

I ended up not doing much with CDEC, which was a pity. This installation was an incredible resource. There were something like a hundred translators in this building, but they only succeeded in translating about 10 percent of the materials that arrived from the field. Even so, some excellent document series were published, and I ended up using one unclassified set, the *Vietnam Documents and Research Notes,* for my Ph.D. dissertation a few years later. I had an office here, but really never used it. But I did manage the payroll, and I also got to the bottom of a recruiting "scandal" since I had to approve all hires. The United States was still funding all these organizations, which, of course, was the leverage behind my various requests. What we Americans lack in finesse, we are usually able to make up for in dollars.

In truth, I am not so sure that I was getting to the bottom of a scandal as much as I was interfering with standard hiring practices. CDEC was somewhat unique in that it was run by a Vietnamese civilian. This is probably why my friend Bill Gausmann had ready access to this outfit even though he was frozen out of all military installations. In any case, this gentleman ran a very tight ship, and I sensed the office staff was intimidated in his presence. Soon after I assumed responsibility, I was called upon to approve a slate of hires from a stack of job applications. It was Lt. Col. Nho, the head of CICV, who suggested that I might take the time to look at all the applications. This little comment reminded me of the practice I had heard of whereby applicants paid an extra fee to the Vietnamese office manager for putting their file on the top of the pile. Sure enough, when I showed up to sign the employment forms, the man told me I only needed to look at the top ten. To his immense consternation, I asked for a cup of coffee and said I would sit down and look at all the files. I told him I was new and wanted to see what the talent pool was like, even though I was sure his evaluations were thorough. As I sifted through the files, some were of very young people with rather minimal educational levels. Certainly they were qualified, but I sensed there were connections that were more primary in gaining them their positions in this pile. At the bottom of the pile, I found several Chinese with college degrees, and beyond, as well as direct experience with translation work. I will have to say here that in all of the Vietnamese offices that I worked, I found that discrimination against Chinese was systemic.

Having found this out, I realized I needed to tread carefully. First of all, CDEC was a highly valued entity in the ARVN intelligence system. It was also invaluable to the U.S. intelligence community—and Bill worked closely with the director in his various projects. So this man was capable, and maybe I was just being used to even some old scores. I decided to split the difference. I signed off on his first five, but then told him I thought for greater continuity we should hire the second set of five who could bring more experience to the table. I apologized for adding this new criterion without consulting him beforehand so that he would have been able to order the files accordingly. This allowed him to save face, though it was not lost on

136   him that among those in the second set were some Chinese. Naturally, this caused quite a ripple in the building. A bit later, Bill told me he had heard that I had done some of my own hiring at CDEC. With a Cheshire Cat smile, he just said, "Timothy. Timothy. Timothy." After this, I basically left CDEC alone.

I was also officially assigned as liaison officer to CMIC (the Combined Military Interrogation Center). In fact, I only got out there once. Eventually, another liaison officer was hired for this installation as well as to another strictly Vietnamese Army intelligence "action" outfit, Unit 101, which this other liaison officer also took on. I wasn't too keen on working with these particular agencies anyway.[3]

One additional organization came into my life and began to assume a greater part of my job. I got a call one day in March from my old superior in the Arc Light Office. He was an Air Force officer from Louisiana and always had me make him chicory coffee in the "good old days" when MACV Headquarters was in Saigon. He told me he was calling from MACV Headquarters in Nakhon Phanom—which he promptly amended to say USSAG—and asked me if I wouldn't mind keeping in touch with all the Vietnamese intelligence offices and their American liaison officers in the four military regions that used to help generate B-52 targets for us. He also wanted me to be on hand to transmit targeting information from them, just in case these Vietnamese folk might want to send in B-52 target nominations. He also insisted that because of the Paris Peace Agreement, I should not let anyone in the embassy know about this. Translation: my local superiors who were now technically embassy employees were no longer strictly in the military chain-of-command and were required, at least technically, to work through embassy channels of authority. Through subsequent rather oblique conversations, it became clear to me that these superiors were well aware of these additional responsibilities of mine anyway.

Running through a typical, or composite, day can add some meat to the bones of these responsibilities. My day began with the American phase. I would come to MACV, now the DAO, and eat my breakfast—something I had been doing for all my military tour. To the Vietnamese women in the cafeteria line, I was a familiar face. As people shuffled through the line, the women were all smiles, giggly, and very chatty. Sure that none of their American patrons knew any Vietnamese, they were free with scurrilous observations, always said with a sweet voice and charming smile. Early on, one of them compared my proboscis to another part of my anatomy in Vietnamese in this sweet voice accompanied by a charming smile, and she then asked me in English how I wanted my eggs cooked. Summoning my best deadpan expression, I replied, in Vietnamese, that I wanted them scrambled just like her hair. The shock was volcanic as her face erupted into a crimson blush that rippled down the entire line.

From then on, I was everyone's friend, and I was beset by constant conversation every time I went through the line. The one who started it all was petite and pretty. She complained about the poor pay, and how she could make much more money in the bars, if she were not such a devout Catholic. As the months wore on, I suspected that her faith might be fraying. One day, she wasn't in the line. When I asked where she was, one of the women looked at me, "Trung-uy, don't ask. You know where she is!"[4] In contrast, the woman who worked beside her was an "older" woman, in her thirties, whose face was pockmarked with small pox scars (like a number of Vietnamese). She reassured me, "Don't worry, Trung-uy. I won't leave the line. I can feed my whole family on what they give me here."

After breakfast, I would head to my American office, which was pretty familiar territory to me. The Office of Intelligence Liaison and the Office of Intelligence Analysis and Estimates occupied much of what had been the famous Tank under MACV. Colonel Walker headed the section that made up these two offices, and he had two civilian subordinates reporting to him who headed the Office of Intelligence Liaison, the same Ray Suarez and Lee Washer mentioned above. A couple of my military friends who stayed on with me worked in the Intelligence Analysis and Estimates Office, and we would continue with our daily bantering and often go out to dinner together. Their civilian boss, from the Defense Intelligence Agency, was someone from Philadelphia. My bosses were Ray and Lee. They were frequently "in the field" somewhere in Saigon, so I seldom saw them. When they were in, they usually had something for me to do. Colonel Walker was mostly busy with the internal bureaucracy of running the two offices and did not have much to do with the liaison part of the business. Nevertheless, he was always friendly to me, and I often had a "sharing old times" conversation with him in the hallway over a cup of coffee.

The more usual drill was that no sooner would I get to my office than I was summoned to Colonel Le Gro's office upstairs. He was the chief of the Intelligence Branch and reported both to the defense attaché and directly to the ambassador. One of his principal responsibilities was to ensure that the stream of intelligence from the countryside into the various intelligence agencies in Saigon continued to flow into the U.S. Defense Intelligence Agency subsumed in Vietnam under the Defense Attaché Office. The Vietnamese, in turn, tried to ensure that the logistical, financial, and even moral support that they had received from MACV would continue under the new DAO. The links in this exchange were intelligence liaison officers like me.

Colonel Le Gro would invariably put me on some special project that he wanted me to get from Colonel Lung at the Military Intelligence Headquarters of the Joint General Staff. His request would be sealed in an envelope he wanted me to courier to his counterpart. Whatever it was I might have been doing for my civilian bosses, he would tell me to drop it. This practice created an awkward relationship with my bosses, who also did not like the direct relationship I was developing with Colonel Le Gro—which, frankly, was understandable. In time, they scarcely bothered me with any further requests of their own as, increasingly, I was turning into an errand boy for the colonel. Part of this, I think, was "cultural." Colonel Le Gro knew I was a former Army officer; and, like me, he was uncomfortable around this new rash of civilians.

At the end of our meetings, he would direct me to pick up a packet from his receptionist, Ellen, in the foyer to his office. Ellen was a striking redhead from West Virginia. For some reason, she never seemed to have the packet quite ready, and she would ask me to help her find some scattered papers in the file cabinet. Once there, she would bend around from drawer to drawer in creative ways that every day offered me a new perspective on her female anatomy. I danced with her at a few of the many new office parties; but, from my own Intel, I knew that she was hooked up with one of President Thieu's bodyguards. Indeed, I saw him at one of these parties, and he looked like a Vietnamese version of a sumo wrestler. From then on, I gave Miss Ellen a wide berth at the file cabinet.

I returned to the office ready to saddle up for the day. In the politics of the Office of Intelligence Liaison, the fact that I had been an intelligence officer "in the war," that I had a direct link to Colonel Le Gro, and that I spent my days in the field among real Vietnamese gave me a certain aura. What added to this mystique was that often when I came down the stairs from the colonel's office, my secretary would whisper to me (so that everyone could hear), "Your other Colonel-friend from Thailand wants you to return his call." The DAO was the only place I had access to a secure phone, so I did all my Thailand business at the DAO.

Naturally, this admiration was not universal. My aforementioned secretary was a willowy platinum blond. She reminded me of Jean Harlow, or some of the other wispy blond movie stars of the 1930s. She was married to a Taiwanese contractor who, if memory serves, was a cargo pilot. She clearly felt she was entitled to her own aura. She knew Chinese, and was constantly etching what I had to concede were beautiful Chinese characters. In moments of agitation, she would gruffly hand me one of these sheets. Like the girls in the cafeteria line, I was sure she was not writing nice things, though with these characters, I was stumped. She had the annoying habit of keeping her gaze riveted on her calligraphy whenever I asked her to do something. On one such occasion of indirection, she replied with the jibe, "OK, I'll do it, but Miss Lan tells me your Vietnamese is terrible!"

Unusual for a Vietnamese, Miss Lan held a high office manager position handling both Vietnamese and American employees. What was also unusual for a Vietnamese woman was that she wore American clothing that, to me anyway, looked odd. In addition, she spoke flawless, unaccented American English. In truth, she was a formidable woman, and she saw it as her role to be the authority on Vietnamese history, culture, and contemporary society to all these newly arrived Americans. That a former lieutenant like me could possibly serve as an alternative source of such information was something she was determined to thwart. Discrediting me seemed to give her immense satisfaction. A particular joy of hers was to launch on some voluminous critique of whatever it was I said in Vietnamese within her earshot, of which my good secretary enjoyed offering me concise summaries. I told myself I was too busy to be bothered by such conspiracies, but in truth they got under my skin.

Something else that got under my skin was the informality of this new civilian office environment. I didn't mind everyone out of uniform and wearing such an incredible variety of clothes—and hairstyles, both male and female. It was the freedom of the conversation that nonplussed me. As a military headquarters, conversation at MACV stayed on a pretty professional level. Beyond this, conversation about family was okay as long as it did not get too detailed or maudlin. War stories and exploits downtown were high entertainment. What was not okay was to talk about politics. If you were in a war headquarters, the assumption was that everyone was there because you supported the Mission. Any free conversation, or debate, on this topic was just not done. Once you settled in, this silence quietly projected war support to everyone in the building. Somehow this silence was comforting, and kept up the morale. In this new DAO, however, everyone felt free to express their political opinions. Not everyone opposed the war, of course, but there was enough of a cacophony to make me wonder why all these civilians had even bothered to come out here. With these contentious attitudes, how could we reassure the Vietnamese of our continued support? As a liaison officer, this unsteadied me.

Needless to say, I was always glad to have this American office scene in my rear-view mirror. The first stop on my daily merry-go-round was Colonel Lung's office at the JGS Compound. Though it seemed forever, I was usually there between 9:30 and 10 o'clock in the morning. The Military Intelligence Headquarters was housed in a high-ceilinged, big-windowed, two-story French colonial building whitewashed a pale yellow. My meetings with Colonel Lung were always very formal. I had to catch myself from saluting. He took his time going over the contents of Colonel Le Gro's daily packet. Once finished, he would call for Colonel Chuong, brief him on the document, and then issue some instructions. These instructions were always conducted in a tone too low for me to hear. After a while, as I became more trusted, both colonels gave me oral messages of amplifications to pass on, which gave me a few inklings on the subjects of these interchanges.

Colonel Lung's office was on the second floor. I had a very large office on the first floor. It was the only office in the building that was air-conditioned, probably at the insistence of one of my more high-ranking predecessors. For the Vietnamese, their breezy windows were enough. Inside my office, a beautiful young Vietnamese secretary, named Co Cho ("Co" means young unmarried woman), presided. Other than sitting in the office and making pleasant conversation (a welcome contrast from the DAO), she really never did anything for me. She was always too busy on the phone to take up any request. She was a Catholic from the North, and was the niece of someone prominent in the military or political world. I could never quite figure this out, but allusions were made to me by some of the officers who came by. Indeed, she was a pretty office ornament, and always attracted the less professionally burdened officers for a visit.

One of them was Major Duc. He was rather portly for a Vietnamese. His English was very good, and, after exchanging pleasantries with Co Cho that always made her laugh, he would talk to me about American sports. He must have been reading beyond *Stars and Stripes* because I was surprised by his detailed knowledge of pro football, basketball, and baseball teams. As mentioned, however, the main purpose of his visits was to ask me to buy him something at the PX. Fending him off was one of my almost daily annoyances.

I was usually able to bring these meetings to a close by the timely arrival of Colonel Chuong, who was clearly Colonel Lung's "go to" man. His arrival would send Major Duc scurrying off, and Colonel Chuong either came to seek clarification on some aspect of Colonel Le Gro's packet, or else to convey some message from Colonel Lung, or even to ask for some information or impression of mine that Colonel Lung would not want to ask me directly. Somehow, he did not want to be seen asking me for anything in the presence of others in his office. Ironically, Chuong was our go-between. Sometimes I could help Colonel Chuong right away. Other times, I had to make it my project back at the DAO to find out. I came to dearly like and respect this mediating colonel. He never asked me for anything personally. His English, however, was not too good, and often I had to call in the other employee in my office, the elderly gentleman who served as my interpreter and translator. This man, who I swear looked like Ho Chi Minh's twin, had a cubbyhole carved out for himself at the back of my office, blocked off from the air-conditioner.

He hated this air, and even outside of it, he wore a heavy sweater to ward off the cold.[5]

Nevertheless, he was unfailing in his courtesy to me. His main responsibility to me was to translate and type up the DISUMs of the Vietnamese Military Intelligence Headquarters so that I could courier them back to Colonel Le Gro for further dissemination throughout the DAO Intelligence Branch. These DISUMs made for pretty standard Intel reading, but there were occasional eye-popping reports of Chinese casualties on the battlefield. What stretched the credibility of these reports some was that there never seemed to be any wounded or prisoners available for confirming interrogations. It did not help that some of these reports came with the further sensation of atomic hand grenades being discovered on these corpses! Despite these incredulous grenades, based on other conversations that I had "around the block," I did not think it was impossible that there may have been some Chinese military advisers or observers attached to North Vietnamese military units.

I always tried to make it to CICV before lunch. In Vietnam, lunches were a full two-hour break. I headed first for the DAO gym to alternate between a weight-lifting day and a running day in which I ran around the DAO building three times. Occasionally, I took off and played tennis at the Cercle Sportif, but I played much less tennis than I did in my Army days. I didn't have any more generals to watch me! After my workout, I gobbled down my lunch at the same buffet line as breakfast, and either returned to CICV or headed there for the first time in the day. It was at CICV that I felt most at home. I would try to spend the rest of the day there, but about half the time I had to go back to my American office to meet with Colonel Le Gro, work on something that had come up at JGS or CICV, and, increasingly, take another of these phone calls from Thailand. Anyway, what made CICV such a haven was my growing friendship with its director, Lieutenant Colonel Vu Van Nho.

At CICV, I had two secretaries to contend with. Co Suong was the more senior one, and was from Sa Dec in the heart of the Mekong Delta. She was also the younger one, probably in her early to mid-twenties, and was vivacious and hyperactive. If I did not have work for her to do, she would flutter around dusting my office until I sent her away with some work. Suong was a devout Buddhist, and had a highly developed belief in ghosts, which she insisted were heavily concentrated at CICV because it had not been properly blessed by a Buddhist bronze when it was built. When she wasn't dusting or typing, she was always warning of a ghost that was lurking somewhere ready to pounce. She helped me get good at avoiding them. Her junior, but older (probably in her mid-thirties) colleague was Nguyen Thi Huong.[6] Huong's family had migrated from the North in 1954, and settled in the heavily Catholic "rocket belt" around Saigon near Bien Hoa.[7] As a Catholic, she had no use for all of Suong's ghosts. Huong was more sedate than Suong, and, though quietly attractive, her face bore some scars from smallpox. Whenever I came to the office at CICV, the faces of both women lit up, but their intense mutual dislike soon clouded the room.

It was at CICV where reality settled over my otherwise surreal existence. Making daily peace between these two women was like being in a family. I mostly resolved things by putting them both to work. It allowed them to ignore each other, and be contented with the pretense that the other was not really there. Suong, in particular, proved to be a very competent secretary. The fact that she was good—and willing to work—made me rely on her for an increasing share of my correspondence and reports, especially since my American "Jean Harlow" could not be pried from her calligraphy. I soon began to use Suong for almost all my work, including my strictly American business, and I grew careless in her competence.

Nho would rescue me from these squabbles by calling me into his office. At first, he was obsessed by my age and prior military experience. Clearly, he did not believe I had been a major. In exasperation, he finally asked me why all the Vietnamese at the MACV building called me "Trung-uy." I really had no choice but to fess up. He was gratified by my confession and told me, "You know, we should be insulted by your appointment, but you are nice, respect our women, and work very hard." This remark made me wonder if all these secretaries were some kind of deliberate character test. In any case, this moment of truth broke the ice. Soon afterward, I was given a Vietnamese name, "Ong Long," which meant Mr. Dragon. Unlike in the West, being a dragon in Vietnam was very auspicious since, in the founding myth of Vietnam, the Vietnamese people are the progeny of the cosmic mating of a divine dragon with a celestial fairy on top of the epicenter of Vietnamese identity, the mythical (and also real) Mount Fan Si Pan. More informally, I was called "Ong

Long-oi." The "oi" meant dear. Finally, one day Nho called me "Anh Long," or "Brother Long." That was one day in Vietnam when the tears welled up.

Nho was an avid reader of *Stars and Stripes*. What particularly caught his eye was the Dear Abby advice column. He would call me in to talk about what she wrote because he felt that this was the way he could really understand American culture, learning how Americans were advised to solve their personal problems. The column would always occasion a contrast as to what advice Vietnamese were likely to offer. The romantic squabbles he understood, and he generally sided with Abby's pragmatic, but principled, advice. But family relations were quite another matter. Sometimes he got quite agitated: "Anh Long, her family advice is crazy," he often decried. "Whenever there are family problems, she treats everyone equally. Just because a father was not attentive enough to a grown son at some party does not mean the father should apologize for the sake of family peace. Parents never apologize to their children! Children need to be filial no matter what their parents do!"

I spent more and more of my day at CICV. The more I stayed there, the more I could almost imagine there wasn't a war going on. But, despite these long, relaxing conversations with Nho, CICV was a very productive Intel shop, and as the war heated up after the sixty-day U.S. troop withdrawal period ended, CICV became the center of a lot of attention—from both Americans and Vietnamese.

In the merry-go-round swirl of "liaising" around this military block, two events stood out. Though officially—and, to a large extent, actually—my job as a liaison officer was to facilitate the exchange of intelligence information between American and Vietnamese military intelligence organizations, I was also supposed to keep my eyes open for "other things." Whatever the ultimate democratic aspirations of the Republic of Vietnam, the truth was that the military remained the source of political power in South Vietnam and in its ruling regimes. Changes in regimes, though they were supposed to come from the ballot box, in fact erupted from military coups d'état. Most of these coups were hatched on the compound of the Joint General Staff, on whose grounds I "liaised." I met frequently, mostly unwittingly, with some of the principals to these plots with whom I pretty exclusively did business over various intelligence reports. Other conversations that they had with each other did not include me. But it was hard to hide the fact from me that such conversations were going on. In these offices where I worked, the Vietnamese secretaries who were supposedly in my employ, in truth, kept a pretty close eye on my comings and goings. I could not have any conversations with any of the Vietnamese in any of these offices without their "reporting" knowledge. Nevertheless, I could report patterns of closed meetings to my American superiors, even though I didn't know what was being said. The secretaries, however, would let me know when I personally was the subject of conversation (in a general way), and they were quite active in at least safeguarding my personal position (since their professional situations were tied to my position in those liaison offices). Thus I learned that some of these closed conversations had to do with wondering whether even having me around all these offices was worth the cost of my compromising their several meetings. Fortunately, I was told that the various reports and services that I provided made my presence worthwhile.

Still, I put them to the test in the first event: my attempt to shed light on some political plotting. One coup rumor I had picked up on was one revolving around a General Manh, and my boss asked me to just find a way to meet him and report on a basic impression. Somehow I managed to arrange a morning coffee to discuss ways in which American intelligence assets might be of service to the Joint General Staff of the Republic of Vietnam Armed Forces. He clearly seemed perplexed by my visit, but he thanked me, and told me he would let me know. As I not so surreptitiously glanced around his office, it was hard not to notice how lavishly it was appointed. As we spoke, I tried to come to an understanding of his responsibilities. He was less than forthcoming in ways that I found underwhelming. The long and short of this encounter was that I filed a report with the basic impression that I deemed this good general to be both corrupt and incompetent. Stupidly, I had Co Suong type this report. It did not take long for me to receive dressings down from both Colonel Lung and Lt. Col Nho about how it was not my place to offer unsolicited comments about Vietnamese officers, particularly generals. This, of course, made clear just what my Vietnamese offices were for. I knew I was skating on very thin ice.

In response, I decided to file a less superficial, and more cerebral, report. This took the form of a much longer analytical essay—much like the papers I used to write in college—in which I laid out the command structure of the Vietnamese Army's intelligence command, and what a tight ship was run by Colonel Lung, and how well he was served by such subordinates as Lt. Col. Nho. I commented on the professionalism of this command, and provided examples of the reliability of this reporting to U.S. commands. I made clear that the commitment of Colonel Lung was to the prosecution of the war itself and, as far as I could tell, was not a source of coup plotting against the Thieu regime, though his loyalty was to the nation first. I concluded that the United States would always find a steady professional ally in Colonel Lung and his command.

Reflecting on this incident, in truth, I really did not know whether this particular general was corrupt or incompetent. Like many folks who get caught up in a war, officials or not, it is a seductive path to carve out for oneself a little private largesse from the bounty that comes with any war machine, and just let the flow of history pass you by. Such a person would hardly be susceptible to a coup conspiracy. The responsibility of rule puts the onus of history on one's back, and ends any little private reverie.

In any case, there is no doubt that corruption was rampant in South Vietnam. Earlier, I noted that Senator Robert Kennedy had turned against the war because of this corruption—and corruption became a rallying cry for the antiwar movement in America. There was plenty of ammunition. A black market thrived on goods pilfered from the PX system and money that could be exchanged far above market rates. The official value of the Vietnamese piaster (or *dong*) was 119 to the dollar. On the streets, GIs could easily get 500, and an estimated $500 million changed hands illegally every year.[8] From 1963 to 1968, one report showed that of the $600 million worth of goods sent to the PX system, $272 million was lost because of corruption. Other reports estimated annual PX losses to corruption at $175 million, or nearly a third of the total goods shipped.[9]

These losses extended to official economic aid from the Agency for International Development (AID) as well. The actual amount was a subject of controversy. One two-month study put losses of all U.S. assistance to Vietnam at from $500 million to $1 billion, or nearly 40 percent at the upper end in the period covered.[10] Another report put the figure at 60 percent.[11] In response, the State Department vigorously sought to refute these figures by insisting that their own reports showed losses to corruption in 1967 to be merely 5 or 6 percent.[12] In any case, as early as 1966, there were 400 Americans "facing charges for theft and black market scandals."[13] The siphoning off of military supplies was on a smaller scale. In April 1975, a General Accounting Office study revealed that $200 million of U.S. military equipment had been "lost" in the past two years, which was pretty much in line with the proportion that the State Department reported as its losses.[14]

The handmaiden to corruption is vice, and that, too, came in spades in Vietnam. In 1971, the Secretary of the Army admitted that 10 to 15 percent of the American troops in Vietnam were chronic users of heroin, to say nothing of marijuana and alcohol.[15] The other fleshly vice, prostitution, was even more lavish in Vietnam. In 1972, there were 300,000 prostitutes in-country, about the same as the number of bureaucrats.[16] And prostitutes made considerably more money than bureaucrats. A bar girl in Saigon could make $40 a night, while a mid-level bureaucrat had to support his family on $30 a month.[17] In the words of former Prime Minister Nguyen Cao Ky, this created "a big upside down" in Vietnamese society.[18] Clearly, these patterns of corruption penetrated high into the ranks of the ruling elite. In October 1974, on the very eve of Saigon's collapse, President Thieu dismissed for corruption four of his cabinet ministers, fired three of his four military region commanders, and demoted 400 field grade officers.[19]

To introduce some perspective, Vietnam is by no means in a stand-alone category on corruption. The economic theorist Edward Van Roy simply states that "corruption is universal."[20] The political scientist Samuel P. Huntington contends that corruption is inherent in the very process of modernization as social norms shift from traditional to modern institutions, and opportunities for private gain proliferate with new sources of wealth. In this process, he defines corruption as the "behavior of public officials which deviates from expected norms in order to serve private ends."[21]

Besides South Vietnam, there are other countries in Asia that fit this bill. Thailand is certainly a strong contender. In a 1976 poll of Thai citizens, 86 percent believed the Thai bureaucracy ran by "teamwork corruption."[22] James C. Scott, the Southeast Asia scholar from Yale, confirms this finding by saying that Thailand's political institutions are run as "clique structures," which is synonymous with corruption. Not to be outdone by South Vietnam, he notes that between 1955 and 1959, 4,602 officials in Thailand were dismissed for corruption.[23]

The blight affects other countries as well. A *New York Times* article observed that "graft is endemic to Asia," and cited the Philippines and Indonesia (and not Vietnam) as being the worst.[24] A survey of Indonesians in the late 1970s showed that nearly half the population saw corruption as the most serious threat to their society.[25] In fact, the largest non-Communist developing country, which was a showcase for Western economic aid, India, was not immune from corruption. On a scale that dwarfed the corruption in Vietnam, the amount of Black Money (money gained from bribes) earned in India from 1947 to 1965 totaled a whopping $7 billion.[26] The point here is that though corruption was something all these countries had in common, only Vietnam had an insurgency.

And, corruption in South Vietnam notwithstanding, the guerrilla insurgency in the South was destroyed by the repulse of the Tet Offensive of 1968. Counterbalancing the corruption in the GVN was the terror the Communists unleashed in their three-week occupation of Hue during this offensive. The systematic slaughter of 3,000 of its citizens inscribed the "bloodbath myth" in the minds of urban residents throughout the country and led to the disillusionment of the radical Buddhists with the Communist cause. What followed in 1973 and 1975 were conventional invasions by the Northern Army against the Southern Army. Corruption does not explain these events. Corruption, in fact, was a constant from 1973 to 1975 in South Vietnam. What was not constant was the deterioration of American support and will that precipitated the collapse of ARVN forces and will on the battlefields of 1975.

Indeed, well after the end of the war, corruption is as endemic under Communism in Vietnam as it was under the old GVN. Transparency International compiles an index of public-sector corruption on a scale of 0 to 10, with zero the most corrupt and ten the least. In 2009, Cambodia's score was 2, Vietnam's 2.7, Indonesia's 2.8, Thailand's 3.4, India's 3.4, the United States' 7.5, and New Zealand's, the most corruption-free, 9.4.[27]

Back to the question of General Manh's alleged plotting: one of the frustrations for those of us in the intelligence business is the compartmentalization of what we are allowed to know based on the "need to know" principle. In order to minimize the damages caused by any penetrations of our intelligence system, all operatives only know what they "need to know" to do their jobs. While this principle is central to damage control in intelligence (like the several water-tight compartments designed to save ocean liners from sinking), it also meant that agents at my level rarely had any sense of the larger picture to anything that we were doing. But some things can trickle down by osmosis.

In this instant case, I was blessed with a few trickles. People from the CIA thanked me for my reports—*both* my reports. Whatever were, or were not, his intentions, there was no coup from General Manh. And from then on, Colonel Lung and Lt. Col. Nho were all smiles. I shortly received dinner invitations from both officers. The ice had thickened considerably under my feet (an apt metaphor, I think, despite its climatic displacement!). Not being in the know of what was going on, even when you were in the middle of what was going on, could make the war often seem very surreal—and my dinner at Colonel Lung's home, the second event, was truly a surreal evening.

Crossing over from a professional to a social relationship with one's Vietnamese counterparts was highly prized, and rare. I felt honored by this invitation, and discovered that my branch chief, Colonel William Le Gro, was also a guest. Colonel Lung and Colonel Le Gro had a very good relationship, and this helped me immensely. I had known the good American colonel a little in my previous military life in Saigon, and I had a good rapport with him. With all the new civilians flooding into the Defense Attaché Office, this prior military connection gave me a huge margin of safety—to wit, from newly arrived intermediate colleagues and superiors. This relative freedom from American office politics offered me much greater rein to pursue my activities with the Vietnamese agencies to which I was liaised. Despite my congenital dislike for military hierarchy, somehow I had grown accustomed to it to the point where I felt uneasy around all these new civilians, Americans or not. In fact, I vastly preferred the military world of my Vietnamese counterparts.

A problem for this dinner was that, in my new capacity as a "senior" liaison officer, I was issued a government car of my own. It was a pretty beat-up nondescript clunker of a Chrysler, but it gave me immense status—and a far too bulky presence on crowded Saigon streets. I cursed this gift several times. On the night in question, my working a little late obliged me to turn down Colonel Le Gro's invitation to go with him to the dinner. This is probably among the most foolish things I have ever done.

I received a terrible set of directions, which was compounded by my indifferent track record at following even a good set of directions. Colonel Lung's quarters were located in a section way to the side of a very sprawling ARVN military base. I found the base itself eventually, but then proceeded to get hopelessly turned around. I came upon a very dark and deserted stretch of this complex, and suddenly there was a guard house and a barbed-wire checkpoint. I did not react very quickly to this unexpected apparition, and three very real ARVN soldiers stumbled out of the house and ordered me to halt, "Dung Lai! [Stop]," which I did. They then noticed that I was a "nguoi My" (American), while I noticed that all three were very drunk.

These twin observations did not help any of us. Somehow this enraged and then frightened them. I, in turn, was startled and frightened like a deer caught in headlights. As I took in just what was going on, from somewhere an icy calm settled over me. I began to speak all the Vietnamese I could think of to keep them distracted from those M-16 rifles that were pointed at me. When, at some point, I explained that I was lost and looking for Colonel Lung's house, the good colonel's name was the "Open Sesame" that lowered their rifles. They grunted, and swung and shook their rifles down the road. As it happened, his house was just a few hundred yards away.

From this dark road, I walked into a living room that was very bright with electric light that reflected off of furniture, carpets, and walls that all seemed white. I almost had to squint. I was clearly late, but everyone was very nice. I explained that I had become lost on the base. Colonel Lung seemed quite concerned that I had gotten lost, and wanted to know why no one had helped me find his house. I reassured him that three young soldiers down the road had helped me find his home.

As my eyes adjusted, I noticed that not everything was white. The living room was very tastefully appointed. I saw an alcove to the side that contained a little altar with large Chinese Mandarin–type paintings around it on the walls. This observation allowed Colonel Lung to talk about his ancestors. He was clearly a Confucian patrician, in the best sense of that word. It was a very well-furnished home, but not lavishly so. In truth, it was fairly small, and not anywhere near the size of all the sprawling villas with high walls in downtown Saigon.

What was unusual was that Mrs. Lung was seated on one of the couches, along with her husband and the guests, and took part in our conversation—and sat with us at the table for the first part of the meal. As the meal progressed and liquor was served, she did retire to the kitchen to supervise the service. But this was still an unusual level of gender equity. More typical is for the wife to greet the guests, remain standing for the living room part, and then serve the guests at the meal, and not sit down. Mrs. Lung was a statuesque beauty, not too much younger than her husband, and like all upper-crust Vietnamese women almost porcelain-white in complexion. The food, an exotic seven-course Chinese meal, was excellent. I really felt I was in the home of an ancient, but modern, Chinese Mandarin.

What was unusual for my hosts is that when we left I asked if I could drive home with Colonel Le Gro, and asked Colonel Lung if he could have one of his soldiers drive my car to me in the morning. I told them that the car had been acting up, and I was not sure it would get me home (this part at least was true). I was very relieved that everyone agreed. The next morning, a soldier knocked on my door, and told me that my car was in the driveway. He also told me that Colonel Lung had sent it to the motor pool and that everything seemed fine. I deflected the soldier's attention by offering him a ride to work. After this service, I took this contemptible vehicle to the American motor pool, and dumped it. It was not a memory I wanted to relive every morning.

My dinners, and a few lunches, in the home of Lt. Colonel Vu Van Nho could not have been more different. The Nho family lived off-base in a middle-class section of Saigon. Their property was walled-in, and I noticed that there was a guard detail at the gate. Inside there was almost a Midwestern American-from-Kansas atmosphere. The house was very open. I really could have wandered throughout the house, as opposed to the almost walled-off area for entertaining visitors in more aristocratic homes. I, of course, did not wander, but one of the kids would drag me into another room, and Lt. Col. Nho would always want to show me something in his office, and another child would take me into the kitchen for a treat. Nho had been to the Army's Command and General Staff Officers course at Fort Leavenworth, Kansas, and he confided that he liked the American way of life.

My visits would always begin with a warm welcome from Nho on the front porch. His wife would quickly follow with her big smile, and then the five children would race out and grab my hands and call out my name, "Ong Long-oi." I would be shown a place on a couch in a very open living room, and each of the children would do a little talent performance for me: one a song, one a piece on a musical instrument, and the little boy always performed some kind of somersault. Then we would eat. His wife served us, and always joined in the conversation. Both Nho and his wife were big on laughter and humor. The wife, whose name I have forgotten, always seemed happy. She was well tanned and was clearly an active woman who was not afraid of the outdoors. There was a congenial, pleasant atmosphere in this home. Nho liked to tell stories and jokes, and then get philosophically expansive as he smoked his pipe. He took this up in Kansas, he explained, because he had come to admire Harry Truman.

For all his humor, Nho could get very serious. In his home, he once asked me, "Why, really, are you here?" I realized he did not mean me personally because he waved his hand when I started talking about growing up on the mission field in India. "No, not you, you Americans. The Chinese came," he lectured, "because they wanted to make us part of their Confucian culture [he then made sure I noticed that there was nothing Chinese in his house—and I wasn't sure there was a contemporary point to this or not], and the French came just because they are greedy and obnoxious. But you Americans do not seem to know what you want here. You've built all these roads, ports, and air fields, but, economically, no big American companies or plantations seem to be coming in. You say you have come to build a democracy and [and he let this point slide without further elaboration] that you are against Communism. If that is so, Communism is something we have to deal with as Vietnamese. It is hard to know if you even like us."

This last point was a not too subtle reference to an American policy that, in a sense, really hurt the Vietnamese. Unlike the Chinese and the French, whose unwanted interveners at least had the social manners to stay involved in Vietnam, the American military in particular sent their people over to Vietnam for just one-year tours. This made it impossible for Vietnamese to establish long-term relationships with American counterparts, and also sent a none-too-subtle message that Vietnam was some kind of undesirable, hellish place. This social asymmetry (the Vietnamese in their various professional positions weren't going anywhere) was at the heart of Vietnamese skepticism over the bona fides of repeated American assertions of a long-term commitment to the future of Vietnam. Both Nho and Col. Lung had asked me, often at the end of long days, if I could offer any real assurances that they could count on us to stay with them for the long haul. They could not understand why we had invested so many troops in the first place and then so quickly took them all away, when the war itself was not correspondingly "drawing down." I lamely repeated Nixon's assurances to President Thieu, and they would look at me—and I would look away. Their skepticism, of course, was contagious, and the intelligence and honor of both men was such that I just could not offer further words as an insult. My growing respect for, and loyalty to, these two men, and growing disillusionment over the incipient realpolitik American abandonment of this whole enterprise, was eating up my soul.[28]

Just before I left Vietnam, and out of Col. Lung's earshot, Nho confided in me: "You know, Mr. Tim, we are all going to have to make accommodation." I didn't say anything because I knew he had to, and did not think that I could.

I Spy 2: The Order-of-Battle Conference

Just before I left Vietnam, I organized an Order-of-Battle (OB) conference at CICV (Combined Intelligence Center, Vietnam) for what I thought would be the culmination of my service as an intelligence liaison officer. Order-of-Battle was at the heart of the mission of CICV. It was also very much the focus of what we all used to do at MACV, and what all my new American civilian analytical counterparts at the Defense Attaché Office (DAO) were attempting to carry on. Essentially, this is the disposition of enemy forces, including the types of units friendly forces faced in each of the military regions (MRs); where they were located; the basic numbers of forces active in each of these units; the quality of the leadership; the quirks of style and strategy emanating from the units; and the training, equipment, morale, and other indicators of fitness like health, state of uniforms, food stocks, and so forth. In other words, there was a host of variables that fed into the Order-of-Battle, but the symbolic essence of OB was the gross number of enemy forces. In the summer of 1973, another numbers crisis was brewing between Vietnamese and American intelligence. I thought it would be a fitting legacy of my service in Vietnam to help resolve this difference.

This difference over enemy forces called to mind the more famous OB dispute between Sam Adams of the CIA and General Westmoreland of MACV in 1968 that was later the subject of a lawsuit by Westmoreland against CBS. He alleged that CBS had defamed his character by insinuating that the general had deliberately falsified these numbers.[1] The dispute between Sam Adams and General Westmoreland was over the true number of VC/NVA forces and the methodologies (assumptions, really) employed in obtaining them. There was also a more pivotal strategic and political issue at stake. In January 1968, on the eve of the Tet Offensive, MACV announced that it had revised its methodology for calculating VC strength and was dropping its total VC/NVA strength from 286,000 to 236,000.[2] It did so by dropping village self-defense forces, secret self-defense forces, and political cadres who were either nonmilitary units or part-time logistical forces that did not play a direct role in Communist combat operations. The CIA, first of all, did not accept either of the MACV figures and insisted on including the full range of enemy organizations in the overall OB figure, specifically mentioning the self-defense militias (overt and covert), administrative services, and political cadre. On January 30, the opening day of the Tet Offensive, the CIA reported that the "organized manpower" of the VC/NVA was between 515,000 and 580,000.

The underlying issue here was that the CIA's interest in the Communist forces encompassed the entire Communist infrastructure in the South, not just the fighters who would go up against American units. Of course, MACV was more focused on what units constituted legitimate military adversaries in the field. James J. Wirtz asserts that the CIA overstepped itself by claiming that these part-time forces took an active combat role in the Tet Offensive. This was contradicted by the lack of prisoners taken from any of these units, and even by their lack of appearance in TIC reports of enemy units encountered in combat.

More strategically for MACV, General Westmoreland had been giving optimistic accounts of the war to the American public in the late fall of 1967 about how "the end was coming into view." His evidence was what he called the "cross-over point" whereby U.S. forces were "attriting" enemy forces (that is, killing them) at a greater rate than these losses were being replaced. Such a metric of victory was possible with MACV's revised OB figures but not with those of the CIA.[3] Thus, there were always greater issues at play with these numbers than simply the numbers themselves.[4]

As these controversies over numbers persisted, it seemed a good idea to call an OB conference between Vietnamese and American intelligence agencies in the summer of 1973. There were two ostensible reasons for the conference. First, from the American point of view, most of the intelligence sources of enemy forces on the ground had dried up. Though a host of different intelligence sources can feed into OB, the most available and reliable source (if properly cross-checked, and the usually vast numbers of these sources statistically permitted this) was TIC (Troops-in-Contact). As mentioned earlier, TIC produces after-action reports, unit battle accounts, and debriefings by commanders and other government agencies of all sorts of missions. In short, TIC is what our guys see, hear, and feel in their encounters with enemy forces. Good intelligence folks exploit this source to the max. The problem was that in the summer of 1973 there was no more American TIC. It was all Vietnamese, and they were no longer sharing their TIC reports. American OB holdings, therefore, were becoming out of date.

The second reason was that the Vietnamese at CICV and the Americans at MACV, first, and then at the Defense Attaché Office, were reporting widely divergent overall numbers for Communist forces in South Vietnam. At the time of the discussions leading up to the Paris Peace Agreement in January 1973, the Vietnamese OB carried a total in-country Communist force structure of 300,000, while the Americans put total Communist forces at 140,000.[5] As in 1968, there was a significant political issue at stake in these numbers. In this case, the issue regarding this divergence was the severity of the American concession of allowing North Vietnamese forces to remain in South Vietnam when Washington had agreed to a total withdrawal of U.S. forces. The 140,000 figure of the Americans suggested that the concession was readily containable by the South Vietnamese military, but the 300,000 total of the Vietnamese insinuated that this American concession constituted a betrayal. Such a conference for the Vietnamese offered the opportunity of nailing down these numbers and embarrassing the Americans into a reconsideration of their precipitous withdrawal.

For me, a more powerful personal motivation constituted a third reason. Apropos of the queries of both Colonels Lung and Nho about the reliability of the American commitment, the question was: Did the Americans even care? An OB conference was one way to show concern and commitment.

Despite these obvious advantages, both sides repeatedly balked whenever I tried to get this conference nailed down. Essentially, the two military sides were wary of holding these discussions in case the results were not as dramatic as both sides officially maintained they would be, namely, that this detailed vetting would vindicate their numbers and not those of their counterparts. When I was able to get State Department and CIA participation, both sides suddenly overcame their objections. The rigid compartmentalization of the intelligence community had kept these groups apart, and the conference served as a temporary reprieve. The catalyst was that I knew the two "foreign" principals from State and the CIA through church (different churches, actually). The man at State was Bill Gausmann, who was one of the embassy's chief "Hanoi watchers." Superiors on all sides were duly notified. How, and on what basis, this conference was approved, I will never know. My immediate American bosses were wary, and their approval was decidedly languid. The intelligence division chief at DAO, Colonel Le Gro, someone whose support I could usually count on, warned me: "Tim, I know you are trying to help your Vietnamese friends, and to improve the 'Intel Cycle' on OB, but this is not going to turn out well for the Vietnamese. But we, at least, can learn quite a bit from this." It was true that I had more than education on my mind.

The conference was an all-day affair. Lt. Colonel Nho handled all the arrangements very well. It was supposed to be a conference of "working echelon" analysts of both sides rubbing shoulders unit-by-unit with their enemy OB files. There were more Vietnamese than Americans because the former had become much more involved with this. Some folks above these working levels were present for most of the time as well. My two civilian chiefs were there, and this was the first time either of them had been at CICV, apart from the initial round of introducing me when I was first hired. There was also my friend from the CIA, Ed Besch. He came with nothing to offer but sure did a lot of "absorbing." There was also a Vietnamese in civilian clothes and sunglasses ("Mr. Sunglasses"), to whom I was never introduced and whose perspective I could never quite see.

The day was Bill Gausmann's show. In fact, the conference was his idea. He had been an in-country Hanoi watcher for four years and had never had an official meeting with South Vietnamese military intelligence officers. He had a deep curiosity about their take on the war itself, beyond their somewhat clinical Intel reports on Communist military forces. I did not want to think that this conference might have been the basis of our friendship. In truth, none of us were supposed to be socializing with each other, but church connections proved difficult to break up. I was, however, warned to have no contacts of any kind with journalists. But church circumvented this as well.

Bill took charge of the conference with what amounted to a keynote address in the morning. He thanked CICV and the VNAF Intelligence Command for this invitation to a member of the State

Department. His message to the South Vietnamese military was to understand the importance of implementing the political provisions of the Paris Peace Agreement (holding elections and establishing a National Council of Reconciliation and Concord), because a long-term American commitment to South Vietnam and the continuation of American military support depended on the history of the Vietnam War shifting to the political arena. Given how the conference turned out, this message at least partly saved the day.

As the working echelons got down to work and pulled out all their charts and files, a pattern of two trends quietly emerged. As files were compared unit by unit, the two sides were pretty close in both their profiles of these units and even their numbers. But the Vietnamese counted many more units as active than the Americans did. Since the Communists were well aware that they were being tracked, they would understandably conduct countermeasures to throw us off. They would move units around to confuse us. Sometimes they would even switch radios between units, and then re-number units that would scramble all sorts of signals. Unless you undertook a regular vetting process, you could end up doubling enemy forces practically overnight, at least in your analytical "books." This clearly appeared to have happened, though the Vietnamese did provide TIC reports that supposedly confirmed all these units.

The second trend needed more careful scrutiny. As you looked at these unit reports, the numbers were suspiciously uniform. It is not normal, for example, for the Third Signal Company of the Viet Cong Ninth Division outside of An Loc to have the same 67 people reported for the past five years, especially since there was a major battle around An Loc in 1972. In other words, this intelligence was over five years old. At least in terms of what we were shown, there did not seem to be an effort on the Vietnamese side to collect current OB intelligence. The Americans were essentially coming to this conference with a blank slate. If the Americans had more up-to-date information, they were not showing it here. My own suspicion is that if we had it anywhere it would be at the relocated MACV Headquarters in Thailand, my secret superiors.

At the end of the day, the working echelon analysts conferred with their superiors and then convened in a concluding plenary session reporting the same disparity in overall numbers: the Vietnamese still insisted there were 300,000 Communist forces in-country while the Americans held to their perpetual 140,000. The real truth, apparent to everyone in the room, was that no one knew how many Communists were in-country. The rigidity and certainty of these figures lay in two different political agendas. In my second year of working in the Intel business in Vietnam, the conference crystallized one lifelong insight: for all the frenetic activities in the "Intel Cycle," there are vast areas of ignorance to intelligence, and this offers politicians a wide-open field to make this ignorance yield whatever certainties they want.

Bill sought to end the conference on a positive note by once again thanking his Vietnamese hosts and insisting that this had been a valuable exchange. He encouraged the Vietnamese Military Intelligence Command to factor the political situation into their military analyses. He then offered to provide State Department liaison officers to CICV and other places to help them work these political variables into their analyses. Mr. Sunglasses almost dropped his shades over this bombshell. To hurriedly change the subject, a photographer was whisked into the room and Bill was presented with a very elegant plaque that celebrated the event in sufficiently dramatic fashion so that it could be promptly forgotten. Such cross-compartmentalized intelligence analysis was forbidden in the American intelligence community, let alone in the Vietnamese Intelligence Command, where such collaboration would provoke volcanic nightmares of coup plotting in the prime minister's office. When everyone had left, Lt. Col. Nho walked me out the door and thanked me for arranging the conference with a look on his face like he had just been through the craziest day in his life.

Despite these dubious results, the conference succeeded in bringing a lot of American attention (and I suspect Vietnamese as well) to the Vietnamese Military Intelligence Command. Colonel Lung and Lt. Col. Nho took advantage of this attention to engage the Americans in another project to stimulate their professed commitment to the future of South Vietnam. I was pressed into service by my Vietnamese friends to bring this project to the attention of as many Americans as I could. In a real sense, I owed this visibility to Bill Gausmann. I will turn to this in chapter 10.

To peel back the OB onion a bit, behind this persistent disparity between the two sets of numbers—the American 140,000 versus the 300,000 of the South Vietnamese—was the question of North

Vietnamese capabilities and intentions. These two factors are essentially what military intelligence is all about. On this pivotal question, the issues were the same to both sets of analysts. They differed in their conclusions. Another huge difference was the differing histories of the development of the Communist war machine that served as the foundation of its Order-of-Battle.

I have spoken earlier of two wars developing on the American side with Nixon's two Linebacker bombing campaigns added to the war run by MACV and ARVN on the ground. Somewhat in parallel, the Communists conducted two wars in the South, or at least ran their operations through two separate commands. Historically, during the war against the French (1946–1954), the Communist Viet Minh divided Vietnam into six "Inter-Zones." Three of them were in Tonkin in the North, where they concentrated their war effort. Two, Inter-Zones 4 and 5, were in Annam (Central Vietnam). Inter-Zone 6 was in Cochin China, the South. Ironically, these zones followed the borders of the three French colonies that subdivided Vietnam: Tonkin, Annam, and Cochin China. Since the French had concentrated their military forces, governing bureaucracy, and economic activities in Cochin China, in 1951 the Viet Minh decided to establish a separate command to run the war there: the Central Office for South Vietnam (COSVN).[6]

Ten years later, in 1961, this same COSVN was reactivated to run the war against the Americans in Cochin China or, as it was known in this war, MACV's Military Regions 3 and 4.[7] The Central Office for South Vietnam reported to the Central Military Committee of the Politburo in Hanoi. The former Inter-Zone 5 comprised most of MR 2 and the southern half of MR 1. The part of old Inter-Zone 4 that ran south of the DMZ was formed into a military district called Tri Thien Hue (and basically covered the cities of Hue and Danang and up to the DMZ). Like old times, both of these regions were directly subordinate to the North Vietnamese High Command in Hanoi.[8] This basic organizational split held throughout the war. Some time before the outbreak of the Easter Invasion, Military Region 5 was split into a coastal zone and a B-3 Front Command in the Central Highlands. The Tri Thien Hue Region remained the same, but territory was added in Laos to coordinate activities along the Ho Chi Minh Trail. The Central Office for South Vietnam, then, was divided into at least seven military districts (there were several additional "sub-regions" around Saigon).[9] To clarify, in their second Communist war, zones became regions.

Under these two commands, the Communists fought different wars. The North Vietnamese High Command deployed conventional military units into Tri Thien Hue and MR 5, first as individual replacements and then as entire units. Both men and equipment came down the Ho Chi Minh Trail network through Laos and Cambodia and fought as conventional military units. On the other hand, COSVN did receive some men and materiel as far as Saigon, or MR 3. But in the Mekong Delta, COSVN relied on a huge flow of supplies transported northward from the Cambodian port of Sihanoukville on a corridor fittingly dubbed the Sihanouk Trail. The Central Office for South Vietnam also procured many of its supplies and manpower locally. It was COSVN that conducted the guerrilla "people's war."

The military fortunes of these two wars were also different. The COSVN suffered three devastating losses. The Tet Offensive, first, gutted the southern guerrilla forces, while the North Vietnamese High Command husbanded its own divisions for a possible American invasion of the North that Hanoi feared was behind the leaked Pentagon request for 206,000 additional troops to be dispatched to Vietnam. Indeed, there were bitter feelings about Tet among southern Communists. One Viet Cong operative, who participated in the offensive, called Hanoi out for making a "grievous miscalculation . . . that had wantonly squandered the southern insurgent movement."[10] The second loss came when the Cambodian Incursion of 1970 scattered COSVN from its headquarters in Mimot and Snuol in Cambodia, even as it just failed to capture the headquarters leadership. Finally, the pro-American Lon Nol Coup in Cambodia that ousted the left-leaning King Norodom Sihanouk in March 1970 shut down the port of Sihanoukville as a source of further supplies for COSVN.[11] After the coup, the CIA unearthed new intelligence revealing that COSVN received 80 percent of its materiel from Sihanoukville. Hence, this loss was grievous.[12]

It is my contention that COSVN essentially was a pretense after this. Functionally, it no longer played an active role in the war since the guerrilla war had been defeated, and Communist forces increasingly were conventional forces from the North. At the end, there was a reversal in the wars of the two sides. While General Abrams's

162   "one war" split in two, one of the Communist commands, COSVN, was sidelined as the North Vietnamese High Command finished the war with two conventional invasions, one in 1972 and the other in 1975. What made this confusing for OB was that to the South Vietnamese, who were a part of the history of the earlier war, Communist intentions were unitary, whatever the organizational splits. Whether from Hanoi or COSVN, all these units were composed of Communists. To the more organizationally minded Americans, the separate commands imposed structural barriers to capabilities that could undermine intentions. The complexity of using OB to gauge Communist intentions was a conceptual paradox of one war historically also becoming four wars organizationally.

With the histories of these two split wars coming to an end in 1973, the crux of the argument over OB still lay in the different intentions that could arise from the capabilities implicit in these two sets of numbers. At 140,000, the reduced capabilities of such numbers allowed the Americans to take some comfort in thinking that the North Vietnamese were unlikely to invade again soon, giving Washington its "decent interval." At 300,000, President Thieu felt that, with all American troops withdrawn, this was a sufficient force for Hanoi to plan another offensive—and soon. Whatever the numbers, President Thieu proved to be a better prophet of these intentions than Henry Kissinger. History was a surer guide than numbers.

I remember in the middle of the Easter Invasion there was a big discussion at one of these command briefings about what the respective numbers were on both sides after a month of heavy fighting, and how ARVN was holding up. For General Creighton Abrams, the key was not the numbers: "I don't think there's any *question* about their *capacity* [ARVNs] to do it. It's simply a question of will. And that's what this is . . . . It's the same goddamn thing. In fact I would say, the way this thing stands right now, it's the same for both sides. It's whose will is going to be broken first. There's nothing fancy left to be done."[13] In the Easter Invasion of 1972, Hanoi was broken first. In 1975, with the Americans gone and Hanoi fully resupplied, it was Saigon's turn.

However, it was the same General Creighton Abrams, again speaking during the Easter Invasion, who had no illusions as to whose will counted the most—and what would seal the tragedy of the Vietnam War: "They [the North Vietnamese] think that the greatest weakness, the greatest weakness in the whole goddamn thing is not here in South Vietnam—it's in the United States— they've put the arrow on the bow and they've aimed it now at the very heart of our weakness, which is *the* United States, *that's* what it's aimed at."[14]

Civilian Life: The *Kieu* and Tay Ninh

Meanwhile, my life in Saigon whirled in circles, surreal circles wheeling around a city that was supposedly undergoing a war. Everyone was trying to carve out a normal life for themselves, but all these little normals could add up to a very weird existence. This certainly was my Saigon in 1972 and 1973.

My military days from March 1972 to January 1973 were more circumspect than my civilian ones from February to August 1973. They were limited by something called work. Since we were in the rear in Saigon, General Abrams (and General Westmoreland before him) had decreed that we should work twelve hours a day, seven days a week. Since I worked a night shift from six at night to six in the morning, there was not much room for night life—or very much else. Still, in the afternoons, I would break away, go downtown, and see a Chinese movie. I became addicted to these Robin Hood–like martial arts movies, and I was always irritated by how one-third of the screen was taken up by English, French, Chinese, and Vietnamese subtitles.

We were always supposed to travel in pairs, and, as an officer, I was issued a .45 caliber pistol (with which I could never hit anything). Mostly, I traveled into town alone, and I always left my "piece" behind. I figured this saved my life on more than one occasion. There were bad people, both Viet Cong agents and common criminals ("cowboys," as they were called), lurking in the shadows of the Saigon streets. If I was unarmed, shooting me would be unprovoked and was likely to trigger at least some popular outcry—maybe even enough for someone to go to a police station—to break the conspiracy of silence on which these subversives depended for survival. Armed, I became a more legitimate target: who would care if an American was shot because he drew a gun on a fellow Vietnamese! This, at least, was my reasoning.

I went alone as well because I liked to practice my Vietnamese, get away from the war, and just melt in. In this latter intention, I was utterly naïve. No matter the street in Saigon, whenever you started walking, a herd of kids would engulf you shoving some tray full of trinkets-for-sale in your face, while countless sets of little hands rifled your pockets and wrists for anything they could rip away. The thing to do was to put your wallet in your shirt pocket and get into a football crouch to stay on your feet. In time, I began to like these kids as I came to realize that they were my protection. Since I always left them stuff to take in my pants pockets, they began to steer me away from places where I shouldn't be walking.

Sometimes I would go to town with my compatriots (we started splitting shifts on weekends with colleagues so that one could get off Friday evening and the other on Saturday). A favorite watering hole for my brothers-in-arms was a place called the "Dragon." The Dragon was at the high end of Saigon's booming flesh trade. There were, of course, bars with beer, prostitutes, and country and western music everywhere. These places quickly settled into well-ordered hierarchies. Different strata of the vast American mission latched onto their own places. Usually, they were set up one-by-one with strolling whores steering the uninitiated to their proper places. There were also whole sections of town devoted to larger sections of the population, like the "Soul City" hangouts of Remus Lamb and the Vietnamese districts by the river.

The Dragon was located just behind the American embassy. It was reserved for military officers, though I did see occasional civilians—probably folks who worked with the military. The place was owned by a pleasant Vietnamese woman in her forties with an expatriate American husband, and he was the one who actually ran the place. He circulated to see if everything was all right. Everything about the place was "quality." I never saw anyone kicked out for being drunk or obnoxious. They served excellent food in American, French, or Chinese cuisine. The drinks were fabulous. Did I forget to mention the women? In this department, the women at the Dragon were the closest thing I knew of in Vietnam to Japanese geisha girls. These women were dressed in elegant, revealing, full-length evening gowns. They all had long black hair and could make pleasant conversation in English. They wafted around the tables and patrons could just talk to them or pursue the conversations more privately upstairs.

Trips to the Dragon settled into a drill. About once a week, a group of us from the office would set out to the Dragon in a fleet of cabs. Once there, we would take up about two tables. Some of us stayed at the tables, and some eventually went upstairs in a rough order as to which hunger had priority. In our group anyway, it was mostly married guys who went upstairs. I never went upstairs, and for those of us who were kept waiting, the American manager always came by with what I called "drinks of virtue." Mostly, I listened to my friends cling to wistful tales of waiting wives and girlfriends. Since I had no one in either category, I came to deeply enjoy a new friend in this surreal war—a snifter of Benedictine and brandy. Thus, with a little help from this friend, I could write home and say that I had walked in this perverse Garden of Eden and not eaten any of the forbidden fruit. Alcohol, in wartime, is an eminently permissible fruit—especially for the rearguard.

For the sake of my conscience, this was fortunate because, ironically enough, near the Dragon was a small French Huguenot chapel—actually, immediately adjacent to the American embassy building. It held services every Sunday afternoon for Lutherans. We were a strange crew of about a dozen people. Our pastor was from the Wisconsin Synod, an offshoot from mainstream Lutheranism that is extremely conservative to the point of not believing in Boy Scouts or any kind of service in government, including the military chaplaincy. This did not preclude Wisconsin clerics from serving the military off base as civilians. Such was the case for our pastor. He was unusually liberal in his theology—so he could live with preaching God's Word in a Calvinist setting—and just as liberal in his delving into libations of the spirit. After each service, we would go out to eat at a restaurant in Cholon. We came to call ourselves the Twelve Apostles. Towards the end of my time in Vietnam, our pastor's wife came to visit for a week, and her unspeakable shock at everything she saw ended his tour in Vietnam along with their marriage.

It was at these Lutheran services that I met Bill Gausmann, whom I introduced in chapter 3. I helped him procure the taxis for the Cholon dinners, and at these tables I developed an appreciation for all his stories. My admiration pleased him to the point where he began having me over to his apartment so he could finish off one story or another that he had just begun at the restaurant because of "all the damn interruptions." I quickly learned that in order to get the full version of these stories, you listened. But the price of listening was to drink right along with him. His liquor cabinet was full and his capacity for consumption rivaled Odin's. To stay upright, I learned the secret of long sips and plenty of ice. One thing about rear-echelon warfare—you learn how to drink, or lie down trying.

As someone just out of college and military training, I realized Bill was the first person I knew who was a real savant. He read voraciously on a wide variety of subjects and had a wealth of worldly experience to boot. He had served in the Resistance in France and received the Croix de Guerre. So, as he liked to remind me, he had stories from the "real war." He was one of the embassy's chief Hanoi watchers, and his knowledge of this adversary was breathtaking to me. I can honestly say that whatever I know about the Vietnam War has been deeply informed and guided by documentary materials he furnished me, but even more by his insights. Furthermore, Bill was my bridge to the civilian world that was off-limits to the military. He introduced me to journalists, a retired Australian general who was a counterinsurgency expert, and several of his State Department colleagues.

I learned that Bill had his passions, and they erupted as the alcohol began to flow more freely. One was Communism, which he hated; another was socialism, which he adored. He hated Communism because it gave socialism a bad name. While socialist and Communist economics were similar, their politics were not. Bill heatedly emphasized that it was socialism that believed in democracy and evolutionary reform, and it was the "Bolsheviks" (what he loved to call Communists of all stripes) that installed repressive dictatorships on the waves of revolutionary violence. He was also bitter about Communist treachery during the Resistance in France during World War II. He was quick to supply numerous instances of similar acts of Communist betrayal in Vietnam of the nationalist movement against the French and, of course, in the current war against the United States. This was a comfortable line of "conversation" for me, and my biases were richly fed.

Another of his passions, however, was capitalism—something he deeply loathed. He knew in fulsome detail the scandals surrounding the Vanderbilts, J. P. Morgan, the Rockefellers, and the other robber barons of the nineteenth century. Bill skewered with relish the greed and inequalities spawned by the excesses of capitalism. Several uncles in my college years had fed me with fervent apologetics of the capitalist system, so this was not a comfortable line of "conversation." However, since I was never required to say anything during these diatribes, I was usually able to steer the discussion to some aspect of Lutheranism, or to propose another foray into Cholon as a way of drawing the evening to a close. I was always grateful that Bill had his driver take me home in his embassy car. I was utterly exhausted after these evenings, and my ability to make it to the car in a reasonably dignified fashion was my final triumph of the day.

With the Paris Peace Agreement in January, and my own release from the military and prompt assumption of civilian status as an intelligence liaison officer in February, I soon developed other civilian connections of my own. As I mentioned in chapter 7, two new civilian bosses came in as my immediate superiors in charge of the Intelligence Liaison Office of the Intelligence Branch of the DAO: Tony Suarez, who had been working with the National Police (and married a police commander's daughter), and Lee Washer, who arrived from some U.S. government agency in either Thailand or Japan. Washer had a Japanese wife. These two bosses were always either having parties at Tony's villa or arranging get-togethers at various restaurants. These parties were good for building morale and establishing camaraderie among a disparate staff.

With these two came a wave of U.S. government civilians. Many of them, of course, were females. As I have mentioned, the Saigon scene became full of "round-eyed" women.[1] It made the whole town come to a stop. I remember in particular a huge Harley-Davidson motorcycle driven by a black man with brawny bare arms, accompanied in the rear by a blond with white thighs that, in the wind, always came clear of any dresses. We called this eighth wonder of the world "the streaking piano."

As a civilian, a whole new world opened up to me. Adapting to a new flow, I went to parties and started to date. But a gap in attitude, behavior, and *weltanschauung* developed between me and this brave new world. Most of these folks were coming to Vietnam on various larks to earn some "hardship duty" bonuses. They were acting like typical American consumers and tourists, getting tailor-made suits and shoes and buying whatever jewelry and jade they could get their hands on. In truth these "newbies" became offensive to me. They had come to this war as if it were a shopping mall. (In retrospect, I think I was a little unfair in this judgment.) To me, there was still a war on, and the Vietnamese, at least, were still in a life-and-death struggle. As an intelligence officer, I knew that outside the boundaries of all these parties, the noose was tightening. So did some of my new colleagues, but they had no plans for staying around until the end. I felt more committed, and I began to withdraw from this *après mois, le déluge* world and return to my war—something I believed in.

Besides the Vietnamese, there was the constant presence of the French. As it happened, the apartment complex I moved into as a newly minted civilian was downtown on a little street called Duy Tan, off the main Mac Dinh Chi street near the American embassy, but also near a French residential section. Indeed, there was a French villa right next to our complex. Somehow, I came to know the Carjeans who lived there. I think it was the mother who introduced herself and brought me over to meet her husband and her daughter, Christine. Christine was lovely, but just seventeen. The mother kept throwing us together, to the evident displeasure of the father. Somehow, we overcame this awkwardness, and I became a regular guest in the household. My French was terrible. Their English was worse, but our Vietnamese was passable. The mother forswore the use of Vietnamese, however, until the servants were dismissed. She said it was too undignified for white people to have to rely on an Oriental language in front of the *Vietnamien*. This was a very *ancien regime–* type colon family.

The Carjeans were my ticket to the French world in Saigon. They took me to the Cercle Sportif where I played tennis with some Vietnamese officers who spoke flawless French, and who were clearly embarrassed by my presence at the club (or by their presence in my presence). I was even invited to a *Quatorze Juillet* party. I remembered to thank my hosts for paying for the American Revolution. There was an implication in my remark that this habit had morphed into paying protection money for a more contemporary and contiguous revolution. It is in the nature of rear-echelon wars that some groups find ways to make wars a very profitable business. Part of my job was to try to trace some of these "hows." When you are in the business of warfare, ways must be found to preserve some normal, or even abnormal, functioning of the economy. But there was nothing normal about the economy in Saigon. I learned that in the business of intelligence, for much of the knowledge revealed, the prudent course of action was silence, especially since I really wasn't sure what was going on. I had suspicions, but they were no more than elusive shadows that kept disappearing whenever you tried to throw some light on them. If you weren't sure of something, it was better to let it lie, lest some overzealous bureaucratic superior in an air-conditioned office far from the Saigon streets wanted to do something zany—like expel all the French from Vietnam.

Regarding my shadowy suspicions, it was my basic conclusion that the French meant us no harm, whatever it was that they were doing. Essentially, they were doing what they had to do to survive— no mean feat in this wartorn land. If there was an underlying psychological reason for my benign perception, I suppose it had to do with my admiration for the British who had hung on in India after independence in 1947. Somehow they helped retain some use for dying colonial habits (for one thing, they did know how to keep businesses profitable and markets functioning), and I did not begrudge them their English clubs nor the French their Cercle Sportif. Besides, I enjoyed the tennis, and I had come to like the Carjean family.

In a war in Vietnam, one should not forget the Vietnamese, which is what I thought all the Americans around me were doing. In addition to my friendships with my Vietnamese associates, particularly Lt. Colonel Nho and Colonel Lung, there was Margaret. Margaret was a flamboyant Southern lady from Atlanta. She always wore a shining white bonnet and white gloves to church. When she walked into the church, she entered like a *Vanity Fair* fashion model cruising down the runway. She had a responsible job in the CIA, but she certainly was not inconspicuous. The church, into which she so elegantly strode, was a large, generic Protestant church, also near the embassy. It felt pretty Southern Baptist, and I did not go often. But when I did, I would invariably meet a CIA couple, Ed and Donna Besch, who introduced me to Margaret. She was glamorous, but definitely at least in her forties.

Margaret was patriotic, moral, and very committed to the Vietnamese. So there were three things we had in common right there. She had a lot of Vietnamese associates, who, I began to understand, all worked for her in some way or other. The person she introduced me to was Nguyen Phu. Phu was a poet and an intellectual, and he was very friendly to me. Ed Besch also told me that Phu had been a decorated ARVN combat officer who had first been recruited by the "Agency" to man listening posts along infiltration trails. I never quite caught what Phu was doing subsequent to these activities. He was also a devout Protestant. Margaret could not get over the fact that I was a missionary kid from India. Seemingly, we three were a fated partnership.

Phu came to my apartment, and he began to teach me what he called "real Vietnamese." He gave me a copy of the epic of Vietnamese literature, *Kim Van Kieu*. Sort of like learning Latin from Caesar's Gallic Wars, he proposed I learn Vietnamese by memorizing the *Kieu*. This epic is a common Chinese folk tale that was nevertheless rendered into beautiful Vietnamese by Nguyen Du shortly before his death in 1820. It is about the length of the New Testament, and Phu knew it by heart. He would recite whole chapters in a trance, and I was always deeply moved. Vietnamese, like Chinese, is a tonal language in which both sounds and tones make different words. The glory of the *Kieu* is that not only do the words rhyme but also the tones of the words are blended in a harmony that is truly musical in effect. Consequently, the full beauty of Vietnamese poetry has to be heard in oral recitations. Sadly, my flat Midwestern atonality always grounded my ability to capture the lyrical heights of this language.

The *Kieu* bears further attention because Vietnamese will tell you that it is their true national epic, and the window to their soul. The story traces the varied fortunes of its heroine, Vuong Thuy Kieu, through the turning of the Buddhist wheel of destiny or fate as she struggles to honor the Confucian demands of filial piety versus the Buddhist claims on a pure heart that is free from passion but full of compassion. (This is the only national epic I can think of in which the central figure and hero is a woman.) In a fifteen-year odyssey, Kieu's vicissitudes are many. Through it all, she keeps her filial vow to her father, even as she does what she must to survive.[2]

Kieu is the eldest child of a mid-ranking mandarin official, an alderman in a village. She has a younger sister, Vuong Thuy Van, and a brother, Vuong Quan, the "last born." Kieu is incomparably beautiful as well as a talented poet and lutenist. A well-bred neighbor, Kim Vuong, who is studying for the Confucian civil service exams, falls in love with her. They spend a chaste evening together, and plight their troth. Before any ceremony can be conducted, Kim is called away to a distant village for a family funeral. While he is away, Kieu's father and brother are arrested by the police on bogus charges. To gain their release, a certain monetary fee is set by a corrupt magistrate, which Kieu procures by selling herself to a Mr. Ma, a supposed scholar, who is actually a pimp. Before Kim returns, Kieu has disappeared into the netherworld of Green Houses (brothels for those of elevated social station).

At first initiated into the life of a courtesan, she manages to escape by writing an elegant poem that attracts the attention of a gentleman patron, Thuc Ky Tam. He brings her into his home as a concubine. Thuc loves her, but, strange to say, his wife, Hoan, does not. Consumed by jealousy, she treats Kieu like a slave, and Thuc professes his powerlessness to intervene. Kieu then flees to a convent, but the corrupt abbess dupes Kieu into returning to a brothel—again for a handsome payoff. This time she is saved from a second round of prostitution by a timely rescue. Her savior is the bandit chieftain Tu Hai.

Tu Hai is all heart and loyalty, but very violent. He is not versed in Confucian proprieties or politics. Nevertheless, the couple spend a blissful five years together, when Kieu is a forest queen. In a significant scene, Tu Hai, who is incensed by Kieu's tragic history, rounds up all her past tormentors and gives Kieu the opportunity to pass judgment on all of them. In this golden opportunity for revenge, or even equal Confucian treatment, she shows true compassion for all of them. In the case of Hoan, she even accepts Hoan's strident and unapologetic defense of her right to be jealous and vindictive. (For some Vietnamese, her pardon of Hoan is seen as an endorsement of monogamous marriage.) The idyll ends, however, when Tu Hai is snared by the wiles of a mandarin general, and he is killed in a treacherous ambush. Dastardly as this deed was, the general proves he is an honorable man with respect to Kieu. He turns her over to a convent. As the wheel of fate would have it, this is a good abbess who also knows Kieu's family, and Kieu is finally reunited with her family.

Her fifteen-year odyssey is over. In the meantime, Kim Vuong has married Kieu's younger sister, Van. Nevertheless, Van offers to stand aside and let the couple reunite, and Kim again pledges his love. Kieu is persuaded to rejoin her lover in marriage, but because of her life of sexual corruption, she insists that the marriage be platonic. She calls on Van to remain married to Kim as well in order to procure an heir for the family. Kieu's own happy ending must await her next life. Thus, in renouncing further desire in this life, while remaining steadfast in her compassion for Kim, she will cleanse her soul for a brighter reincarnation in the next life.

In a direct sense, the story reflects the ups-and-downs in Nguyen Du's own life. As a young man, he served as a mandarin official in the court of the ruling Le Dynasty, to which he was impeccably loyal. The wheel for him turned when he spent most of the middle years of his life surviving the upheavals of the Tay Son Rebellion (1771–1792), in which an upstart but charismatic band of soldierly brothers swept the Les from power. Nguyen Du was aware of the virtues of the Tay Sons, despite their lack of proper Confucian breeding, even though he decried the consequences of such an upheaval. In the *Kieu*, Tu Hai is modeled after Nguyen Hue, the leader of the Tay Sons, for whom Nguyen Du had a particular admiration. When the Tay Sons, in turn, were driven from power by Nguyen Anh, Du was given a position in the court of the new Nguyen Dynasty. Since this dynasty came to power with the help of foreigners, the French, he held his place in this order with reluctance and resignation. Indeed, he is said to have written the *Kieu* under a grip of melancholy.[3]

For Vietnamese, the *Kieu* is a story of who they are, and is emblematic of their troubled history, whether under exploitation by the Chinese, French, Americans, or even the Communists. The story highlights the dual character to their political, social, and religious beliefs. This duality is a tension between Confucian principles and conventions and Buddhist beliefs and morals. The *Kieu* borrows its structure from a Chinese romance, and it is laced with Chinese literary clichés and scriptural references. Kieu's deepest motivations, however, are Buddhist. She is conscious of the blight her sins have put on her soul, and of their weight on her reincarnation (a Buddhist belief, not a Confucian one), and also of the *nirvana* (enlightenment) that comes with detachment and the renunciation of passion. The *Kieu* reflects the outward observance of Confucian conventions, but the inner cultivation of a Buddhist soul. Hence, in this duality, what is essentially Vietnamese is distinctly Buddhist.

Since Buddhism is as foreign to Vietnam as Confucianism, the identification of Buddhism with Vietnameseness requires explanation. Confucianism came to Vietnam from China as part of the thousand years of Chinese domination and was a set of ideals and a moral code that were expressive of this domination. To emphasize this foreignness, Confucian ideas and principles were always expressed in Chinese-language borrowed nouns, not in indigenous Vietnamese words. Buddhism, specifically the Mahayana Buddhism that came to Vietnam, was a religious path to salvation that could rely on, and accommodate, gods of anyone's choice. It did not come, then, as any part of a foreign political order. Hence, the folk religions of China, Japan, Korea, and Vietnam could insert their culture's gods and myths into this Buddhism, and call it their own. Accordingly, in Vietnam, the hearth god, Ong Tao, was incorporated into Buddhism so that it became, thereby, the national religion. To make the distinction clear as to what is essentially Vietnamese, Buddhist terms and concepts are always expressed in indigenous Vietnamese words. The true Vietnamese soul is Buddhist.[4]

In this sense, Communism remains a foreign graft on the national soul of Vietnam. In their histories, Communists give prior place to Confucianism over Buddhism because it is materialist, not spiritual like Buddhism, and has more "progressive" political ideas. Communist historians impose the rhetoric of class struggle by asserting a dialectical conflict between Confucianism and Buddhism with the gradual victory of Confucianism over Buddhism in preparation for the final Communist synthesis. As much as Communists succumb to the national admiration for the *Kieu*, one such writer cannot refrain from the dismissive observation that it "falls back on Buddhist themes."[5]

Regarding desired qualities among people, the *Kieu* centers on destiny or fate (the cosmic wheel that turns the near-endless cycle of births, deaths, and rebirths), and the reaction of talent and heart to it. My friend Phu would always comment on how talented the Americans were. I asked him once about the Communists, and he replied, "In this respect, the Communists are like the Americans, they are talented. As for Kieu, and the rest of us Vietnamese, we have heart." I didn't know quite how to take this. With Phu, I was memorizing the *Kieu*, not translating it. Later, in graduate school, I read it in translation. When I came to the poem's close, I understood:

All things are fixed by Heaven, first and last.
Heaven appoints each creature to a place.
If we are marked for grief, we'll come to grief.
We'll sit on high when destined for high seats.
And Heaven with an even hand will give

talent to some, to others happiness.
In talent, take no overweening pride—
Great talent and misfortune make a pair.
A Karma each of us has to live out:
let's stop decrying Heaven's quirks and whims.
Within us each there lies the root of good:
the heart means more than all talents on earth.[6]

Phu, clearly, was a man with heart. In my view, so also was the Communist major I met at Camp Davis.

Despite my poor command of the language, Phu and I hit it off in other ways. He took me to restaurants in the Vietnamese parts of Saigon. These were always nerve-racking excursions. We would take a taxi into the deep labyrinths of the slums around the river where you would never see a Caucasian face. Phu would always be paying off somebody or other as we went deeper into this enigma. Finally, we would end up in a restaurant along a garbage-blackened sludge of a canal. The roofs were always so low that I almost felt I had to crawl to the table. The food was actually very good—always some sort of fish and rice combination. Phu never let me contribute to this trail of money that followed us in and out to this real Vietnam. I relaxed when I came to realize that one way or another this money came from Margaret.

What was also becoming clear to me was that Margaret was grimly aware of where events in Vietnam were heading, and she was intimately involved in preparing a network of "stay behinds" that would be embedded in whatever New Order came into being in Indochina. Phu clearly was one of her linchpins. A realization that was also emerging was that Margaret had designs on me in this endeavor. I hardly ever saw her, except for occasional and superficial encounters in church, but Phu was obviously keeping me very close, and we were becoming very good friends.

Phu's desire to acquaint me with the "real Vietnam" took us beyond the *Kieu*. He wanted me to see a part of Vietnam unaffected by the war. He first thought of a visit to the famous Buddhist bonze of Can Tho, a monk of the Mekong Delta's Hoa Hao sect, whom pilgrims of all faiths sought out to question about the meaning of life. A day trip to the Mekong Delta, however, was out of the question, so Phu proposed instead a trip to the "Holy See" of the Cao Dai sect in Tay Ninh. Tay Ninh was only 60 miles northwest of Saigon. It was doable, and I leapt at the chance.

Part of my enthusiasm was nostalgic. The first novel I read about Vietnam was Graham Greene's *The Quiet American*, and it made a deep impression on me. One of the key moments was the trip the two main figures—Thomas Fowler, the older English journalist, and Alden Pyle, the younger American CIA operative—took to what Greene called "Tanyin" (transposing the two middle letters of Tay Ninh).[7] They had just had a fight over Phuong (the story's love interest) and went on the trip to clear the air. Greene used this jaunt as a "Heart of Darkness" quest to a surreal interior that revealed a bizarre synthesis of Eastern and Western civilization in the "Heavenly Eye" of the Cao Dai Holy See. On the way back, Fowler's car ran out of gas, so they spent the night in a French watchtower manned by two terrified Vietnamese soldiers. In these claustrophobic quarters, they engaged in a fervent political debate that served as a platform for Greene's venomous anti-American views. The nocturnal seminar was interrupted by a Viet Minh attack, and Pyle saved Fowler's life as they escaped into a rice field. For me, it was a dream come true to reenact this fictional journey in real life.

For our journey, in yet another mysterious coup, Phu had procured a car. We took off on a Saturday in June, I believe. We started to drive on the famous Highway One, but it branched off to continue south to the Mekong Delta. We took a less famous road northwest to Tay Ninh. The countryside was open with rice fields and rubber plantations alongside the road until they yielded to the occasional hamlet that seemed to crop up about every 10 kilometers. The rubber plantations were impressive with their trees in uniform rows and heights. They were incongruous fields of impeccable order in the chaos of a war. One of them might have been the famous French-owned Michelin Plantation, but, wisely, there were no signs. This order, nevertheless, was disrupted by sections of jungle, and my training at Fort Belvoir triggered images of ideal ambush sites. Thinking like this made me uneasy. Along the way, we stopped at a Cao Dai roadside shrine. I hoped the Good Lord would tolerate my supplication from a place with a "seeing eye" symbol, rather than a cross.

We arrived in Tay Ninh in time for lunch. Phu, of course, knew just the place for it. As usual, he insisted on paying (silently, I thanked

Margaret). The weather was throbbing hot, but the food was hotter. Under an egg-boiling tropical sun, there is nothing like spicy food to sweat out the heat. Thus fortified and acclimated, we strolled to the town square where the Cao Dai Holy See is planted in the center. It is a tall (three or four stories) octagonal church-like building with the walls painted yellow.

Once inside, I realized we had entered into a world I could never have imagined. There is an outer hallway along the perimeter of the octagon that has mural paintings, along the outer wall in each octagonal section, of the Cao Dai Saints: Confucius, Lao Tzu, Moses, Mohammed, Buddha, Victor Hugo, Joan of Arc, and Jesus Christ (none is Vietnamese, interestingly). The inner part of this hallway consists of pillars. In between the pillars, the hallway opens to a huge chamber with pews, giving it a cathedral-like aspect. At one end is a painting of a triangle with a single "Heavenly Eye" that looks very Masonic, and whose vision seems to suffuse the entire chamber. At the other end is an imposing pulpit best described by Graham Greene: "The dragons with lion-like heads climbed the pulpit: on the roof Christ exposed his bleeding heart. Buddha sat, as Buddha always sits, with his lap empty. Confucius' beard hung meagerly down like a waterfall in the dry season."[8] As we stumbled along, transfixed by what we saw, willowy figures in robes of yellow, blue, and red flitted among the pillars in some kind of devotional ritual. On the way out, I picked up several brochures in a foyer.

The Cao Dai (literally, the supreme being) is one of many syncretical movements that sprung up in an Asia trying to sort out, and come to terms with, the onslaught of modernization ushered in by the Western colonial presence. Key events included the Taiping Rebellion in China in the nineteenth century, which tried to blend Christianity with Confucianism; the Sakdalist Uprising in the Philippines in the 1930s, which sought to combine agrarian socialism with Christianity; in Burma, the Saya Sen movement, also in the 1930s, which tried to revive Buddhism with the declaration that Nirvana was not possible under Christian rule; and finally there were the Hoa Hao and Cao Dai sects that sprang up in Vietnam. Though all these movements proved to be historical culs-de-sac, they nevertheless represented heartfelt attempts by traditional societies to merge their own values with what they perceived to be the spiritual energies of the West.

The Cao Dai was founded by Ngo Minh Chieu in 1926. He was a mid-level bureaucrat in the French colonial administration of Cochin China. He appears to have been influenced by the Dai Yuan (Hall of the Way) movement of the 1920s in northern China, which saw itself as the sixth, and most universal, religion of mankind. In a founding letter to the French authorities, Chieu introduced his new religion as the perfect blending of the three religions of Vietnam—Confucianism, Buddhism, and Daoism—with the Christianity of the West. In this fusion, he was a spiritualist who conducted séances to receive insights from the "heavenly eye," which could see everything—past, present, and future—and guide the journey of its adherents along its heavenly way.

Chieu quickly attracted a number of followers from his fellow Vietnamese officials, and raised money to build his Holy See in Tay Ninh. With his church built, he established an institution organized like the Catholic Church with a pope, cardinals, archbishops, and bishops hierarchically presiding over parishes that fanned out into the countryside. It became hugely popular with the peasantry, and by 1928 it had 200,000 members.[9]

The other sect, the Hoa Hao, was a reform Buddhism that started in 1939. Its founder, Huynh Phu So, preached a simple form of Buddhism that shunned temples and their financial obligations. He further insisted on simple and inexpensive marriage and funeral ceremonies. It, too, was widely popular in the Mekong Delta. Both sects were ambivalent about the West, but virulently anti-Communist because of the atheism of Communism and the unsuccessful attempts by the Communist Viet Minh to suppress them.[10]

By 1973, both sects had become significant features in the sociopolitical mosaic of South Vietnam. There were some three million adherents of the Cao Dai in Vietnam and Cambodia, and over a million followers of the Hoa Hao in the Mekong Delta. Together they represented about a third of the South Vietnamese population. If one considers the radical Buddhists already alienated from the Communists, and the hostility of the two million Catholics toward Communism, then, in political terms, by no means did the Communists "own" the South. Never mind that the government of South Vietnam probably didn't either. Turning to the country as a whole, the little island of the "universal way" in Tay Ninh had a stark future. Wars force politics into either/or choices away from the natural muddle of the middle, the fertile soil of compromise. By 1973, the politics on the ground in South Vietnam no longer mattered. In yet another dimension to the tragedy of the Vietnam War, the fate of Vietnam was being decided far away from Tay Ninh, and with little reference to the *Kieu*.

We returned to Saigon that afternoon without incident. Our car did not break down, and we were not ambushed in any nonexistent French watchtower. Nevertheless, the trip ambushed me with a deep sadness. As I returned to the cacophony of Saigon and reflected on the naïve universalism of Tay Ninh, I realized that everyone was trying to remake Vietnam in their own image. As the putty of outsiders, I recalled Susan Sontag's comment on a radio show about her own reaction to reading the *Kieu* as the reflection of "a culture of sadness."

The Unraveling: An Overblown Medal

Whatever the Paris Peace Agreement accomplished, it did not bring peace to Vietnam. After the sixty-day withdrawal period, virtually all U.S. military personnel were withdrawn from Vietnam, and Hanoi released 591 U.S. prisoners (including 10 from Laos). Whether these constituted all prisoners held, particularly those in Laos, is still a matter of controversy, but the U.S. government was officially satisfied. Still, the agreement did call for the full cooperation of the North Vietnamese in accounting for all of the U.S. Missing in Action (MIAs). These numbers have been a contentious moving target, but before the Pentagon started declaring large numbers of these missing as dead, the official count was 1,392.[1] A Joint Casualty Resolution Center was set up in the old MACV Headquarters building, now the Defense Attaché Office. One accomplishment of this agreement, then, was the severance of the American military from its longest war. The U.S. government held on to its commitment to Vietnam through a vast logistical system supervised from the new Defense Attaché Office and supported by a stream of U.S. military assistance. How long this was going to last was a matter of widely divergent opinions. But in 1973 it looked like everything was set up to keep ARVN going for a good while.

That was fortunate because, aside from the provisions concerning the U.S. withdrawal, the rest of the agreement was honored uniformly in the breach. This uniformity was based on the mutual insincerity of all involved. The Americans professed their continued commitment to the integrity of South Vietnam, even as they essentially wanted out. The North Vietnamese were only too happy to oblige them, the better to turn on Thieu after the Americans were safely gone. The South Vietnamese accepted the agreement because they had no choice, but they were determined to find a way to bring the Americans back into the fight.

To begin with, there was no de facto ceasefire in place. The shooting went on uninterrupted, although both sides refrained from making major moves until after the sixty-day U.S. troop withdrawal period. Though Nguyen Van Thieu remained in power as the South Vietnamese president, his regime was supposed to convene a National Council of Reconciliation and Concord to be composed of three delegations: one chosen by the regime, one by the National Liberation Front, and one by these two factions in equal numbers that would be so-called neutralists. This council was to work out a formula for a single national government. As such, it avoided the onus of mandated elections detested by the Communists or of a dictated coalition government despised by President Thieu. The built-in ambiguity of this council seemed like a skillful proposal of diplomatic finesse at the conference table in Paris. On the ground in Saigon, however, the lack of specifics as to how to set it up beyond just these three sets of numbers made it something easy to perpetually haggle about and never quite get done.

From the American and South Vietnamese perspective, the most egregious violations of the Paris Peace Agreement had to do with the one-for-one replacement provisions of North Vietnamese troops and equipment. Though the North Vietnamese were allowed to keep in place their forces and equipment as they existed at the signing of the agreement, they were only allowed to replenish these forces at those levels. To ensure compliance with these provisions, six sites were designated as replacement "harbors," which would be supervised by an International Commission of Control and Supervision (ICCS) composed of Hungarian, Polish, Canadian, and Indonesian forces. Although the United States was successful in setting the numbers for this commission at 1,160 (Hanoi had wanted the ICCS limited to 250), this was hardly a robust force.[2] Further, these sites were never really established, and their monitoring by the ICCS was spotty at best.

This was because the whole system was ignored by the North Vietnamese. Instead, they transformed the Ho Chi Minh Trail from a clandestine network of trails for infiltrating men and materiel to the southern battle fronts into an overt superhighway. This state of affairs was not ignored by the American military. Because of the U.S. preoccupation with these violations, my principal job, among the three Vietnamese intelligence agencies to which I served as a liaison officer, increasingly became to keep relations tight with CICV. It was at CICV where South Vietnamese intelligence laid out the evidence, in some very convincing aerial photography, of the extent of these resupply activities. I was not sure where the South Vietnamese were getting all these pictures (though I had my hunches), but these efforts were attracting a lot of outside attention.

In addition to getting permission to put an American DAO civilian into the photo reconnaissance shop at CICV, we had some high-level visitors. Besides the Order-of-Battle conference detailed in chapter 8, the deputy chief of the Defense Attaché Office, Air Force Brigadier General Ralph Maglione, paid an initial visit on June 6. This was followed by the visit of Major General John Murray (who succeeded General Fred Weyand, the last commander of MACV), the "commander" of the DAO, on June 14. These visits provided CICV with a golden opportunity to impress high-level American military leaders not only with their professional competence but also with the gravity of the threat that was building. Lieutenant Colonel Nho wanted me to help bring this project to the attention of the DAO. During the period from February to June 1973, aerial photography revealed the construction of a system of roads, pipelines, and airfields clearly designed to support another offensive. Hanoi had not wasted any time. Over this network in this period, 400 tanks rumbled south, as did 170 pieces of 122 mm and 130 mm artillery. The activities around Khe Sanh airfield in MR I were so intense, and protected by such a dense pack of anti-aircraft artillery, that reconnaissance overflights proved impossible.[3]

Lt. Colonel Nho had put together an impressive poster-board display of this network of roads as well as vivid photos of the tank and artillery convoys. Particularly impressive to the visitors was a detailed map of a pipeline for gasoline slicing along the Ho Chi Minh Trail. Aerial photography of sections of this pipeline made it clear that next time, unless this system was severely disrupted, the common expectation in any Communist offensive that they would run out of gas would no longer hold true. I had played a small part in procuring some of the supplies for these displays and getting a large copy machine fixed to make the acetate overlays, but my greatest satisfaction was helping an ethnic Chinese captain play an important role in explaining some of the maps and photographs. In any case, these visits were immensely reassuring to the Vietnamese; and, as the liaison officer to CICV, I was flying high.

Despite the massive peace agreement violations by the North
Vietnamese, in 1973 ARVN was doing well in the field. American
aid to this American military machine was flowing in and ARVN
went on the offensive, embarking on land-grabbing operations all
over the country. In truth, these were violations of the agreement
as well, since it had called for a ceasefire in place. Vietnamization,
in effect, meant the Americanization of the Vietnamese military. At
one level, this was fortunate because the departing American military was making its exit just before its own disintegration could be
revealed. In the late 1970s, this decline showed up half a world away
in Germany, where a garrisoned American army was rife with drug
use, racial tensions, and a general breakdown in discipline.

Meanwhile, in 1973, everything in this offloaded American military system was perking along. Parts flowed in for all the helicopters, tanks, and airplanes that routinely break down in sophisticated
conventional military machines. The Vietnamese Air Force (VNAF)
provided cover for ARVN forces fighting not yet fully replenished
North Vietnamese forces. Throughout the year, ARVN was recover-
ing much of the territory lost in previous offensives. In these land-
grabbing operations, what the Vietnamese were not grasping was
the rapid deterioration of the American will for this Vietnamese
venture.

On another level, the Americanization of South Vietnam's military turned tragic because, absent actual American troops on the
ground, the "virtual American" Vietnamese could not count on
the lavish flow of the American logistical system to continue. This
tragic truth would hit home in two short years. But no one, not
even the North Vietnamese, knew this in 1973. Indeed, in support
of these operations, even if they became overextended and disinte-
grated sometimes, the South Vietnamese clung to their umbilical
cord: Nixon's assurance "guaranteeing their safety."

★   ★   ★

The biggest day of my life began one very hot day in early April.[4]
Throughout February and March of 1973, as the extent of North
Vietnamese violations of the terms of the Paris Peace Agreement
became graphically (and photographically) clear on an escalating
daily basis, the question of Nixon's promised retaliation for these

violations loomed increasingly large. This became acute after March 28, which marked the end of the sixty-day withdrawal period and the official time when the various provisions of the agreement were to be implemented. During this period of rising tension, I kept getting mildly annoying calls from my secret superiors at USSAG in NKP, who seemed to regard me more and more as a direct employee. Cordial requests were turning into crisp orders to keep the B-52 targeting lines open with the four regional headquarters of the South Vietnamese military, and especially with the American Intel "contact personnel." I thought they were crazy with this obsession, but I obliged them. If there would be a renewed campaign like the Christmas Bombing, I figured it would all come from CINCPAC (Commander-in-Chief, Pacific Forces) and SAC (Strategic Air Command) Headquarters, as before.

Still, my bosses wanted me to be ready to show how quickly this could work in a surprise drill. That morning, I took my usual run around the Defense Attaché Office building, a little earlier than normal. It also seemed a little hotter than usual that day. I distinctly remember taking a longer shower because I just could not stop sweating—a common affliction in Vietnam. As I was attempting to paste on my clothes, an out-of-breath sergeant burst into the locker room and told me that Colonel Le Gro wanted to see me in his office pronto. This got my attention.

Once in his office, he told me that today was the day they wanted to run the practice operation. (I did not realize he was in the loop on this matter, but, since he was in charge of military intelligence for the DAO, I was also not too shocked.) I was to get sets of B-52 target nominations from each regional military headquarters into Saigon by the end of the day. Also, I was to do this personally because they did not want the intelligence compromised, and I was to only contact American Intel people, not Vietnamese. We had long suspected that the whole B-52 targeting process had somehow been penetrated and that Communist units were being tipped off.[5] Up to now the only preparation I experienced was in the form of occasional phone calls ensuring that target nomination procedures were in place, so these instructions came as a shock. As we discussed the logistics, it became clear that I could not get to MR I in Hue (the First Regional Assistance Command, or FRAC), as well as the other three in a single day, so this leg got shaved off the exercise. Whether it was just dropped or someone else did it, I never knew. Anyway, an Air America plane was waiting at next door Tan Son Nhut Air Base to take me to Pleiku and SRAC (the Second Regional Assistance Command and old MR II). After being returned to Saigon, a helicopter would take me to Long Binh to the Third Regional Assistance Command (TRAC and old MR III, in which Saigon was in the geographic middle). Once I brought these targets back to Saigon, another plane would take me to the Mekong Delta and the Delta Regional Advisory Command (DRAC and old MR IV) in Can Tho. It was going to be a full day.

It was heady having a single plane, however small, chartered for my exclusive use. As I boarded this plane for the Boonies, I fancied myself as Marlow in Joseph Conrad's novel *Heart of Darkness* on a quest for the mythical Kurtz. I was after targets, though, not ivory. Whatever my fanciful notions, the pilot was nonchalant, and he projected an image as if missions like this were routine. Air America, after all, was a CIA-chartered company and had a fleet of small planes throughout the Indo-China theater dedicated to all sorts of miscellaneous and multipurpose flights. The former II Corps in the Central Highlands, SRAC, had the unusual distinction of having had the only civilian in command of a U.S. military mission, the colorful John Paul Vann,[6] who was killed in a helicopter crash in June 1972.

Instead, I was met at the "airport" by an "operative" in shorts, sandals, and a T-shirt, who said he worked for AID. He said he had a packet of target nominations for me in his apartment. Given the time constraints I was under, I expressed some irritation at this. Unfazed, he noted that it looked like I could use some lunch, and he would have a quick one for me there as a bonus for taking these "damned targets" off his hands.

When I got to his apartment, it was clear that it was more than lunch he wanted to show me. I was introduced to a young, comely local woman, whom he called his cook. And I do remember that it was a good lunch. But mostly I remember the beaming pride of this somewhat over-the-hill "bureaucrat" eager to show off the prize someone like him had managed to pull off in this very strange war. I was glad to be on my way, but I was entranced by the little kingdom this disciple of the mythical Lord Kurtz had carved out for himself in the forgotten highlands of Pleiku.[7] Lavish American logistics, the pride of our military, was spread like thick gravy across all of

Indochina, and provided a "field of dreams" for entrepreneurial bureaucrats. Many of them were "prior-service" veterans who, having served their country, were now serving themselves.

When I got back on my own temporary little Air America plane, I took out the file and looked at the target nominations. Supposedly, these targets were developed jointly with the Vietnamese, but the Intel was from pretty sophisticated sources, and I suspected my "secret" friends had a hand in these nominations as well as with all the photo intelligence that was coming into CICV. There was another thing that was also clear: these were very lucrative targets. Colonel Le Gro was pleased when I brought them back to him in Saigon, as he promptly sent me off on a waiting helicopter that flew me to Bien Hoa, not to Long Binh, the TRAC Headquarters. For reasons that were never explained to me, I was to meet an American major in Bien Hoa (the town next to Long Binh, and the location of a major air base), who would give me the MR 3 targets.

Bien Hoa was just 20 miles away, so it was a quick flight. Once again, the Huey helicopter was at my exclusive disposal for this leg of my mission. Exercise or not, it was a heady experience. Once on the ground, I was not taken, as I expected, to the sprawling bases that at one time were the concentrated core of the U.S. military presence in Vietnam—the air base at Bien Hoa, where most of the GIs arrived on Jail Birds and left on Freedom Birds, and the Army's massive base at nearby Long Binh, which contained, at one time, the largest American military prison in the world. Instead, I went to a relatively quiet street in Bien Hoa town where I was met by an American army major, who was thrilled to see me and be a part of this adventure. Unlike his laconic civilian predecessor in Pleiku, he could not wait to show me all the targets. Again, as someone who had been processing these nominations for over a year, I couldn't help but notice that this was shockingly good stuff. The North Vietnamese must have thought they were conducting Warsaw Pact maneuvers.

On the flight back, the pilot let me sit on the floor by the window so I could pretend to be a door gunner. The breeze was refreshing, and the tangled jungles looked like a warm green comforter from the air. Suddenly, I heard the "Whomp, Whomp" of artillery. The pilot veered away to the point where I thought I might slide out of the chopper. Breathlessly, I asked him if we were under fire. "Naw," he

said, "that's just ARVN firing off artillery rounds at nothing hoping
to fend off nonexistent VC attacks, but we need to give these guns
some space." I was a little disappointed. But I brought my packet
back to Colonel Le Gro in his DAO office. Again, he expressed his
pleasure, and sent me off to Tan Son Nhut to board another Air
America chartered plane for Can Tho, the largest city in the teeming
Mekong Delta, which also served as DRAC Headquarters.

This was the last leg of my little adventure, but the Can Tho jaunt
did not follow the script of the first two. Instead of being met by a
military jeep, I was met by an employee of the consul general's office
and whisked to a small enclave in what passed for a limousine. Upon
my arrival into this gated compound containing a three- or four-
story building with a big U.S. embassy seal at the front, I was ushered
into the office of the new consul general for the Delta, a Mr. Harrison. He quickly demanded to know what I was doing in Can Tho.

I knew I had a problem on my hands. I had been given strict orders not to discuss my mission with anyone who was not a part of
this exercise, whether Vietnamese or American. I told Mr. Harrison
that I could not tell him about my mission without the express permission of my boss, Colonel Le Gro. He replied that I wasn't leaving the building until he found out. I said that I would then have to
phone the colonel. He replied that I wasn't going to use a phone,
but would have to use a Telex, so he could read what I said. He did
not want to get pulled into a phone conversation with my colonel
(who outranked him) nor to permit any subliminal "tone of voice"
communications between us. So, I typed up a request for the Telex,
and we waited for a reply.

While we waited, I decided to make small talk. Somehow it came
up that I had grown up in India as a missionary kid and went to
Kodaikanal boarding school in Madras Province (now Tamilnadu).
To our mutual surprise, so had he; but he was an "embassy kid"
(meaning that his parents worked for the U.S. government). For
some reason, this made me an immediate confidant (actually, I was
a little suspicious), and he proceeded to tell me that he was part of
a new band of consular officers brought into Vietnam to finally re-
claim control of the American Mission. Technically, the ambassador
is the chief-of-mission of all U.S. government agencies operating in
a given country. With a full war going on since 1964, MACV had
de facto independence, as military officials came and went as they

liked, and military operations were conducted exclusively from the chain-of-command. But the stand-down of MACV on March 28, and its replacement by the Defense Attaché Office, brought us under the embassy. None of us, however, was in the habit of getting permission from the embassy for any of our trips. And, clearly, no one had bothered to get clearance for this exercise from the new consular officer in Can Tho.[8]

I asked Mr. Harrison how he had come to such a coveted assignment. He told me that he had spent most of his career in Latin America, as had many of his colleagues in this new influx, and he wanted to be a part of shutting down this immoral war. He also suspected that the whole DAO edifice was nothing but a bureaucratic war-machine to restart the war. "So," he then asked, "what are you here for?" This was not turning into a fruitful conversation.

"Let's see what Colonel Le Gro says," I replied. When the Telex came, it said that I was to leave those premises immediately and not tell this gentleman anything. He countered that nothing was going to happen until the ambassador weighed in on the matter. I then insisted that it was only fair that I let my superiors know that this had moved to the "ambassadorial level." After some hesitation, he allowed me to Telex this new wrinkle. My reply came back from Brigadier General Maglione, the Deputy Defense Attaché, telling me to leave immediately and not to tell Mr. Harrison anything.

"Not until we hear from the ambassador," snarled Mr. Harrison.

Pretending severe stress—made convincing by the fact that it was pretty genuine—I asked to be excused to the bathroom to gain some composure. Taken aback, he gestured to a room that happened to be near the door, something I had noticed. I waited long enough to catch him off guard, and then I opened the door and bolted like a jaguar (remembering, of course, not to step on the big black ant that had made it to the top of the sink and then fallen to the floor). Mr. Harrison screamed, "Stop," and then "Stop him!" I made it out of his office and out of the building. There were two Vietnamese guards who were typically preoccupied, and I got past the gate despite their belated "Dung Lais! [Stop!]" I heard sharp reports, which I imagined to be gunfire. What they really were, I never looked back to find out, but they certainly gave wings to my feet. At the end of the first block, there just happened to be a military jeep with an American in it, who stepped down and said, "Here, Tim, get in." As we drove out of town, he asked me, "The Colonel wants to know if you told that guy anything?" I told him that I had not. He relaxed and took out an attaché case and said, "Here are your targets." He looked mighty pleased with himself.

I returned to Saigon in the early evening, around 7 P.M., I think, and was met by Colonel Le Gro. He took the attaché case and opened it. After looking over some of the nominations, he expressed his pleasure. He said, "Well, you did it all in a day, and these show that we've got very good targets in this system." He told me not to worry about what happened in Can Tho, that it would all be handled at higher levels without any repercussions for me. Then he gave me a pat on the back.

But my day was not over. I returned to my office to get transportation back to my apartment. A very distraught Lt. Col. Nho met me, and just as quickly as at Can Tho, he whisked me over to Colonel Lung's office at the JGS compound. Colonel Lung was clearly anguished and upset. He wanted to know what I had been doing all day. He had reports of me in Pleiku, then in Bien Hoa, and finally in Can Tho picking up attaché cases, without the knowledge of any of his officers in the Intelligence Command. To my horror, I realized that somehow the Vietnamese had been kept out of the loop. I had to tell Colonel Lung the same thing I told Mr. Harrison. This time, however, I could use the phone.

In explaining the situation to Colonel Le Gro, I told him that I felt my own position as a liaison officer was in serious jeopardy unless he intervened and explained this all personally. The good colonel came over at once and went into Colonel Lung's office. Lt. Col. Nho stayed in the office with him. When the door finally opened, I saw a smile on Colonel Lung's face. After Colonel Le Gro left, the two Vietnamese officers invited me into the office and told me what a good liaison officer I had been, that I had worked very hard for them, and that they were very appreciative.

I smiled and thanked them, but writhed in an existential guilt and deep personal sorrow. Not only was it a very hot, full day; it had also been a very long day, in a very long war.

★   ★   ★

This bizarre event quickly became buried in the continual violations of the ceasefire provisions and the efforts of all of us to bring this to the attention of anyone who would listen. For me, it lay in various endeavors to get the Vietnamese intelligence case before the appropriate American agencies, whether it was an Order-of-Battle Conference or in setting up visits to CICV by the remaining American general officers left in-country. So just as much a surprise as the exercise itself was the announcement by Lt. Col. Nho in the middle of July that I was to be awarded the Vietnamese Army Staff Medal First Class in a ceremony in the Joint General Staff's Intelligence Headquarters. Colonel Lung pinned on the medal, but most of the official photographs were with Lt. Col. Nho, who was clearly being given credit for this medal as well. Colonel Le Gro looked on, as my American superior. It seemed like a hell of a lot of fuss for just an exercise, but I initially just chalked it up to my own personal encounter with, and memory of, this very strange war.

Part III

Coming to Terms

Conclusion: Going Native and Going Home

Life really did not return to normal for me after this strange episode. The question of what this was all about became part of a larger questioning on my part of what our further involvement in Vietnam was all about. On top of this, I had a new American boss who piled on so many projects that it distracted me from my alienation and only made it worse. When I had time to think, I couldn't get Colonel Lung's smile out of my mind. What was bothering me was a growing unease over the trend of historical events in Vietnam. Like all of my REMF colleagues, I wanted to believe that ARVN could go it alone, and that Vietnamization would pass its final test. But I became worried about the natural set of separating interests between Washington and Saigon in the face of the singular obstinacy of Hanoi. In personal terms, it became increasingly clear that I would have to betray that smile if I remained in Vietnam. I submitted my resignation effective July 31 and prepared myself to look forward to entering graduate school in the fall at the Johns Hopkins University School of Advanced International Studies (SAIS) in Washington, D.C. I had made my own "accommodation" in January by reactivating my application file of four years earlier.[1]

My Intelligence Section Chief, Colonel Walker (Colonel Le Gro was the Intelligence Division Chief), accepted my resignation with disconcerting grace. Privately, he told me: "Tim, if you had not done this, I was going to send you home for three months. You needed this to clear your head because you are starting to go native on us. Remember, you work for us, not the Vietnamese. With these misplaced loyalties of yours, it is better this way. You have worked very hard for your Vietnamese friends." This last comment about my Vietnamese friends he said kindly, but it was not a compliment. Spiritually, I was separating from this receding American mission, and in any set of final "withdrawing" moments, this was not going to be helpful. Curiously, in this rejection/acceptance by Colonel

194   Walker, my respect for him grew. To his country—and mine—he was more true than I was.

The evidence of these transferring loyalties was increasingly obvious to my American colleagues. I was less and less successful in hiding my annoyance with these "newbie" arrivals. They all seemed more intent on their own little private schemes and interests, whether it was great deals on tailor-made clothes, incredible buys in jade jewelry, or even larger entrepreneurial ambitions, than in the desperately urgent mission of ensuring the success of Vietnamization. The American way of war is lavish, both in firepower and logistics. This means that we throw a lot of money into these ventures with the accounting never too strict. The opportunities, as I "discovered" in my trip to Pleiku, to serve oneself either during or after one's service to one's country were legion. As I mentioned earlier, one of my immediate civilian bosses was married to the daughter of a high-ranking commander in the South Vietnamese National Police (what we called the "white mice"). He lived in a lavish villa with a huge retinue of functionaries at his beck and call. The other boss who had transferred in from Japan became very cozy with this colleague. This coziness, I soon discovered, was as much extracurricular as it was professional. One morning, I was called in by one of these two and offered an opportunity to participate in a business venture of theirs in Thailand. I demurred, saying that I was probably headed back to graduate school in the fall and would not have the time to invest in this venture. Okay, he said, but then he asked me to stay out of their way. I didn't quite know what he meant by this, but I gave the two of them a very wide berth after that, and I never really had any idea of what they were up to.

Indeed, the venality of this war pressed in on me from multiple fronts. I mentioned earlier that I kept finding excuses for not going to the Intelligence Headquarters of the JGS Compound (Colonel Lung's shop) because of the badgering I received from some of the officers for goods from the PX. After "things" cooled with Christine Carjean under the withering glare of her disapproving father, and with conversation limited because of our poor command of our respective languages, the Madame of the family started overwhelming me with similar requests. In fact, she began to keep track of my every movement (or so I thought), and I began to suspect that her family owned the building in which I and several of my colleagues rented our flats. I was beginning to feel hemmed in.

Wars are brutalizing, ennobling, and corrupting all at the same time. Unfortunately, in REMF Land, all we saw was the corruption. Just as with post-traumatic stress syndrome for the combat veteran, this corruption for the REMF carried the danger of becoming a lifelong addiction and nightmare. The things I very self-consciously stayed away from—the easy women, ready drugs, and sleazy money—were nevertheless alluring and habit-forming. All this, I could see. I had to leave.

The casus belli of my resignation, however, was this new boss. I still had my two liaison office chiefs discussed above, but this new one worked in Intelligence Collection. She was an officious woman in her forties who was your classic, efficient bureaucrat par excellence. She had direct access to me in that she could levy "SICRs" on me (Special Intelligence Collection Requirements, pronounced "sickers"). She did this in spades, and was utterly clueless about the diplomatic costs to me in procuring them. A SICR originated somewhere in the military intelligence system requesting information on various things, most of which seemed utterly trivial to me, like what NVA units were currently on R and R leave in Laos or how many NVA trucks were currently parked just outside the Angel's Wing (a part of the South Vietnamese border northwest of Saigon). None of it ever seemed to be big picture stuff like what I was interested in.

Why anyone ever wanted this stuff, I was never told; I was just ordered to get it. Since I did not know any of this myself, I had to ask someone from the various Vietnamese agencies with whom I "liaised," usually Lt. Col. Nho or Colonel Lung himself. These were two very nice gentlemen, but there were limits to their patience. To answer too many of these requests would make it look like they were working for the Americans rather than for their own military—which is why I wanted a prioritized scheme for rationing these SICRs. Furthermore, none of these requests really came for free. For every set of ARVN-generated Intel reports, I could eventually count on a request for my "good offices" to secure this or that. To handle this in an omnibus way, my big coup was to arrange a deal with Pacific Architects and Engineers (PAE, a U.S. contractor) to handle the cleaning and maintenance of the CICV building.

Everyone in the building loved to have these PAE maids cleaning their floors and bathrooms every day. My office suddenly glowed with repeated dusting of the walls, my desk, and all the rest of the furniture. As a building originally constructed for Americans, it was built for air conditioners (meaning it was windowless). Now whenever an air conditioner broke down, it was fixed in a half an hour. But even this was not enough to quench this boss's appetite.

I had the further difficulty of other American agencies returning to the hunt. Since so many American Intel agencies had shut down, CICV was one of the few primary Intel production centers left, and these agencies were offering money for reports that I had long been getting for "free." When I asked this female boss for a prioritization scheme of SICRs, she became intensely frosty, and loftily proclaimed that they all came from Washington (which I doubted) and had equal priority. At one level, I realized that the woman was just doing her job, but my world was unraveling.

As my job unraveled in June and July, I turned more and more to my personal life. Not all of my American colleagues were schmucks. At the nondenominational Protestant church, I met up with several of them who would go to an orphanage on Saturday mornings, and I was invited to go along. We would give money for food and play with the children for a couple of hours. This was a Catholic orphanage supported, I believe, by some order in Belgium. Many of the children were from very large families, and the parents would rotate their children through the orphanage every month, usually three at a time, basically to keep them fed. There were also a lot of abandoned GI kids, the so-called Amer-Asians. These were the children waiting forever for adoptions from the West, which was a little like boys from the Dominican Republic making it into professional baseball. A few of these children were the offspring of a Vietnamese mother and an African American father. These particular children were viciously shunned by the other children, and by most of the nuns, as well. As a result, most of them were virtually autistic. I played with one such little girl who was about nine, who would just hang on to my leg, and she cried like it was the end of the world every time I left. In fact, going to the orphanage became excruciating because here I could see that we Americans were literally betraying our own children.

Indeed, with each visit, I felt increasingly responsible for the plight of these children. My countrymen had brought these children into the world and then abandoned them. The fate of this nine-year-old pierced me deeply, and I began to have thoughts of adopting her. As these thoughts became more concrete, they ran into two barriers. One was the impossibility of a single parent bound for graduate school really being able to handle the responsibility. The other was the agony of the choice itself. Even though my nine-year-old leg hugger seemed the most desperate, there were many other children in equally compelling circumstances. How could I play God and choose just one, and leave a hundred others behind?

Here again, the individual versus collective moral dilemma hit me. How could the United States invest so much of its treasure and talent in one little country like Vietnam, and mostly ignore the equally compelling needs of so many other poor, violence-beset countries. What was more, for all this effort, America was abandoning even this one orphan country it had chosen—just as I was going to leave Colonels Lung and Nho.

Back in Saigon, though I cherished my weekly dinners with Bill Gausmann, it was clear we were both coming to the same depressing conclusion—something we never directly addressed. He became more withdrawn, and academic. He no longer talked about contemporary politics in Hanoi or Saigon, but launched out on general discourses on nationalism versus Communism. He drank more, and so did I—to keep up. So my memories of the contents of these later conversations have become more vague. But he talked of his family, and of mine, and of his Croix de Guerre, and of the Resistance in France in World War II. He also talked of returning to Washington for a last assignment, and of our keeping in touch while I was in grad school. So it was over—but it was a reality we dared not verbalize—lest our unbelief fry us in a spiritual Hell.

I also continued to see Phu. His recitations of the *Kieu* grew more rhapsodic. He closed his eyes more while he recited, as if he were shutting out the present and evoking the time in Vietnam before any of this had happened. The more rhapsodic he became, the more any chance of my grasping any of the inner and deeper spirit of this lyrical language disappeared. Phu spoke less of politics and more of his Christian faith, and how we would probably not be brothers-in-arms but eternal brothers in the faith. The ethereal Margaret lost substance for me as well. Though I would still see her in church, instead of a quick but pleasant conversation over coffee after the service, I would get a smile and a wave and then she would vanish. Whatever she may have had in mind for me with Phu had also vanished.[2]

The real agony of this unraveling came with my continued and regular contacts with my two good Vietnamese colonels. I tried as hard as I could to support them in their mission of defeating the Communists in what had clearly become an uninterrupted war, Paris Peace Agreement or not. They still showed their appreciation, and I thought their dedication to their mission was unwavering. What they really felt was inscrutable, which, in a way, was fine, because I don't think I really wanted to know.

At heart, my resignation did not come from any of these frustrations. It came from the realization of a truth, the truth that Saigon in July 1973 was embroiled in a classic Greek tragedy. As I mentioned in chapter 1, the key to the ability of the Vietnamese to hold off the Communists lay in the success of a program of Vietnamization whereby the South Vietnamese would be able to continue to fight against the Communists with an American-trained and -equipped military, backed up by a legitimate South Vietnamese political system that, in some last resort extremis, could count on U.S. support in a tangible political and military way that would serve as a bulwark against Communist victory. This the United States had done in 1965, 1968, and 1972. Despite all of our efforts to ensure this Vietnamese capacity—and, in 1973, the South Vietnamese were managing nicely—this bulwark was as much a psychological necessity of morale to the Vietnamese as it was material. Though it hadn't quite happened yet, in July I knew that this bulwark was disappearing. And this was the tragedy: with the bulwark gone, nothing that we or the Vietnamese did in Saigon would make any difference.

Knowing this, I left Vietnam on August 3 in deep moral despair. Personally, I would have given anything to stay on and give my loyalty to South Vietnam, but as an official representative of the United States government, however lowly, this loyalty was not mine to give individually, absent that of the collective support of my country. What was killing me was that, however much I rationally understood these "macro" moral and geostrategic imperatives, in my soul

I felt I owed nothing to my American superiors—and everything to my Vietnamese charges. Yes, I had gone native. I had to go "home," if there were to be anything American left in me.

Just before I left Vietnam, I committed the greatest act of folly in my life (and there are many candidates for this honor) that nearly ended my career in Southeast Asia—and beyond. I quit work on a Friday, and did not fly out until Monday or Tuesday of the next week. This gave me one last weekend as a real, unemployed civilian in Vietnam. I decided to try being a real tourist and fly up to Hue to see the sights of the Imperial Capital. I purchased a regular commercial ticket on Air Vietnam, but contracted to stay in some U.S. government quarters for my one night there.

During the flight, I could almost imagine a postwar capitalist Vietnam. The stewardesses were dressed in gorgeous satin azure-colored *ao dais,* and were all smiles and attentive to all my little requests. But landing in Hue was a shock. The city was incredibly seedy and rundown. My tour of the citadel was depressing. The scale of the place was incredibly small—reminding me, as I was leaving, that this really was a very small country. All of the brick courtyards were besmirched by eruptions of weeds. Many of the walls and pagoda-like structures still bore the marks of all the fighting in Tet '68. The tales of past splendors and glories by the tour guides were clearly just that—in the past. President Thieu always had as a backdrop, for his press conferences and speeches, the tower in Hue celebrating the victory of the South over the North in the sixteenth century. Seeing the actual tower as a pile of bricks crumbling into sand was just too symbolic for me.

That evening I went out to find a restaurant. It was an eerie experience. When I finally found a place that looked somewhat safe, I found I was the only patron. I felt like a Rip Van Winkle who had woken up a long way from the Hudson Valley. I left the restaurant determined to find some kind of tourist memory. I walked along the famous Perfume River on the way back to my quarters. Whoever named this river had a very sick sense of humor. The place stank—and it was very dark. Down an embankment there were a set of sampans tied up for the night.

Someone from one of these noble vessels shouted out offering me a ride to see the city by night. Holy shades of Amsterdam or Venice: why not!? I tumbled down the hill, scrambled aboard, and asked how much for a half-hour ride. He said only 1,000 piasters (about $10) to start out with. As he shoved off, this puzzled me a bit. As we got to the middle of the river, my quandary lifted. Out from the bowels of this craft emerged a young lovely; who, but for some frontal equipage, might have passed for nine years old! Contracting some horrendous disease was not how I wanted to spend my last night in Vietnam. Like the incident at the Guard Post, I began to engage the owner of the vessel in a conversation using about every Vietnamese word I ever knew. I actually succeeded in making him laugh a couple of times. However, he was very determined to extract some more lucre from me, and kept bringing up the girl whom he called his "daughter." I reassured him that his daughter was simply too beautiful, and that I am sure he wanted to save her virtue for some high-ranking officer in the army (I felt it important to leave the question of which army a little vague). Though he did not seem to be overly concerned about this matter of virtue, he also did not know exactly how to get me off this.

At this point, I thought it might be prudent to accept a slightly more benign form of illness as a possible way out of this incredible mess. I mentioned that I thought I was smelling some very good food emanating from the bowels of this sampan and that I bet his wife was a very good cook. This I declared rather loudly, and the good cook heard my prayer and emerged with a big smile and a pot of rice and *nuoc mam,* the Vietnamese fish sauce that is so odoriferous that I even smelled it above the Perfume River. Fortunately, the extreme darkness permitted me to exclaim on its delicacy with what at least sounded like relish, and I gave the good woman—directly— another 2,000 piasters. She was thrilled, and the husband was caught off guard.

Thus fortified, I at least had the presence of mind to ask to be left off at a place different from our point of embarkation. When the man started veering back to this spot anyway, I demanded that hospitality required him to honor my wish, and I grabbed the till from him and beached the boat at least 50 yards before this previous point. He recovered his composure and wished me a good night. As I disembarked, there was a lot of scrambling in the bushes at this earlier spot. As I raced up the hill, I heard my good pilot call out, "This stupid American didn't do anything except eat *nuoc mam.*" I don't know how persuasive he was because at least some of this scuttling continued closer; but, in extremis, I am a very fast scrambler, and I crested the bank well ahead of this scuttling and burst into a sprint to my quarters. All my running had paid off after all. It is possible that all of what I heard was just a herd of goats—that spoke Vietnamese. I left Hue, and Vietnam, without inquiring further.

★ ★ ★

I had escaped, but Vietnam did not. When I returned to the States in early August, Watergate was all the rage. The Senate's Select Committee on Presidential Campaign Activities, under Senator Sam Ervin of North Carolina, was holding hearings about a coverup of illicit campaign activities by Nixon operatives at the Watergate condominium complex during the 1972 presidential campaign. Nixon was forced to appoint a public prosecutor, Archibald Cox, whom he promptly fired in October. This set the stage for a battle with Congress over access to White House documents. Nixon's intransigence, and the revelations of increasingly damaging details, led to the clamoring for an impeachment trial. On August 9, 1974, Nixon resigned the presidency.

As part of this struggle, Nixon's opponents in Congress took out their frustrations on Vietnam. Despite the continued high level of fighting in Vietnam in 1973, Congress, in the Cooper-Church Amendment to a defense appropriations bill, forced an ending to U.S. bombing in Indo-China by August 15, 1973, which was extended to all American combat activities in Indo-China by November 1973. South Vietnam was truly on its own. What it had left on hand was an American-supplied and -supported military machine, now without any Americans. However Vietnamized this machine had become, it still required American logistical support to keep it running. This reliance on outside support was just as true for the North Vietnamese. It is worth remembering that, as nonindustrialized lesser-developed countries, neither South nor North Vietnam had the industries to produce the tanks, artillery pieces, planes, and helicopters of modern militaries. Saigon relied on Washington for these provisions, and Hanoi on Moscow and Beijing. In any case, by 1973 South Vietnam had turned into a battlefield of two foreign-fed conventional armies. What there was of a Communist guerrilla war had perished in the flames of the Tet Offensive of 1968.

It was during these two years that the pivotal imbalance occurred that precipitated the disastrous defeat of 1975. In 1973, Congress approved $2.2 billion in military aid to South Vietnam. This was slashed to $900 million in 1974, and cut to $700 million in 1975, with the actual funds for this last amount totaling only $500 million.[3] In two short years, U.S. military support in 1975 was less than a fourth of what it had been in 1973. Meanwhile, the buildup of Communist forces, and support for them, continued unabated. In their own version of Enhance Plus, international Communist assistance in 1972 permitted a doubling of supplies shipped to the South over the previous year.[4] Russian military assistance to Hanoi stayed steady during these subsequent three years at $650 million per annum.[5] Throughout the war, North Vietnam could also count on a flow of Chinese support that totaled between $10 and $20 billion overall, which included a large number of logistical troops sent to North Vietnam to free North Vietnamese troops for "liberation" duties in the South.[6]

These commitments, of course, permitted a huge buildup of Communist forces. Since the ceasefire in 1973 to the end of 1974, the Defense Attaché Office reported that 200,000 replacement troops moved south, raising North Vietnamese forces there to over 300,000. During this same period, armored vehicles, mostly tanks, had ballooned from 100 to over 700. This was double the number of tanks available to ARVN. As this DAO study concluded: "Significantly, the RVNAF were, for the first time in the war, in an inferior position."[7] Then, according to the journalist Robert Shaplen, a Soviet military mission to Hanoi in December 1974 pledged a fourfold increase in military assistance in support of this upcoming offensive.[8]

What added to this inferiority were the tremendous pressures of these cutbacks on top of a highly inflated economy. The quadrupling of oil prices in October 1973 contributed to a 100 percent rise in basic commodity prices by 1974, while the basic pay for a soldier only grew by 25 percent. This turned into a crisis of supply when an explosion set off by Communist sappers in December 1973 of the main POL (Petroleum, Oil, and Lubricants) storage facility near Bien Hoa burned up half the national stocks—which were not replenished by the United States. These twin blows made the continuation of ARVN land-grabbing operations economically ruinous, and caused about 150,000 ARVN troops to become "flower pot" and "ghost soldiers" (troops who slipped away to take civilian jobs to make ends meet), and another 240,000 to desert outright (a rate double the level of desertions before the ceasefire).[9] Although President Thieu can be justly criticized for dangerously overextending his forces beyond their now dramatically reduced capabilities, it is hardly fair to criticize the gardener for a dying garden when his water supply has been cut off.

And die the garden of South Vietnam did. In December 1974 and January 1975, North Vietnamese forces attacked Phuoc Long Province (a border province in the Northeast corner of MR 3) as a probe of American intentions. Of course, there was no response militarily, but President Ford did ask Congress for $300 million in supplementary military aid in light of this flagrant violation of the ceasefire agreement. Congress dithered, and after two congressional trips to Vietnam in February, no action was taken. Now convinced that no American help would be forthcoming, the North Vietnamese launched what would be their final offensive to the "liberation" of the South on March 10. For the opening of this campaign in the Central Highlands, they had amassed a force in this area that had achieved against ARVN a ratio of 5.5 to 1 in troops, 1.2 to 1 in tanks, and 2.1 to 1 in artillery.[10] At the launch pad for this final campaign, then, the South Vietnamese were outnumbered and outgunned.

The Central Highlands "capital" of the highland Montagnards, Ban Me Thuot, fell the next day, the same day Congress voted down Ford's supplemental request. The North Vietnamese then implemented a strategy, quite roughly equivalent to a Pentagon contingency scenario mapped out in the mid-1950s as it contemplated a plan to salvage the deteriorating French position in Indochina, to attack along a prong across the Central Highlands and another one straight south from the north along the coast on Highway One. With the joining of these two prongs, together they would turn south for the final advance on Saigon.[11]

Things unraveled dramatically from this loss. President Thieu contributed to this debacle by a series of disastrous decisions. He ordered the simultaneous recapture of Ban Me Thuot and a withdrawal from the two other Central Highland towns of Pleiku and Kontum. The result was chaos. In the north, in MR 1, the legendary General Truong was attempting to draw up a defense of Hue and Danang, but Thieu ordered him to release the Airborne Division to Saigon for its final defense. With this, ARVN positions in the

North collapsed, and the withdrawal turned into a general rout of ARVN forces. As one reporter put it, ARVN began "losing the war faster than the Communists could win it."[12] By March 18, the Central Highlands were overwhelmed; and, in the North, Hue Fell on March 28 and Danang on the 30. The two prongs had joined.

From March 30 to April 7, General Fred Weyand, Army Chief of Staff, came to Saigon, at the behest of President Ford, to draft a plan for South Vietnam's survival. It called for the re-outfitting of eight ARVN divisions to hold a line at the northern border of MR III, 75 miles northeast of Saigon. The president promptly asked Congress on April 10 for $722 million to do this. Congress denied the request on April 17, the day the capital city of Cambodia, Phnom Penh, fell to Communist Khmer Rouge forces.

On April 3, the North Vietnamese juggernaut crossed into MR III, already breaching General Weyand's nonexistent line. Between these forces and the prize of Saigon lay the little town Xuan Loc, some 60 miles northeast of Saigon. It was defended by the 25,000 troops of the Eighteenth ARVN Division. At the start of the war, LBJ had proclaimed that South Vietnam was "just like the Alamo."[13] Little Xuan Loc now acted like it really was. These 25,000 troops held off four North Vietnamese divisions for eleven days (ironically enough, the same time frame as the Christmas bombing in 1972) from April 10 to 21. This division's heroic defense was a bittersweet, small piece of proof of the potential of Vietnamization, but there was no relieving force from a "Sam Houston" to save this "Texas," and President Thieu resigned the day this local Alamo fell. Saigon itself succumbed on April 30.[14]

The key provision of the January 27, 1973, "Paris Peace Agreement on Vietnam" was Chapter 5, "The Reunification of Viet Nam and the Relationship between North And South Viet Nam." Article 15 of this chapter opens with the following preamble: "The reunification of Viet Nam shall be carried out step by step through peaceful means on the basis of discussions and agreements between North and South Vietnam, without coercion or annexation by either party, and without foreign interference. The time for reunification will be agreed upon by North and South Viet Nam."[15]

The only phrase in this solemn declaration that proved to be subsequently true was the "without foreign interference" from Washington. I submit that this lack of American interference with the fall of Saigon was not a "decent interval," but a betrayal. It was a betrayal by Nixon for the moral lapse of Watergate, and more grotesquely for the clumsy attempted coverup of it, which politically prevented him from redeeming his frequent written pledges to the South Vietnamese to come to their military assistance in the face of the massive Communist violations of the Peace Agreement. Of these violations and fundamental Communist treachery toward this agreement, there can be no question. It was a betrayal by the U.S. Congress for its failure to honor administrative requests for this assistance to South Vietnam at appropriate levels, especially for failing to give the Vietnamese, and Vietnamization, a last chance with the Weyand Plan.[16] Ultimately, it was a betrayal by the American people for not caring. It was this last betrayal that ensured the inevitable conclusion to this tragedy.

Epilogue: Secret Mission Revealed—and Its Liberation

But was this tragedy inevitable? This is the question I pursued in my years of graduate school back in the States. Every course I took at both Johns Hopkins for my master's degree and at Duke for my Ph.D. had to do, in some way or other, with figuring out what had happened in Vietnam. Naturally, the politics of this conflict were complex. South Vietnam seemed to have a hard time establishing a legitimate national political system. The Communists had a long record of trying to claim the mantle of nationalism for themselves. Most of my professors appeared to be sympathetic with their efforts. I was skeptical. Having grown up on the mission field in India, I remembered the atheism of Communism, and the tyrannical politics that were, to me, a natural outgrowth of this godlessness. I remember reading about the treachery of Ho Chi Minh toward Phan Boi Chau, the "father" of modern Vietnam; the Communist betrayal of the Catholics in the North; their dependence on the Chinese in the final siege against the French at Dienbienphu in 1954; and their relentless campaign to conquer/reunify the South, regardless of the human costs, and of dishonoring the terms of the Paris Peace Agreement they had pledged to honor.

There were other nationalist groups in modern Vietnamese history, but in World War II they chose to withdraw from the country to American and Chinese protection in southern China, leaving the Communists to carry on the fight alone against the Japanese in defense of the Vietnamese Fatherland. For many Western academics, this record entitled Ho Chi Minh and his ruling Communist circle to a reputation as the leader of an independent Communist nationalist movement that was comparable to Marshal Tito of Yugoslavia. My own study of Ho Chi Minh revealed him rather to be a loyal servant of the Comintern, and as committed a Communist as he was a nationalist. If there were an Asian Communist who had earned a Tito-like independence from Moscow, it would be Mao Zedong of China, not Ho. Indeed, Ho's steadfast loyalty to both Moscow and

Beijing gained the North Vietnamese a steady flow of military assistance to the very end of the war.

The non-Communist nationalist record, however, remained sul-
lied. The first president of South Vietnam in 1954, Ngo Dinh Diem,
was a committed nationalist, whose credentials even Ho respected.
Diem espoused a nationalist ideology, but he married it to something called "personalism," which, in Vietnam, he equated with loyalty to his regime. Though rhetorically committed to democracy,
his primary concern was to provide Vietnam with a strong moral
foundation first. The twin pillars to his personalist credo was the
intellectual loyalty and moral obligation to one's god, nation, fellow
citizens, and one's self (what he called *Thanh*); and the dutiful practice of these obligations, no matter how grievous (what he called
Tin). It was reminiscent of Chiang Kai-Shek's New Life Movement
in China in the 1930s. Like Communism, then, personalism in Vietnam had a Confucian, rather than a Buddhist, foundation. As events
turned out, the Communists were better motivated, and had more
reliable patrons.[1] In any case, Diem soon became autocratic, and
as a minority Roman Catholic, his rule aroused the antagonism of
Buddhist militants. On November 1, 1963, Diem was overthrown in
a military coup with the tacit approval of the United States.

Without American approval, Diem and his brother, Ngo Dinh
Nhu, almost a co-regent with Diem, were killed. This set in motion
a merry-go-round of further coups and political chaos that lasted
until 1965. In this interregnum, the Communists would have seized
power, except for the commitment of American ground combat
troops to save this fledging "democracy." Nguyen Van Thieu, a field
officer who had secured the presidential palace in the Diem Coup,
eventually took power, and he won a presidential election in 1967. In
the midst of what was termed the "Big Unit War," President Thieu
presided over what might be charitably called a "limited democracy." His record, as both a military commander and political leader,
was mixed. The military part has already been noted. Politically, he
did implement a major land reform measure in 1970 that effectively
ended tenancy in Vietnam and earned his regime thereafter a strong
reservoir of rural support. A convert to Catholicism, he nevertheless
reached out to the Buddhist majority in ways that Diem had not.
He championed a Buddhist chaplaincy in the military, for example.
He also made overtures to the same popular, mass-based sects—the

Cao Dai of Tay Ninh and the Hoa Hao of the Mekong Delta—that Diem had tried to suppress. In the swirl of urban politics, however, he alienated progressive circles of opinion, both in Vietnam and in the United States, by his reelection as president in 1971 in which he intimidated his two electoral opponents into withdrawing from the race.[2]

Meanwhile, the costs to the United States of this murky intervention had escalated. By the end of the Johnson administration in 1968, the United States had committed to Vietnam 40 percent of its combat-ready divisions, 50 percent of its tactical airpower, and 33 percent of its naval forces.[3] Clearly, such a skewing of American global obligations in the larger Cold War could not be sustained indefinitely. Richard Nixon was elected to the presidency on a pledge to bring an end to this intervention. His plan to do this was by a war policy of phased American troop withdrawals supposedly being replaced by equivalently capable South Vietnamese forces under the rubric of Vietnamization, and secured by secret negotiations with the North Vietnamese aimed at achieving a ceasefire and commitment to a peaceful solution to the national reunification of Vietnam.

However complex all of these politics were, none of them, to me anyway, justified the betrayal at the end—of South Vietnam more generally, and of my two good colonels personally, Vu Van Nho and Hoang Ngoc Lung. Indeed, in all my years of study and research, my thoughts frequently turn to these two men, and to the blazoned memory in my mind of their smiles on that fateful day at the end of my "exercise."

One very cold day in the winter of 1979, in a windowless carrel in the subterranean depths of Duke University's Perkins Library, I was poring over books and manuscripts for my dissertation on the "lessons of Vietnam," much as I had been doing on any other cold winter day, when I stumbled across the following passage in Guenter Lewy's *America in Vietnam:*

> No sooner had the agreement been signed than North Vietnam started violating its provisions. Large numbers of NVA troops were infiltrated into South Vietnam via Laos and Cambodia and SAM-2 missiles were installed at the rebuilt airstrip of Khe Sanh. . . .
>
> On 29 March [in 1973] the last American prisoners were released in

Hanoi and the final installment of American troops left South Vietnam. Also, on that day, in a nationwide address, Nixon hailed the completion of the American withdrawal from Vietnam. . . . [But he noted that] some problems such as continued infiltration remained, and he warned that "we shall insist that North Vietnam comply with the agreement and the leaders of North Vietnam should have no doubt as to the consequences if they fail to comply with the agreement." Less than a month later, . . . the president had just about decided to follow through on these threats and resume the bombing of North Vietnam when the floodgates of Watergate opened up: Nixon learned that his counsel, John Dean, had begun to talk to the Watergate prosecutors. Realizing that the renewed bombing would spur violent criticism and knowing that Dean's testimony could tie him directly to the Watergate scandal, Nixon refrained from approving the raids.[4]

That very hot day in April 1973 had been real! It was no exercise! Only what was also real was that John Dean had spilled the beans about the Watergate coverup to Congress, and Nixon canceled a massive bombing campaign against the huge North Vietnamese "trail" system and new combat base at Khe Sanh by B-52s—"my" B-52s! I was a mouse in the cockpit with my paws briefly on the bomb bay of history. It was, indeed, my brief moment of glory. But the Watergate cat slapped me off the joystick. My moment was lost, and I was relegated to the life of a college professor tilting my lance against academic windmills with the folly of my dissertation thesis: this was the war we could have won.

But could we? Among those who think we could is Marshall L. Michel, who has written a definitive account of the Linebacker II Christmas Bombing in 1972. In this work, he contends: "Had Nixon remained in power and the U.S. kept a significant B-52 presence in Asia, it is at least questionable if the North Vietnamese would have risked a conventional invasion of South Vietnam. It was only after the fall of Nixon that the fall of South Vietnam became inevitable."[5]

Michel's contention lands us in the middle of "counterfactual analysis." As explained by Joseph Nye, a counterfactual is to imagine a situation "in which one thing changes while other things are held constant," in this case: Watergate doesn't happen so that Richard Nixon remains in office, and he carries out a B-52 bombing campaign (the targets for which being "heroically" provided by yours

210   truly) against the North Vietnamese in fulfillment of his promise to Thieu, and the North Vietnamese are beaten back, like they were in 1972. To avoid making a case for any imaginary scenario we want, counterfactual analysts require that, for such an assertion to be analytically useful, it must meet four tests: plausibility, proximity in time, relation to accepted theory, and relation to known facts.[6]

For the sake of my claim to have undertaken a secret heroic mission to win the war, it is my sad conclusion that under the rigor of these four tests, Michel's counterfactual contention falls away. Though this option was certainly proximate in time, it simply was not plausible because of the context of American politics (accepted theory), and ran into difficulty with one profound known fact. Even before Watergate, by 1973, 60 percent of the American public felt Vietnam was a mistake.[7] More than this general "malaise," in February 1975, while the final Communist offensive was just getting underway, a Gallup poll found that "among the 79% of the public who said they were following the issue, fully 72% of Republicans opposed such a move [that is, to send additional military aid to South Vietnam and Cambodia], as did 80% of Democrats."[8] American patience with the Indochina War broadly speaking had run its course, and there would clearly be no "rally around the flag" effect to any dramatic reintroduction of American military power.

As I stated in chapter 1 of this book, the basic deal of Vietnamization lay in the following principles. In response to a North Vietnamese will that was utterly resolute and fully supported without any slowdowns or cutoffs by its two international patrons (Moscow and Beijing), the basic will and motivation of the South Vietnamese depended on an assurance that the American support to their Americanized war effort (what we called Vietnamization) would be foundational. Certainly, this meant the continuance of the material support necessary to keep this American military machine running. More importantly, without an innate nationalism to call upon, this meant that ARVN morale and motivation drew its essential sustenance from the honor and secure dependency that came from superpower support. That is, if there weren't domestic reasons to keep on fighting, the fact that the whole world deemed this civil war important, and the major power of the "free world" was with them, served as a motivational compensation. With this as the essential deal, what sealed this tragedy was Andrew Mack's prescient

observation that in any Big Nation with a parliamentary or congressional system of policy ratification, the unity behind the commitment to such Small Wars will eventually fray apart in the normal
political process of partisan give-and-take—and division. Though
Watergate may have been the proximate cause of the collapse of
South Vietnam, the more basic responsibility for the betrayal of this
deal lay with the American people. Indeed, it was the stark recognition of this fact that led Leslie Gelb and Richard Betts to conclude
in their study of Vietnam that "American public opinion was the
essential domino."[9]

It is fashionable, among conservatives at least, to blame the media for the collapse to this support. Indeed, in an exhaustive study of
media coverage of the war through 1968, Peter Braestrup found the
record to be mixed, but during the Tet Offensive there was a clear
shift in perspective to a more openly critical stance from mainstream
media outlets.[10] Nevertheless, in the Army's own official account of
media coverage, William Hammond concluded that the fault in this
reporting—or "misreporting"—lay as much with the military in its
less than successful attempts to manipulate press accounts into favorable portraits of the war's progress.[11] I think it is fair to say that
media coverage of the war was reflective of this downward slope in
support, rather than its cause.

One counterfactual that might have worked at the Paris Peace
Agreement of 1973 was an alternative to the "secret" threat to unleash the B-52s in response to violations of the agreement. This
would have been to tie the continuance of North Vietnamese troops
in the South to an American advisory presence of 10,000 military advisers dispersed throughout major ARVN units in the four military
regions. This network of advisers, linked to call-in capabilities of
Tactical and Strategic (B-52s) U.S. air support from offshore carrier
battle groups and land bases in Thailand and the Philippines, could
have remained in South Vietnam as a guarantee of a U.S. commitment to the integrity of South Vietnam until such time as they were
no longer needed; namely, when the North Vietnamese pulled out
their remaining troops from South Vietnam. If this provision had
been part of the formal agreement, there would have been no subsequent congressional proscriptions against the use of U.S. military
force in Indochina, since there would have been vulnerable American advisory forces remaining on the ground.

When I considered this alternative in an earlier work, I found that however appealing it might seem in hindsight, at the time all of the options that were seen as "fainthearted" were shelved in favor of the ones that seemed more "macho" and forceful. One such debate was over a "phase four" thrust across the DMZ by American forces into North Vietnam after Tet 1968, rather than the more modest McNamara Line of a blocking force across the Ho Chi Minh Trail into Laos (in the event, neither was done). Another was the insistence of championing a right-wing pro-American South Vietnamese government, rather than risking a coalition government that would nevertheless draw on more comprehensive political constituencies. Finally, in the instant case of securing compliance with the Paris Peace Agreement, Kissinger and Nixon opted for the more "macho" threat of B-52 bombings, rather than a tepid stay-behind network of military advisers.[12]

The force envelope of U.S. air power was built on four levels, and all four were needed for it to work effectively. From the ground up, the first level was the helicopters that moved troops rapidly and could apply firepower quickly to specific targets. The second level were the Specter C-130 Gunships and A-3s, slow-moving, armor-plated, propeller-driven airplanes that could provide almost continuous fire coverage over a battlefield. The third level was provided by TACAIR, the air force fighter bombers, pre-eminently the Phantoms (F-4s) as well as F-105s, that could blast hardened sources of enemy fire emanating from such places as bunker complexes. Finally, there were the B-52s that could knock out major conventional targets like warehouses, truck parks, and ammunition storage centers. Only the first three levels could be applied directly to the fluid situation of any battlefield, and for these levels, you needed advisers in the field. You did not need advisers for the B-52s, but their utility for turning back fluid troop formations was limited, because in my day the time from intelligence nomination to target selection to bombs-over-target was a twenty-four-hour process. Absent Watergate, Washington might have insisted, with perhaps sufficient domestic support, on a network of U.S. military advisers to monitor the North Vietnamese troops left in-county by the agreement. Indeed, Henry Kissinger himself has acknowledged that not providing for any American military residual force in Vietnam was the key U.S. concession made in the peace negotiations and the one about which he has had the most second thoughts.[13] It is still likely, however, that the North Vietnamese would have tried another offensive anyway, and ARVN would have required a sustained level of U.S. military and economic support that was already declining sharply before Watergate. This is the only sliver of hope that I see offering a counterfactual scenario of hope for Saigon, but it is a very slender thread.

The most seductive of these counterfactuals is that we fought the war with "one hand tied behind our back." This hawkish mantra insists that if we had unleashed the full might of our military in an invasion of the North, the war could have been brought to a swift conclusion. Colonel Harry Summers popularized this prospect in his best-selling book, *On Strategy*.[14] More somberly, General Westmoreland made it clear in his memoir that going North was a move he had always assumed would be available for a final, "phase four" push to victory.[15] Indeed, embedded in the 206,000 troop request that Westmoreland forwarded to Washington during the Tet Offensive was the plan to finish off Communist forces decimated in Tet by striking across the North Vietnamese panhandle in a copy of the dramatic Inchon Landings that turned the tide of the Korean War. This force would storm the beaches and swarm across the Annamite Mountains into Laos and shut down the Ho Chi Minh Trail once and for all.[16] Politically, however, Westmoreland overreached in this request. Sending over these 206,000 additional troops would have required an expansion of the draft and a large mobilization of the reserves—a political price President Johnson was not willing to pay. And there was another large obstacle in the way of this "victory": China.

As I just noted in chapter 11, China had made a huge investment in support of North Vietnam and was deeply committed to its survival as a state within the Communist camp. During the years of the American bombing, over 300,000 Chinese support troops poured into North Vietnam to keep its logistical system functioning, thereby freeing more PAVN troops for duty in the southern front. China also provided Hanoi with supplies from a massive storage complex on Hainan Island, across the Along Bay from the North Vietnamese port of Haiphong, and it kept the Viet Cong in the Mekong Delta provisioned through the Cambodian port of Sihanoukville (formerly Kampong Song). China also set up its own version of the NATO trip-wire[17] in its construction of a Chinese military base at Yen Bay, which sits astride the twentieth parallel of latitude. This parallel marks the strategic northern tip of the North Vietnamese panhandle and the base of the Red River Delta, the economic and demographic heartland of North Vietnam. As American ground forces streamed into South Vietnam in 1965, the Chinese premier Zhou Enlai issued Washington a stern warning not to disturb any of these Chinese activities because China was prepared to go to war with the United States. Further, "Once a war breaks out, it will have no boundaries."[18]

This warning had a sobering effect on Washington. In 1965, memories of the Korean War were only twelve years old. It surfaced the nightmare of the "flashpoint," the point that would trigger a massive Chinese intervention such as occurred in November 1950 in the Korean War.[19] There were voices that insisted that—in light of both the planning for, and turmoil of, the Cultural Revolution (1966–1970)—these Chinese threats did not have to be taken seriously. Charles Parker has argued that during the Cultural Revolution, the ruling circles were split. Mao Zedong and his supporters were just as opposed to the Soviet Union as to the American presence in Vietnam, and were inclined to dismiss an American threat to China proper. His opponents, however, Liu Shaoqi and Deng Xsiaoping, were much more concerned about an American threat. Parker contends that the issue was decided in Mao's favor when Washington, in effect, publicly "abandoned victory" in President Johnson's refusal to honor Westmoreland's 206,000 troop request during the Tet Offensive.[20] Since Mao did not regain his ascendancy over Chinese politics until 1970, when I came to Vietnam in 1972 the specter of a Chinese intervention in response to any American repeat of the Inchon Landings in North Vietnam was not lightly dismissed.

President Nixon certainly pushed the envelope to this nightmare by his Linebacker I and II bombing campaigns, but he did not launch an attack on the North with ground forces. Parenthetically, whenever the possibility of an offensive by Chinese military forces was discussed in the Tank at MACV informally around the desks of analysts (never in formal briefings), the common assumption was that only nuclear weapons could stop such an attack. In fact, by not using ground forces in his bombing campaigns—in one of the supreme ironies of the war—Nixon followed in the way of his opening to China. In the resultant Shanghai Communiqué of February

1972, he changed the fortunes of the Cold War fundamentally in Washington's favor. It effectively turned China into an informal ally of the United States against the Soviet Union. It is my assessment that the alternative path of confrontation through a ground invasion of the North was not worth the certain costs and grave risks.

In the genuine fear of this Chinese flashpoint, however, Washington fell into a trap. On the larger global level, the war in Vietnam was part of the foreign policy of containment; in Asia, of China. In response to Zhou Enlai's warning, the United States assured Beijing that it had no plans to destroy North Vietnam or to invade it. This meant that in containing China, the war itself had to be contained. The success of this policy, then, depended on a victory denied to the United States, at least for any conventional way of achieving it against North Vietnam. In essence, to avoid the risk of triggering the Chinese flashpoint, Washington promised not to win the war. It was this Chinese connection—or unbreachable obstacle—that sealed the Greek tragedy of the Vietnam War.

★   ★   ★

All in all, it was just a bad war. World War II was fought for the unconditional surrender of our three tyrannical adversaries. With such a surrender in 1945 of Berlin and Tokyo (and of Rome two years earlier), to Tom Brokaw, and many others, this made it the "good war" fought by America's "greatest generation."[21] On the other hand, if, as Leslie Gelb and Richard Betts have concluded, the goal set by the American people in Vietnam was just not to lose,[22] it made Vietnam the bad war on two counts. First, it is not very ennobling to die for a cause whose objective is just not to lose. Second, in moral terms, it is bad to engage in such a war in the first place if you are just going to leave so that your erstwhile client is obliged to lose the war for you.

Coming home from this bad war, I slowly came to two conclusions. The first made me sullen. I had lost my faith in the distinctive goodness of America. As I noted in chapter 1, I came to Vietnam armored by my belief in the tradition of American exceptionalism, and that if any country was the "last best hope of the world" (in the words of Abraham Lincoln), it was America. Certainly good once again would come out of this struggle against Communist tyranny, and my own small involvement in this crusade would help secure my own place in the history of this great land. Instead, of course,

216   I found a United States that turned its back on and betrayed a client state, requiring me in the process to betray my two Vietnamese colonels. In this war, I saw an America that fell off its perch of
uniqueness into the morass of generality—of an America no better
than anyone else. I probably should not have believed the myth in
the first place, but it was a hard fall.

Indeed, it has been a hard fall for the whole Baby Boom generation. Rather than achieving a generational unity and common
national and personal purpose, this bad war has torn us apart. Following World War II, the Cold War was "fought" and won by this
greatest generation that ruled the destiny of America from Presidents Eisenhower, Kennedy, Johnson, Nixon, Ford, Carter, Reagan,
and George H. W. Bush all the way up to 1992. Of these postwar
presidents, Truman, Eisenhower, Kennedy, and George H. W. Bush
were combat veterans. The Baby Boom presidents, William Jef-
ferson Clinton (1992–2000) and George W. Bush (2000–2008) both
avoided war service (the former through an artful letter to his draft
board and the latter through service in the Alabama Air National
Guard) and triggered unprecedented partisan rancor.

But this rancor is merely emblematic of the generation as a
whole. I remember participating in a conference on the literature of
the Vietnam War sponsored by The Asia Society ten years after the
fall of Saigon in 1985. What I remember was the screaming, crying,
and utterly contrary views on the war and of its tragic impact on
the lives of the participants.[23] Indeed, in a recent speech on Vietnam
at the State Department, Henry Kissinger himself lamented the destructive persistence of this rancor: "Most of what went wrong in
Vietnam we did to ourselves. . . . To me, the tragedy of the Vietnam
War was not that there were disagreements . . . but that the faith of
Americans in each other became destroyed in the process."[24]

Sadly, this loss of faith in each other could make us shrill, as at
this conference, or more often sullen and withdrawn. These mood
swings were reflected in my subsequent professional world as a professor in North Carolina. I certainly had my sullenness, but I devoted my scholarship to figuring out the war, and taught courses
about it. In other words, I talked. I had a colleague right across the
hall from me who was a combat veteran of the war. He was mede-
vacked from the field, and never talked. I nevertheless gleaned from
him in stray remarks that he was antiwar, served as an enlisted man,

was anti-officer, and disrespected my REMFness. My views were different than his, and I had been an officer. Between us, Vietnam was no bond. The rest of my colleagues were certainly aware of my Vietnam service but did not know how to handle it. Ambivalence over whatever inner turmoil the war had provoked in them came out, once in a while, in shrill comments on the few occasions that I presented my research. I struck some raw nerves.

In this North Carolina world, the University of North Carolina Press editor, Lew Bateman, befriended me. He began his involvement with this issue sympathetic to the antiwar movement, particularly with the views of the SDS (Students for a Democratic Society). But he became increasingly turned off by the antitroop behavior of the movement. In his post-student career in publishing, he found himself more and more in the role of championing the works of scholars who had more balanced perspectives on the war, and then even to publishing more "revisionist" works—like mine![25]

In my own case, as time moved on, my sullenness was gradually replaced by my second conclusion that led me to a feeling of liberation. As I gained some perspective, I came to realize that my problem with this bad war was not with America, but with politics itself. If America were no better—or worse—than anything else, then what this war had succumbed to was politics. Among the many definitions of "politics" is that it is the process whereby problems of human relations are solved by accommodating multiple interests and imperatives with the balance of resources available. In other words, in a world of scarce resources, politics is the process whereby these tradeoffs are made in which a society or country charts its course through this sea of compromise.

These compromises have formed the basic dramas, tragedies, and blessings of human history. Agamemnon sacrificed his daughter Iphigenia so that the Greek fleet could sail to Troy. When he returned home triumphant, his wife, Jocasta, murdered him. That's politics. Bhima, in India's epic *Mahabharata,* was ordered by the gods to cheat in the final battle of Kurukshetra so that victory could be won. He cheated. The victory was won. And, at the end of his life, when he appeared at Heaven's Gate (Mount Meru), he was denied entrance by the gods for cheating. That's politics. Vietnam had become a war far out of proportion to larger American global responsibilities in the Cold War. Somehow it had to be jettisoned. As I looked at the overgrown weeds in the citadel at Hue, viscerally I understood this. So, as an operative of this collective cost-benefit analysis, I had to sell my two colonels down the river. That's politics.

Inevitably, tradeoffs have to be made. The utilitarians called the fruit of these tradeoffs "the greatest good for the greatest number." In extricating itself from Vietnam after a "decent interval," Washington gained a geopolitical ally in Mao's China, and went on to win the Cold War itself. The "reasonable" cost was the abandonment of the twenty million people of South Vietnam—to say nothing of the honor of its word. Indeed, the central theater of the Cold War was built on the larger strategic tradeoff between the security and prosperity of the 300 million people of Western Europe under a NATO umbrella in exchange for the 100 million people of Eastern Europe left standing out in the rain of Soviet tyranny. That's politics.

And politics, I concluded, was something I could no longer do. This pull between the individual and the collective was something I realized I just could not compartmentalize. I had trouble when I first encountered it at Fort Huachuca in Arizona and had to take the "ethical drop" during my training in "area studies" in 1971. And I had trouble when this same issue assumed flesh and blood in my responsibilities to my government versus my personal loyalties to Colonels Vu Van Nho and Hoang Ngoc Lung in South Vietnam in 1973. Politics I could not do.

I began to realize that it was this reluctance that drew me to the monastery of academia. Here I could study and explain politics, but I did not have to practice them. As a political scientist, there is a natural seduction into opportunities of what is termed "public service." And I did pursue some of these opportunities, but not very energetically, and certainly not with the same enthusiasm that I have sought out academic opportunities.

When I first expressed my political ambitions as a high school youth, I was dismayed that my parents pursed their lips. They had felt strongly called to the India mission field in Christian service to another kingdom, not of this world. To them, there was a world far beyond, and better than, the limitations of the politics that tied us to this world. But I had thought this same kingdom could also be served by politics—as long as the politics were good in a special place like America. Yes, my parents had acknowledged, as long as you don't lose sight of the ultimate prize, and of its limitless possibilities.

A Middle Kingdom for me had rested in the conversation between Pilate and Jesus at the "trial" before His crucifixion in the Gospel of John. Pilate, in this sequence, wanted to know if Jesus were a king. Jesus replied that His kingdom was not of this world. So, what, Pilate wanted to know, was it? The reply by Jesus was that His kingdom was Truth. For a long time, I thought, in answer to my parents, the pursuit of truth fearlessly was how I was keeping my eye on the prize as a college professor. But, as a professor, I was equating this truth with reason, which fit my world fine, until in so many ways, in academia and elsewhere, I kept rubbing up against the limits to reason in truly grasping, understanding, and helping people cope with the realities of the human condition.

In this so-called Middle Kingdom of Truth built on reason, not only was I finding truth to be elusive through reason alone, but I was also discovering the return of the bayonet to my soul in this pursuit. Maybe intellectual battles were just pugil sticks encased in pillows, but they could become vicious nevertheless. Arguments, however rationally conducted, can become combats, if your motives descend to defeating arguments, and their proponents, more personally.[26] For humans, truth has to be a common pursuit rooted in mutual respect, and even charity,[27] so that egos are not invested and thereby bolstered or diminished. In my own academic writing, especially on Vietnam, I found my motivation too often evocative of the cry of "Kill! Kill! Kill!" I thought I had repudiated on the training fields of Fort Belvoir.

As the living out of my life pulled me further away from this war, and I read the Bible more deeply and studied it with fellow church members, I came to understand that this Kingdom of Truth was rooted in God's Love, not His reason. Furthermore, in this Kingdom, there are no scarce resources. God's love is freely there for everyone in limitless amounts. There is enough for me, my family, my friends, my country, my enemies, and, yes, for Colonels Vu Van Nho and Hoang Ngoc Lung, too. In God's Kingdom, there are no tradeoffs—and no politics—there is just His limitless love. In this second conclusion of forsaking my political ambitions, I have found my own *giai phuong,* or liberation. Like Kieu, in her renunciation of desire, I have discovered my heart in the embrace of the Kingdom of God. And this is not such a bad thing from this bad war. From this story and study of war, I have found my peace.

Chronology

Note: In this chronology, regular typeface refers to global events pertinent to the Vietnam War, while entries in italics indicate events in my life in this enfolding drama. Entries in the period central to this memoir, 1972–1973, are put in bold typeface.

1946
Winston Churchill's "Iron Curtain" speech in February signals the beginning of the Cold War. In December, fighting breaks out in Hanoi between French and Viet Minh forces starting the French Indochina War as Paris tries to reassert control over this restive colony. *Amid Independence riots in India, my parents, Clarence Lomperis and Marjorie Larsen, both from Illinois, are married in Calcutta, India, in April.*

1947
George Kennan's "X" article on "The Sources of Soviet Conduct," published in the July issue of *Foreign Affairs*, outlines a foreign policy of containment for the Cold War. Kennan warns that halting Communism would occur in "rapidly shifting points" across the globe. In contrast to the French, the British grant independence to India, Pakistan, Burma, and Ceylon as a wave of rapid decolonization in Asia and Africa sets in that continues at a high pace until 1960. *I am born in March in South India to The Rev. and Mrs. Clarence Lomperis, Lutheran missionaries.*

October 1949
Communist forces under Mao Zedong win the civil war with the nationalist Guomindang army and take control of China. This victory brings the Cold War to Asia, as the United States struggles to counter Communist revolutionaries with a Third Force democratic nationalism in the wave of European colonial withdrawals as part of a global foreign policy of containment. *The Christian church in China goes underground as Western missionaries flee or are imprisoned. Ties among Lutheran missionaries to China, Hong Kong, Taiwan, Japan, Malaya, and India are close, and prayers are lifted up for our "oppressed and imprisoned brethren in China."*

1950–1953
The United States repels a North Korean invasion of South Korea and fights the Communist Chinese intervention to preserve North Korea to a stalemate in the Korean War. The division of the two halves of Korea at the thirty-eighth parallel remains "permanent."

1954

A French garrison of elite paratroopers and legionnaires at the remote outpost of Dienbienphu falls in May to Communist Viet Minh forces, advised
and supplied by Communist China. In July, the Geneva Accords provide for
the withdrawal of French forces and the temporary division of Vietnam
at the seventeenth parallel, pending nationwide elections. The Communist Viet Minh are given control of the North, and an as yet unspecified
entity was to take control in the South. Following the defeat of France in
Indochina, the Southeast Asia Treaty Organization (SEATO) is an alliance
formed to contain the further expansion of Communism in Southeast
Asia. The signatories are the United States, Britain, France, Pakistan, Australia, New Zealand, the Philippines, and Thailand. The central purpose of
SEATO was to defend against "aggression and subversion" directed against
member states and other "designated nations." Specifically mentioned as
such were South Vietnam, Cambodia, and Laos. This treaty commitment
became the official justification for the United States to send its combat
forces into South Vietnam. Australia, New Zealand, and Thailand also
sent forces and permitted U.S. forces the use of bases in their countries. *I
entered boarding school at Kodaikanal School ("Kodai" for short), an American
missionary school located near the southern tip of India in Madras State (now
Tamilnadu).*

1956 and 1957

To the surprise of many, Vietnamese nationalist Ngo Dinh Diem succeeds
in establishing a republic in South Vietnam. Both sides of the seventeenth
parallel refuse to hold elections in their territory, and division at this parallel becomes "permanent." In giving up the struggle in Indochina, the
French go on to a war to hold onto Algeria. The Cold War heats up with
the Hungarian Uprising and the Suez Crisis. During these years in Asia, the
United States is involved in a major counterinsurgency against Communist
insurgents in the Philippines, and the British are engaged in a similar fight
in Malaya. *In 1957, we return to the United States for a year's furlough in Hart-
ford, Connecticut. I arrive as a convinced Cold Warrior at the tender age of ten.*

1959 and 1960

Having failed to dislodge South Vietnamese President Diem "peacefully,"
the Communist North begins "armed struggle" in the South through the
reinfiltration of guerrilla cadres into the South. The United States begins
its "Advisor War" (1960–1963) through a series of programs unveiled as
"nation building." *The fall of 1960 sees a controversial presidential election in
the Andhra Evangelical Lutheran Church of South India turn ugly in a near riot
with chants of "white missionaries with black hearts," which I observe from a
rooftop. My father and others attribute the outbursts to rabble-rousers and even*

to Communists, but Westerners essentially give up control of "native" churches
throughout India during this period.

October 1962

The Cuban Missile Crisis is the ultimate crisis of the Cold War in which a nuclear exchange between the United States and the Soviet Union is avoided by the Soviets withdrawing missiles it had secretly installed in Cuba. During this distraction, Communist China attacks India in both Kashmir and the northeast Province of Assam and seizes a fair amount of territory. The United States provides a massive amount of military assistance. *To me, these two events are proof positive of the perfidy of the Soviet Union, and of Communism more generally. This is further etched in my mind by reading Arthur Koestler's* Darkness at Noon, *which detailed the psychological horrors of the Stalinist purges of the 1930s. George Orwell's* 1984, *which I also read in high school, served to reinforce this point.*

November 1963

Having become increasingly autocratic, President Diem is overthrown in a coup launched on November 1 in which he and his brother are assassinated, despite American attempts to ensure their safety. This touches off an interregnum of chaos in which there are numerous changes of government between 1963 and 1965, while the situation in the countryside deteriorates. On November 22, Lee Harvey Oswald assassinates President John F. Kennedy in Dallas, Texas. *We are back in Illinois on furlough, and I was in a French class in high school when news of this tragedy broke.*

August 2–4, 1964

Two sets of Communist attacks on U.S. Naval vessels in the Gulf of Tonkin (the waters off the coast of North Vietnam) occurred on these dates and led to the Gulf of Tonkin Resolution in which Congress granted the president the power to use all means necessary to restore peace in Southeast Asia, "including the use of armed force." This became the equivalent to a declaration of war and started direct combat operations by U.S. units in Vietnam. Considerable controversy has surrounded these attacks. Several investigations have concluded that the first attack did take place, even though the North Vietnamese may have mistaken the American ships for a more clandestine South Vietnamese infiltration operation. The second attack probably was bogus.

1965–1967

Guenter Lewy termed this period the "Big Unit War" in which large conventional American combat units engaged "main force" Viet Cong and conventional North Vietnamese forces to reverse the Communist momentum and prevent a Communist takeover of the country. United States forces in Vietnam surge to half a million servicemen and -women by 1969. *These are the first two and half years of my college career at Augustana College in Rock Island, Illinois, and debate over Vietnam is intense. I lead a counterdemonstration in support of the war drawn from friends on the football team.*

January–end of March 1968
This is the duration of the Tet Offensive, a critical turning point in the war. It is an all-out Communist offensive to seize power in the South. Southern Communist forces were utterly decimated in this assault, but its dramatic scope triggered a precipitous decline in support for the war by the American public. On March 25, President Lyndon Johnson announces he will not run for reelection. *I am in Washington, D.C., participating in the Washington Semester Program of American University. While there, I get caught up in the Martin Luther King riots following his assassination in April, and I observe the Eighty-second Airborne Division reestablish order. Seeing the nation's capital under military occupation and the television clips of carnage in Vietnam is deeply depressing.*

April 30–June 30, 1970
This period ushered in what the Nixon administration termed the "Cambodian Incursion" in which 20,000 U.S. and 30,000 ARVN forces blitz into Cambodia to clear out Communist sanctuaries of supplies and command headquarters. It is also launched to give a breather for large U.S. troop withdrawals as part of "Vietnamization." The Cambodian Incursion touches off massive protests nationwide, including one at Kent State University in which four college students are killed. *Having joined the army in the fall of 1969, I finish my Basic and AIT training, and then I attend Officer Candidate School at Fort Belvoir, Virginia. This is just outside Washington, D.C., which became the site of further war protests. We are trained quickly for riot control, but are not needed.*

1970–1971
President Richard M. Nixon embarks on his plan to end the war through U.S. troop withdrawals accompanied by the upgrading of South Vietnamese forces under the rubric of Vietnamization, all the while conducting secret negotiations with Hanoi on a deal for a final U.S. withdrawal. *I am in Vietnamese language school followed by intelligence school in training for deployment to Vietnam, in the fond hope that the length of these training programs will delay me from actually having to go.*

June 1972
President Nixon announces that henceforth only volunteers will be sent to Vietnam. *I arrived in-country three months before this announcement. I am hired to work in the "Tank" as an analyst on the MR 3 Desk.*

April–September 1972
This period marks the Easter Invasion, and was an all-out conventional assault by fourteen North Vietnamese divisions to conquer the South. Through the massive use of U.S. air power, including a mining and bombing campaign over North Vietnam called "Linebacker," and some tenacious fighting on the ground by South Vietnamese forces, it was turned back by September. *During this invasion, I am transferred to the Air Intelligence Division to process/analyze the Intel on Arc Light B-52 bomber target nominations for daily briefing to the Arc Light Panel.*

October 1972
Secretary of State Henry Kissinger gives his premature "Peace Is at Hand" speech.

November–December 1972
These two months see the huge influx of $2 billion worth of military equipment to South Vietnam called "Enhance Plus." Its goal is to secure South Vietnamese support for the impending peace agreement by providing supposedly enough materiel to fight the North Vietnamese on their own.

December 18–29, 1972
These twelve days (minus one day for a Christmas halt) mark the Christmas Bombing or Linebacker II, which is a "saturation" bombing campaign, mostly by B-52 bombers, against the infrastructure of North Vietnam. One way or other, it induces the North Vietnamese to return to the bargaining table in early January 1973.

January 27, 1973
The day the Paris Peace Agreement is signed between North Vietnam, the United States, South Vietnam, and the PRG. It calls for a complete withdrawal of U.S. forces in sixty days, the return of U.S. prisoners, a ceasefire in place, and the peaceful reunification of Vietnam by mutual consent of the parties.

February 1973
I am discharged from the Army in-country and begin work for the Defense Intelligence Agency in the Defense Attaché Office as an Intelligence Liaison Officer to the ARVN Joint General Staff Intelligence Headquarters, the Combined Intelligence Center, Vietnam, and the Combined Document Exploitation Center, Vietnam.

March 28, 1973
This date marks the end of the sixty-day withdrawal period for all but fifty U.S. forces from Vietnam. Over five hundred U.S. prisoners are returned to the United States.

late March–mid-April 1973

This period marks massive Communist resupply operations, a clear violation of the ceasefire in place provision of the Paris Peace Agreement.

mid-April 1973

White House counsel John Dean informs Watergate prosecutors that the coverup involved the White House. *This is also when I conducted my "target exercise" in three Military Regions.*

June 1973

This is the month I hold the Order-of-Battle Conference at CICV. From this event, I host two high-level visits by U.S. general officers to examine targeting intelligence at CICV.

August 1–3, 1973

In these three fateful days, I resign my position, go on a last trip to Hue, and return to the United States.

August 15, 1973

The Cooper-Church Amendment bars all further U.S. bombing in Southeast Asia.

November 1973

This ban is extended to all U.S. military activity in November. Also, the War Powers Act (of dubious constitutionality since it is passed as a joint resolution rather than as two bills from each chamber first) is passed over a presidential veto.

1973–1974

United States military assistance to South Vietnam is cut back in each year.

August 1974

Under threat of impeachment, Richard Nixon resigns the presidency, and Vice President Gerald Ford is sworn into the office.

December 1974–January 1975

North Vietnamese forces probe the border province of Phuoc Long for a possible U.S. response. There is none.

February 1975

Two congressional visits to Vietnam produce only acrimony, and President Gerald Ford's attempts to secure emergency funding for Vietnam fail.

March 10, 1975
North Vietnamese troops launch their final assault on South Vietnam called the "Ho Chi Minh Campaign."

late March–early April 1975
This period marks the formulation of a last-ditch round of U.S. military assistance, the Weyand Plan, to hold the line at the northern border of MR 3.

April 10, 1975
Communist forces cross into MR 3 and begin the siege of Xuan Loc.

April 17, 1975
The U.S. Congress rejects the Weyand Plan, the same day the nearby capital of Cambodia, Phnom Penh, falls to Communist Khmer Rouge forces.

April 21, 1975
Xuan Loc, the "little Alamo," falls; and South Vietnamese President Nguyen Van Thieu resigns.

April 30, 1975
North Vietnamese tanks slam into the grounds of the Presidential Palace in Saigon. This marks the fall/liberation of South Vietnam.

December 4, 1975
King Savang Vatthana abdicates, and the Communist Pathet Lao take over Laos. All of former Indochina is now under Communist rule. Also in 1975, Thailand does not renew agreements for the use of Thai bases by U.S. military forces.

May 15, 1976
I marry Ana Maria Turner, a fellow student at the Johns Hopkins University School of Advanced International Studies.

1976–1980
My wife and I are both at work on our Ph.D. programs, mine in political science at Duke and hers in economics at UNC–Chapel Hill.

1977
The Southeast Asia Treaty Organization (SEATO) is dissolved.

1979–1980
A Vietnamese invasion and occupation of Cambodia puts an end to a four-year bloodbath in Cambodia. As allies of the Khmer Rouge, the Chinese launch a series of punitive border attacks in North Vietnam. *In the middle of*

228   *all this, while researching my doctoral dissertation, I make my discovery about my 1973 "exercise" in the basement of Perkins Library of Duke University.*

1989

Vietnam withdraws its forces from Cambodia ending its occupation. Ironically enough, this is the same year the Soviet Union pulls out of Afghanistan, and the Cold War officially comes to an end with the collapse of the Berlin Wall in November.

1992

The United States returns Clark Air Force Base and the Subic Bay Naval Installation to the Philippines, ending a direct American military presence in Southeast Asia. The United States retains over-the-horizon capabilities with the Seventh Fleet in Japan and the Fifth Fleet in the Indian Ocean, as well as defense guarantees to the ASEAN Regional Forum (ARF) of the Association of Southeast Asian Nations (ASEAN), something of a successor organization to SEATO.

Acronyms and "Nam Speak"

AID   Agency for International Development. One of the three main entities of the U.S. State Department, the others being the Foreign Service and the United States Information Agency. The agency was part of the pacification effort, so other government agencies often had their employees work under an AID rubric.

AIT   Advanced Individual Training. Follow-on training to Basic and the second stage to the sixteen-week package of military training in the Army before joining an active duty unit.

Arc Light   A conventional bombing strike by a B-52 bomber.

Arc Light Panel   The panel or board of officers at MACV Headquarters that selected the daily targets for Arc Light strikes to be approved by the COMUS MACV (see below).

ARVN   Army of the Republic of Vietnam (South). Pronounced "arven."

ASEAN   Association of Southeast Asian Nations. See Chronology for further details.

B-52   The largest and most lethal bomber in the inventory of the U.S. Air Force. Its primary mission is the delivery of nuclear ordnance, but it can be used to deliver conventional bombs as well, for which it was employed in Vietnam.

Basic   The first eight weeks of military training that all army recruits undergo.

Battalion   An army unit composed of three or four companies ranging from 600 to 800 soldiers. Communist battalions in Vietnam numbered around 300 men.

Boonies or Boondocks   Rustic locales far from creature comforts. For soldiers, this was usually where combat took place. The Boonies are the opposite of REMF Land.

BOQ   Bachelor Officers Quarters.

Brigade   An army unit whose size can range from 3,000 to 5,000 soldiers. Generally, three battalions comprise a brigade, and divisions are made up of three brigades.

BUFF   Big Ugly Fat "Fellow," a B-52.

BX   Base Exchange in the Air Force (PX, or Post Exchange, in the Army). Commercial retail outlets on a U.S. military installation that run the gamut from a "7/11" equivalent to a Super Wal-Mart. The base exchanges do not charge sales taxes and prices are usually heavily discounted.

CDEC   Combined Document Exploitation Center. Pronounced "see deck." A combined activity of MACV and the Vietnamese Joint General Staff. One of the three installations to which I "liaised." The other two were CICV and the JGS Intelligence Headquarters.

CIA   Central Intelligence Agency.

CICV   Combined Intelligence Center, Vietnam. Pronounced "sick V." A joint U.S. and Vietnamese intelligence facility in which Intel and analysis were to be shared. This is where I spent the bulk of my time as a liaison officer.

CINCPAC   Commander-in-Chief, U.S. Pacific Command. Pronounced "sink pack." CINCPAC Headquarters was in Hawaii.

CMIC   Combined Military Interrogation Center. Pronounced "see mick." I was originally assigned to this installation, but another liaison officer took up this assignment and Unit 101, an ARVN intelligence unit engaged in secret operations.

Company   An army unit of about 200 soldiers consisting of four platoons. Commanded by captains, companies are the basic "small unit" of the U.S. Army.

COMUS MACV   The U.S. Commander of MACV. The first one was General Westmoreland (1964–1968), followed by General Abrams (1968–1972), and concluded by General Weyand (1972–1973).

CONUS   The Continental United States. This was the more or less official term for what GIs called "the world."

CORDS   Civil Operations and Revolutionary Development Support. It
was the massive bureaucratic umbrella organization that was tasked with
making "pacification" work. On the U.S. side, such agencies as AID, the
CIA, and the military were involved. For the South Vietnamese, CORDS
"interfaced" with agencies working with rural concerns like land reform
and refugees as well as with locally recruited militias, such as the Regional
Forces/Popular Forces, which were affectionately called "Ruff Puffs" by
U.S. advisers.

COSVN   Central Office for South Viet Nam. This was an office that directly reported to the politburo in Hanoi, and was responsible for the war
on the Communist side in the equivalents of MR 3 and 4. From the American perspective, this was the highest southern, or Viet Cong, entity in the
Communist chain-of-command.

DAO   Defense Attaché Office. Successor organization to MACV, and
nominally under the control of the U.S. embassy.

The dap   An elaborate greeting ritual performed by black soldiers toward the end of the war. It consisted of many handshakes punctuated by
the smacking of fists and improvised body-shaking resembling a dance that
could go on for as long as five minutes. It was an exclusive "black thing"
that not too subtly was a poke in the eye at hierarchical military courtesy—
namely, the salute. It became increasingly common in REMF Land but was
relatively rare among combat units in the Boonies.

DEROS   Date of Estimated Return from Over Seas. Pronounced "dee-
ros." The date when a soldier's tour of duty in Vietnam was completed and
he could take a Freedom Bird home.

DI   Drill Instructor, or, more properly, the Drill Sergeant that provided
basic military instruction in Basic and Advanced Individual Training in the
Army. Pronounced "dee eye."

DIA   Defense Intelligence Agency. The U.S. Department of Defense's
in-house civilian intelligence agency. Bureaucratically, it became a rival to
the more free-standing Central Intelligence Agency.

DISUMs   Daily Intelligence Summaries. This was the basic Intel prod-
uct of the Tank in MACV during the Vietnam War.

Division   An army unit of 10,000 to 15,000 soldiers. The division is
the basic maneuver element in the U.S. Army consisting of nine combat

battalions and other support units. Communist divisions were smaller, usually about 10,000 soldiers.

DMZ   Demilitarized Zone. The demarcation line between North and South Vietnam established "temporarily" at the seventeenth parallel by the Geneva Accords of 1954.

DOD   U.S. Department of Defense.

Draftee   Someone who was conscripted into military service, rather than volunteering or enlisting. The usual tour of active duty for a conscript, or draftee, during the Vietnam era (1960–1975) was two years.

DRV   Democratic Republic of Vietnam (North).

Enhance Plus   A massive $2 billion military aid package dispatched to South Vietnam in November and December 1972 aimed at securing President Thieu's support for the upcoming Paris Peace Agreement and giving the South Vietnamese military forces the equipment it needed to defend against North Vietnamese military forces without the assistance of U.S. forces.

ETS   Estimated Termination of Service. The scheduled date for a soldier's formal discharge from active duty. For a draftee in Vietnam, this was usually about six months after his DEROS. Such soldiers were given temporary assignments in a military installation back in the "world," and were decidedly "short."

FRAC, SRAC, TRAC, and DRAC   First Regional Assistance Command (Hue), Second Regional Assistance Command (Pleiku), Third Regional Assistance Command (Bien Hoa), and Delta Regional Assistance Command (Can Tho). These are the third iteration of terms for the four military regions or districts of South Vietnam, the others being the four corps and the four military regions. This set was employed by the Defense Attaché Office in 1973–1975.

Fragging   The practice late in the war of enlisted ranks rolling fragmentation grenades (hence, "fragging") into the tents of officers who insisted on offensive combat patrols. With the program of U.S. troop withdrawals adopted by President Nixon, a defensive mindset began to permeate ground combat units, whose soldiers only wanted to go on patrols to defend their perimeters so they would not be "the last soldier to die in Vietnam."

Freedom Birds   Planes that took soldiers back home to the States after their tours of duty in Vietnam. The planes flew from Bien Hoa to Travis Air Force Base outside of Sacramento, California. Earlier in the war, an alternate route was from Cam Ranh (in MR 2) to McChord Air Force Base near Tacoma, Washington. In the military vernacular, "I am going to DEROS back to the world on a Freedom Bird." The opposite was the Jail Bird.

GI   Generic term for a member of the U.S. Armed Forces. Originally, it meant soldiers in the army, but by Vietnam the term had been generalized. It was one of the few terms left over from World War II. The initials, like all the equipment lavished on the American military, highlighted the fact that its soldiers as well were "Government Issue."

Grunts   Troopers who humped the Boonies; that is, who went on long patrols along the rice paddy dikes of MR IV, in the jungles of MR III, or on the treacherous hills and ridges of MR II; they also manned the fire support bases of MR I. Grunts were heavy combat soldiers. In REMF Land, they were either treated like gods, or given a very wide berth.

GVN   Government of Vietnam (South).

HUMINT   Human Intelligence. Intelligence gained from human sources. Most often Humint comes from agents, but it can also come from diplomatic and liaison activities.

I Corps, II Corps, III Corps, and IV Corps   The four corps tactical zones into which the U.S. Army divided Vietnam. They were in a North-South progression headquartered in Hue, Pleiku, Bien Hoa, and Can Tho, respectively. Each Corps was typically commanded by a two-star general. Pronounced "eye core, two core, three core, four core." The IV Corps was often just called "the Delta," referring to the Mekong Delta in which it was situated. Strictly speaking, the corps zones referred to the U.S. command structure (USARV).

In-country   This term simply meant "Vietnam." Freedom Birds landed soldiers in-country. Other places were "the world" and "R and R."

INR   Bureau of Intelligence and Research. The INR is the State Department shop responsible for analytical intelligence reporting.

Intel   A generic term for all the intelligence emanating from the intelligence community operating in Vietnam. The term was also used for basic information on any situation, as in the question, "What's the Intel?"

Jail Bird   The plane that brought a soldier in-country from the world—again, usually from Travis Air Force Base to Bien Hoa. The term was seldom invoked without inferring having been sent to Vietnam, as in, "I'm so short that I can't even remember when that damned Jail Bird dumped me here." This term was less common than Freedom Bird, and was used more at the end of the war.

JGS   Joint General Staff of the Vietnam Armed Forces. The South Vietnamese equivalent to the Pentagon. Its compound was located in the suburbs of Saigon adjacent to both Tan Son Nhut airport and MACV Headquarters.

JUSPAO   Joint United States Public Affairs Office. Most of the employees of JUSPAO were with USIA, which was in charge of the U.S. Mission's public relations activities, such as relating to the media. The JUSPAO also put out a batch of reports and studies on the war, as well as publishing captured documents translated at CDEC.

KIA   Killed in Action.

Lifer   As opposed to a draftee, a lifer was someone who volunteered or enlisted in the military for "life" as a professional career. A life term actually meant a twenty-year "hitch" (period of service), after which a lifer was eligible for full pension, and thereby enabled to take up a "second career." In Vietnam, there were certainly some tensions between draftees and lifers, but they were greatly exaggerated by movies such as *Platoon*.

MACV   Military Assistance Command, Vietnam. The formal command structure overseeing the U.S. war effort in Vietnam. Its headquarters was located in Tan Son Nhut, a suburb north of Saigon. The MACV was commanded by a four-star army general, the COMUS MACV.

Medevac   "Medical evacuation by helicopter." In Vietnam, the United States set up a comprehensive fleet of medical evacuation helicopters that would speed casualties to nearby Mobile Army Surgical Hospitals, or MASH units. The military boasted that no casualty was any farther than 20 minutes from a MASH unit. Systems of domestic medevacs have been established since in all fifty American states.

MI   Military Intelligence.

MIA   Missing in Action. At the end of the war, about 2,000 U.S. military personnel were listed as missing in action.

MIEUS   Monthly Intelligence Estimate Updates. Pronounced "moos."   235
This was the big "dog and pony show" put on by MACV's intelligence shop
for the benefit of the intelligence community in Vietnam, namely, the State
Department, the CIA, and visiting congressional delegations.

MPs   Military Policemen.

MR 1, 2, 3, 4   Military regions 1, 2, 3, and 4. The MRs coincided exactly
with the four corps tactical zones (CTZs), and replaced them in official us-
age on July 1, 1970. See I Corps, II Corps, III Corps, IV Corps above.

Nam, or The Nam   Term used by veterans for Vietnam largely in the
past tense, as in "When I was in the Nam." Vietnam in the present tense
was referred to as "in-country."

NKP   Nakhon Phanom, Thailand. Town on the Mekong River in Northeast Thailand where the United States had an Air Force base. In 1973–1975,
it had a U.S. Support Activities Group (USSAG) that, in effect, continued
many of the activities conducted by MACV when that command stood
down on March 28, 1973.

NLF   National Liberation Front. Its formation was announced in December 1959 as part of the "armed struggle" proclaimed by Hanoi that
would be carried out in the South under the auspices of this proclaimed
southern Communist movement. To Communists, it was the successor organization to the Viet Minh that fought against the French (1946–1954). To
Americans, it was the political arm of the VC (Viet Cong).

NVA   Term used by the United States for the North Vietnamese Army.

OB   Order-of-Battle. The disposition of enemy forces held by intelligence services. This is a critical metric in guerrilla war, and the subject of
much controversy.

OCS   Officer Candidate School. For the United States, the third source
of commissioned officers, the other two being the Service Academies and
the Reserve Officer Training Corps (ROTC) programs in the nation's colleges
and universities. The OCS was intended as an in-service route to commissioning for the enlisted ranks, but during Vietnam many college graduates
(like myself) availed themselves of the OCS option. In 1970 there were three
Officer Candidate Schools: Infantry OCS at Fort Benning, Artillery OCS at
Fort Sill, and Branch Immaterial OCS at Fort Belvoir. I went to the latter,
which, to my great disadvantage, had an engineering curriculum.

PAVN People's Army of Vietnam. The North Vietnamese army, and the term preferred by Hanoi. The term for all Communist forces was PLAF, People's Liberation Armed Forces.

Pentagon East Slang term for MACV Headquarters, but a recognition that many important wartime decisions were actually made in Saigon.

Phoenix Program The counterterror program run by the CIA, as part of pacification under CORDS, which was designed to root out the Viet Cong infrastructure. It was a joint program with the South Vietnamese government, ultimately with the National Police. The Vietnamese called the program "Phung Hoang."

Platoon An army unit of about forty-five to fifty soldiers consisting of two sections, or four squads. Platoons were commanded by first lieutenants, or sometimes by first sergeants.

POL Petroleum, Oil, and Lubricants. Acronym for the vital fluids necessary for the fueling and greasing of a modern military machine.

POWs Prisoners of War. The release of American POWs at the Paris Peace Agreement was the principal concession gained by the United States in this agreement.

PRG Provisional Revolutionary Government. This was the political arm of the National Liberation Front. Formally, it housed the delegation of the "government-in-exile" of the National Liberation Front that participated in the official peace talks in Paris that began in 1968 as four-party talks: the United States, the DRV, the GVN, and the PRG. After the Easter Invasion, it maintained a capital in the District Town of Loc Ninh. It was peremptorily ignored by Hanoi in the final 1975 offensive.

Purple Heart A decoration (ribbon or medal) earned by any military personnel wounded in combat.

PX See BX.

REMF Rear Echelon Mother F—kers. Military personnel who worked in locales where there were creature comforts, and combat was just a "distant thunder." Pronounced "remph."

REMF Land Where the REMF locales were. If you were in the Army, you wore khaki uniforms, rather than fatigues. Saigon was the preeminent bastion of REMF Land.

R and R   Rest and Recreation. All troops stationed in Vietnam were entitled to one week's R and R. Unlike the two-week leave that could be taken at home, the R and R leave had to be taken at a designated R and R center. At their own expense, family members could join troopers on their R and R. When I was in Vietnam, the only designated centers were Hawaii and Bangkok. At the height of the war, R and R leaves could be taken in Australia, Taiwan, Japan, and Hong Kong, as well.

RVN   Republic of Vietnam (South).

RVNAF   Republic of Vietnam Armed Forces (South). Pronounced "arvenaff." As opposed to ARVN, this term includes all branches of the armed services.

SAC   Strategic Air Command. Its headquarters was at Offut Air Force Base, just outside of Omaha, Nebraska. The SAC was in charge of the strategic nuclear delivery systems: the B-52 bombers, Minuteman Intercontinental Ballistic Missiles (ICBMs), and Submarine Launched Ballistic Missiles (SLBMs). This mix of delivery systems was, and is, known as the Strategic Triad. In the 1960s and 1970s, SLBMs were Polaris Missiles. Today, they are Trident D-5s. The Air Force directly controlled the B-52s and the ICBMs, and the Navy the SLBMs. The release of some of these B-52s for conventional bombing duties in Vietnam was a source of considerable unhappiness in the Air Force. The Eighth Air Force, a unit under SAC, commanded the B-52s used in Vietnam from their bases on Guam and U Tapao in Thailand. Very reluctantly, the selection of daily targets for B-52 strikes was delegated to the Arc Light Panel at MACV.

SEATO   Southeast Asia Treaty Organization. See Chronology for further details.

Short   Anyone whose tour of duty in Vietnam (or elsewhere) was nearly up. Short-timers were generally pulled away from heavy combat, if they were in the Boonies; and eased out of their responsibilities, if they were in REMF Land.

SICR   Special Intelligence Collection Requirement. Pronounced "sicker." A point of origin in the intelligence cycle in which an intelligence agency requires a "piece" of information, which is forwarded to a relevant agency, which, then, "tasks" a field operative to procure it.

SIGINT   Signal Intelligence. Intelligence derived from enemy communications. A highly classified and reliable source of intelligence.

Single Didget Midget   This was the ultimate in "shortness." Folks in this exalted state had less than ten days to their DEROS.

SOG   Studies and Observation Group. This was the cover term for a unit of clandestine operations that both gathered intelligence and disrupted activities in the enemy's rear. Its primary focus of activity lay along the Ho Chi Minh Trail. It drew personnel from all services. In today's military, this unit would fall under the Special Operations Command.

Spec Four   Specialist Four. An enlisted rank in the pay grade of an E-4 (enlisted, fourth level). At this level, Spec Fours did technical or support assignments. The Corporal, also an E-4, held command, usually of a Squad (consisting of ten to twelve soldiers).

Squadron   An armored unit in the Army equivalent to a battalion. A squadron will have about twenty tanks. In the Air Force, a squadron is its basic tactical unit, and consists of eight planes.

Strack   Someone who always had a spit-polish military appearance and carriage. In Vietnam, General Westmoreland was strack. General Abrams was not.

Tac   A shortened form of Tactical Officer (pronounced "tack"). This is what a drill instructor was called in OCS. Tacs were usually First Lieutenants.

The Tank   The nerve center of MACV Headquarters. This was in the middle of the building, and only personnel with the highest security clearances could work in it. It was where General Abrams and his staff deliberated and communicated their decisions. Initially, I got a job as a briefer in the Tank.

Target Cell   B-52 target nominations came in from field headquarters in geographic "target boxes" on a military map with grid coordinates, which the nomination asserted contained such lucrative targets as bunker complexes, truck parks, staging areas, cave networks, ammunition dumps, transportation chokepoints, and the like. If this target were selected for strike, a Target Cell of usually three B-52 bombers would saturate this target box with conventional ordnance.

TIC   Troops-in-Contact. Intelligence information that came directly from troops that had been in recent contact with enemy forces. The TIC was considered to be a critical Intel source for OB.

Troop   An armored unit in the Army equivalent to a company and consisting of four to six tanks. The term was also used for an individual soldier,
usually a combat soldier.

USARV   United States Army, Vietnam. Pronounced "use areV." This
designation highlights a quirk to Vietnam service. The campaign command
for the Vietnam War was MACV; hence, all military personnel in-country
were assigned to some activity of MACV, in my case the Air Intelligence
Division of MACV Headquarters. However, everyone was also still attached to a U.S. military unit that had deployed to MACV as part of the
U.S. Army, Vietnam. At least officially, your USARV assignment was your
primary one. This was not a problem in the Boonies where troops directly
served in their American combat units, but it did pose problems in REMF
Land. In my case, I was assigned to the 525 Military Intelligence Group.
Whenever I needed official paperwork, such as to go on leave or R and R, I
had to go to this unit's headquarters, which was in a ramshackle Quonset
hut somewhere in the larger MACV Compound that I could never seem
to find.

USIA   United States Information Agency. The USIA was one of the
three branches of the State Department. Its personnel were responsible
for all of the public information activities of the U.S. Mission in-country.
In Cold War parlance, this was the propaganda arm of U.S. foreign policy. It held major PR events, ran libraries (information centers), and set
up "Vietnamese-American Friendship Associations." In Vietnam, JUSPAO
was a USIA-supported activity. Internationally, the radio network, Voice of
America, was a major outlet of its activities. The USIA was disbanded in
1999, and most of its activities assumed by the Under Secretary of State for
Public Affairs and Public Diplomacy.

USSAG   United States Support Activities Group. This was a headquarters unit established on the U.S. Air Force base in Nakhon Phanom,
Thailand, to assume control over some of the activities of MACV when it
officially stood down on March 28, 1973. It was called "MACV-in-exile."

VC   Viet Cong. The term literally means "Vietnamese Communist"
(the Vietnamese term is Cong San). It illustrates another quirk. To the
South Vietnamese, the term simply meant a Communist, North or South.
Like northerners, they did not see their country as separated in ways that
made them different as Vietnamese because of the division at the seventeenth parallel. To the Americans, however, the term VC referred strictly to
southern Communists, as opposed to Communist infiltrators from North
Vietnam. In its OB, then, the Americans were sticklers for designating

units as either VC or NVA. To the South Vietnamese, they were all Cong San, which created complications in reconciling OB holdings between the Americans and Vietnamese.

VNAF   Vietnamese Air Force (South).

White Mice   Slang term for the National Police of South Vietnam. This refers to the white shirts worn by these forces and their small physical size in the eyes of Americans. Despite this somewhat derogatory term and a marginally deserved reputation for corruption, this force, formed under the advice of the "Police Academy" advisory group at Michigan State University, was quite effective in preventing terrorist attacks in the cities and in keeping the urban Viet Cong infrastructure underground.

WIA   Wounded in Action. Thanks to the efficacy of the medevac system, this category greatly outnumbered the KIAs. In previous American wars, the killed to wounded ratio was one to three. In Vietnam, it was one to six.

WIEUS   Weekly Intelligence Estimate Updates. Pronounced "woos." Intelligence briefings held weekly in the MACV Tank on Saturdays. There was more analysis in this briefing than in the DISUMs but less long-term projection than in the MIEUS.

The world   The good old USA. The world meant home. For troopers in-country, this is where their real lives were, and what they would easily pick up, when they returned home. While in-country, then, troopers were sure that Vietnam was something that would quickly recede in their minds, like a bad dream, once they got back to the world. For all returning veterans, including me, it was never quite that easy.

Notes

Preface: "What Did You Do in the War, Daddy?"

1. Among the many ambiguities of this war is that editors cannot agree on whether the name of this Southeast Asian country is one word or two words. Louisiana State University Press had me spell it as two words, and UNC Press as one.

2. John Clark Pratt, comp., *Vietnam Voices: Perspectives on the War Years, 1941–1982* (New York: Viking Penguin, 1984).

3. This question was initially presented by J. David Singer, "'The Level-of-Analysis Problem in International Relations," *World Politics* 14, no. 1 (October 1961): 77–92.

4. He sets forth his case most thoroughly in Kenneth A. Waltz, *A Theory of International Relations* (Reading, MA: Addison-Wesley, 1979).

5. Jack L. Snyder, *Myths of Empire: Domestic Politics and International Ambition* (Ithaca, NY: Cornell University Press, 1991).

6. Robert Eric Frykenberg, *Guntur District, 1788–1848: A History of Local Influence and Central Authority* (Oxford, UK: Clarendon Press, 1965). This is where I grew up in India, and I gained my first exposure to a Ph.D. dissertation when I was permitted to carry Professor Frykenberg's note-card box as he went on interview trips throughout the district.

7. Stephen Dando-Collins, *Caesar's Legion: The Epic Saga of Julius Caesar's Elite Tenth Legion and the Armies of Rome* (Hoboken, NJ: John Wiley and Sons, 2002).

8. Jeffrey Race, *War Comes to Long An: Revolutionary Conflict in a Vietnamese Province* (Berkeley, CA: University of California Press, 1972).

9. Jonathan Shay, *Achilles in Vietnam: Combat Trauma and the Undoing of Character* (New York: Touchstone Books, 1994), 31.

10. "Afghanistan: Never Mind," *St. Louis Post-Dispatch*, November 11, 2010, A16. For a full account of this strategy review, see Bob Woodward, *Obama's Wars* (New York: Simon and Schuster, 2010).

Chapter 1. Prelude to the War's End: The Years 1972–1973

1. This is the title of the most widely read account of the siege. See Bernard B. Fall, *Hell in a Very Small Place* (Philadelphia: J. P. Lippincott, 1967). This title soon became emblematic of the Vietnam War itself. For this brief historical account, unless otherwise noted in other notes, I rely on my previous book *The War Everyone Lost—and Won: America's Intervention in Viet Nam's Twin Struggles*, rev. ed. (Washington, DC: Congressional Quarterly Press, 1993).

2. The British gave independence to India, Pakistan, Ceylon, and Burma; the Dutch to Indonesia; and the Americans to the Philippines.

3. X [George F. Kennan], "The Sources of Soviet Conduct," *Foreign Affairs* 25 (July 1947): 566–582. This is the only article the editors of this outlet have permitted to be published anonymously, hence the "X."

4. George C. Herring, *America's Longest War: The United States and Vietnam, 1950–1975*, 2nd ed. (New York: Alfred A. Knopf, 1986), 25–26. The provision for

nationwide elections was only part of the Final Declaration of the Geneva Accords, which was not signed by any of the parties. Most observers at the time expected the Communists to win these elections, so Diem's grounds for refusing to hold elections in the South because of this northern intransigence can be seen as a convenient excuse. Nevertheless, it is fair to say that any elections held in the North would have been under highly controlled conditions. See Philippe Devillers and Jean Lacouture, *End of a War: Indochina, 1954* (New York: Frederick A. Praeger, 1969), 303, 309–311, and 320. The definitive account of the Geneva Accords is by Robert F. Randle. He notes that the heart of the South's refusal was the North's equivocation on agreeing to UN supervision of these elections in their zone. See his *Geneva, 1954: The Settlement of the Indochinese War* (Princeton, NJ: Princeton University Press, 1969), 432–433, 445–448. In truth, both sides saw elections as the mere ratification of prearranged political deals.

5. U.S. Army, Chief Office of Information, *Special Warfare, U.S. Army* (Washington, DC: U.S. Government Printing Office, 1962), 22.

6. For a full account of this Buddhist revolt and its suppression, see Robert J. Topmiller, *Lotus Unleashed: The Buddhist Peace Movement in South Vietnam, 1964–1966* (Lexington: University Press of Kentucky, 2002).

7. On this controversy, see Joseph C. Goulden, *Truth Is the First Casualty: The Gulf of Tonkin Affair—Illusion and Reality* (Chicago: Rand-McNally, 1969); Eugene G. Winchey, *Tonkin Gulf* (Garden City, NY: Doubleday, 1971); and Edwin Moise, *Tonkin Gulf: The Escalation of the Vietnam War* (Chapel Hill: University of North Carolina Press, 1996).

8. The best articulation and defense of this strategy still comes from Westmoreland himself. See William C. Westmoreland, *A Soldier Reports* (New York: Doubleday, 1976).

9. Timothy J. Lomperis, *From People's War to People's Rule: Insurgency, Intervention, and the Lessons of Vietnam* (Chapel Hill: University of North Carolina Press, 1996), 100–101, 104.

10. Guenter Lewy, *America in Vietnam* (New York: Oxford University Press, 1978), 42–51.

11. Herring, *America's Longest War*, 201–202.

12. Though an embarrassment to Americans, it is not surprising that the senior officers of the South Vietnamese military were drawn more to French ideas of modern politics, since most of them trained and began their careers under French command. See Donald Kirk, "The Thieu Presidential Campaign: Background and Consequences of the Single Candidacy Phenomenon," *Asian Survey* 12 (July 1972): 609–627.

13. Richard A. Hunt, *Pacification: The American Struggle for Vietnam's Hearts and Minds* (Boulder, CO: Westview Press, 1995), 263–264.

14. The Australian scholar of Vietnam, Alexander Woodside, has called the modern South Vietnamese society too fragmented to have developed a coherent rallying ideology. See Alexander B. Woodside, *Community and Revolution in Modern Vietnam* (Boston: Houghton Mifflin, 1976), 277–301.

15. Robert K. Brigham, *ARVN: Life and Death in the South Vietnamese Army*

(Lawrence: University Press of Kansas, 2002), 47. While this thesis of a lack of nationalism in the South Vietnamese army is provocative, Brigham's study is confined to interviews drawn from the enlisted ranks. A more complete verdict on this important question must come from further studies of the ARVN officer corps and senior leadership. From my personal perspective, impressionistic as it was, I found a high level of nationalism among the Vietnamese intelligence officers with whom I served.

16. In her analysis of South Vietnamese society, Frances FitzGerald saw this as the perpetuation of a collaborationist mentality fostered by the colonial era. See Frances FitzGerald, *Fire in the Lake: The Vietnamese and the Americans in Vietnam* (New York: Vintage Books, 1972), 365–379. In a provocative work, the noted China scholar Lucian Pye argued that such politics of dependence are endemic to Asian understandings of political power. See Lucian Pye, *Asian Power and Politics: The Cultural Dimensions to Authority* (Cambridge, MA: Belknap Press, 1985), chap. 11.

17. FitzGerald, *Fire in the Lake,* 400.

18. Andrew Mack, "Why Big Nations Lose Small Wars: The Politics of Asymmetric Conflict," *World Politics* 27, no. 2 (January 1975): 175–200. In a more recent statistical study, Jonathan Caverley confirms Mack's analysis by reporting that democracies are much less likely to win protracted insurgencies than nondemocracies. See Jonathan D. Caverley, "The Myth of Military Myopia: Democracy, Small Wars, and Vietnam," *International Security* 34, no. 3 (Winter 2009/10): 122–124. An obvious exception is the Soviet defeat in Afghanistan from 1979–1989.

19. Lewy, *America in Vietnam,* 147.

20. Indeed, in his graduate studies at the University of Wisconsin, my father wrote a seminar paper in which he concluded that the Christians in Guntur District built on the gains in status achieved largely through Christian missionary schools under the British by forming political organizations in Independent India to lobby against caste discrimination. See Clarence G. Lomperis, "Social Mobility of Protestant Christians in Andhra Pradesh," unpublished seminar paper, University of Wisconsin–Madison, 1969.

Chapter 2. Nixon's "Secret" Plan and How I Got to Vietnam

1. Neil Sheehan, *A Bright Shining Lie: John Paul Vann and America in Vietnam* (New York: Random House, 1988), 730.

2. Nixon was perhaps unaware of an ironic legacy to this matter. For both Presidents Lyndon Johnson and Richard Nixon, the North Vietnamese proved to be intractable negotiators. Just as American and European statesmen had a "never again" legacy about Munich in appeasing Hitler's aggression in the 1930s, the North Vietnamese remember feeling betrayed by both their Chinese and Russian benefactors at the Geneva Accords of 1954 but also by the American refusal to even sign them. "Never again" would they allow themselves to be cajoled into signing an agreement that stripped them from what they had won on the battlefield.

3. "The Bitter End, 1969–1975," *The History Place: Vietnam War,* 3, http://www.historyplace.com/unitedstates/vietnam/bw-index-1969.html, accessed February 4, 2010.

4. Decades later, when I came to work at Saint Louis University in 1996, a Jesuit Catholic institution, I had a much more comprehensive exposure to Catholicism and have come to appreciate the sincerity of its teachings and beliefs, Protestant though I remain.

5. Jonathan Shay, *Achilles in Vietnam: Combat Trauma and the Undoing of Character* (New York: Touchstone Books, 1994), 77–102. The most chilling account of going berserk in Vietnam that I have read is in Nelson Demille's novel *Up Country*, in which the protagonist goes berserk against a North Vietnamese soldier in individual combat with his bayonet. His more taciturn comrades rebuke him, pointing out that a single rifle shot was all that was necessary. Demille is a Vietnam veteran of heavy combat. See Nelson Demille, *Up Country* (New York: Warner Books, 2002), 403–410.

6. Guenter Lewy, *America in Vietnam* (New York: Oxford University Press, 1978), 325–326. The revelation of this massacre by the journalist Seymour Hersh in March 1970, juxtaposed against the Cambodian Incursion in April 1970, could not have come at a worse time for Nixon's war policies. A whole cottage industry of war crimes accusations sprang up, and Guenter Lewy has taken pains to show that, whatever else may have occurred elsewhere, nothing was on the scale of My Lai. See ibid., 326–343. For full-length accounts of My Lai, see Seymour Hersh, *My Lai 4* (New York: Random House, 1970), and *Cover-Up: The Army's Secret Investigation of the Massacre at My Lai* (New York: Random House, 1972); and U.S. Army, *Report of the Army Review of the Preliminary Investigation into the My Lai Incident* (Washington, DC: Government Printing Office, 1970). This document is more commonly referred to as the "Peers Report."

7. This is a lead-in phrase that Garrison Keillor uses in his tales of "Guy Noir, Private Eye" on his *Prairie Home Companion* PBS radio show.

8. In interviewing a planeload of soldiers bound for Vietnam in September 1972, Kay Bartlett found that some of the soldiers had signed up "hoping that Nixon's secret plan would end the war before they were sent over." So I was not alone. See Kay Bartlett, "Vietnam: Who Will Be the Last to Go?" *Free Lance Star* (Fredericksburg, Va.), September 9, 1972, 14.

9. The installation had been moved from Fort Holabird, Maryland, because this location in the populous Northeast corridor made it too susceptible to penetration by Soviet intelligence agents.

10. Robert B. Semple Jr., "Nixon Rules Out Duty in Vietnam for New Draftees, Only Volunteers Will Be Sent but Order Does Not Affect 4,000 Already There," *New York Times*, June 29, 1972, 1. I was one of these "unlucky" 4,000.

Chapter 3. My Arrival In-Country

1. Raphael Littauer and Norman Uphoff, eds., *The Air War in Indochina*, rev. ed. (Boston: Beacon Press, 1972), 172.

2. These problems have been aired extensively in the memoirs of these two service commanders. See William C. Westmoreland, *A Soldier Reports* (New York: Doubleday, 1976); and Lewis W. Walt, *A General's Report on Vietnam* (New York: Funk, 1970). Indeed, the CINCPAC commander at the time called these arrangements

"the most asinine way to fight a war that could possibly be imagined." See Ulysses S. Grant Sharp, *Strategy for Defeat: Vietnam in Retrospect* (San Rafael, CA: Presidio Press, 1978), 233.

3. For a detailed breakdown of these South Vietnamese forces, see Richard Dean Burns and Milton Leitenberg, *The Wars in Vietnam, Cambodia and Laos, 1945–1982: A Bibliographic Guide* (Santa Barbara, CA: ABC-Clio Information Services, 1984), 143. On the number of U.S. military advisers, see Dale Andrade, *America's Last Vietnam Battle: Halting Hanoi's Easter Offensive* (Lawrence: University Press of Kansas, 2001), 484.

4. Shelby L. Stanton, *The Rise and Fall of an American Army: U.S. Ground Forces in Vietnam, 1965–1973* (Novato, CA: Presidio Press, 1985), 78–80.

5. Two accounts of these activities are Kenneth Conboy and Dale Andrade, *Spies and Commandos: How America Lost the Secret War in North Vietnam* (Lawrence: University Press of Kansas, 2000); and Richard H. Shultz Jr., *The Secret War against Hanoi: The Untold Story of Spies, Saboteurs, and Covert Warriors in North Vietnam* (New York: Perennial Books, 1999).

6. William E. Le Gro, *Vietnam from Cease-Fire to Capitulation* (Washington, DC: U.S. Army Center of Military History, 1981), 19.

7. Anthony S. Campagna, *The Economic Consequences of the Vietnam War* (New York: Praeger, 1991), 83, 96. I mention this time frame to emphasize the long and extensive economic involvement in Vietnam. By the end of the French Indochina War, the United States was underwriting three-fourths of the French war effort, and in the "second" American war, this economic assistance was subsidizing a similar proportion of the war costs of the Saigon regime.

8. These classes were highlighted in the 1987 movie *Good Morning, Vietnam*.

9. One of the most valuable of these sources was the *Viet-Nam Documents and Research Notes*. These were a series of translated documents from CDEC on key enemy decisions and analytical essays done by JUSPAO researchers. Many of them were done by Bill Gausmann. I relied on them heavily for my Ph.D. dissertation.

10. Guenter Lewy, *America in Vietnam* (New York: Oxford University Press, 1978), 124.

11. Malcolm Browne, "Deep Recession Grips Saigon," *New York Times,* June 4, 1972, 1–2.

12. This contrast was revealed to the public in the Pentagon Papers. For those of us in the business, this disparity was classic. Though MACV might be accused, with some justification, for being axiomatically positive, in my view this does not mean that some of the negativism coming out of the CIA was therefore automatically correct.

13. Neil Sheehan et al., eds., *The Pentagon Papers as Published by the New York Times* (New York: Bantam Books, 1971), 130–138; and Martin E. Goldstein, *American Policy toward Laos* (Rutherford, NJ: Fairleigh Dickinson University Press, 1973), 198, 313, and 317.

14. Richard A Hunt, *Pacification: The American Struggle for Vietnam's Hearts and Minds* (Boulder, CO: Westview Press, 1995), 249. Hunt offers a sharply critical assessment of Phoenix. See ibid., 247–251. A spirited defender of it is William Colby

with James McCarger, *Lost Victory: A Firsthand Account of America's Sixteen Year Involvement in Vietnam* (Chicago: Contemporary Books, 1989).

15. I later learned that this hospital used to be the American International School, the school run by the U.S. embassy for dependent children in the 1950s and early 1960s. Ironically, one of my classmates in the Washington Semester Program at American University in 1968 had attended the school.

16. "William Gausmann, USIA Official, Dies," *Washington Post*, September 28, 1977, C6.

17. We both returned from Vietnam to Washington, D.C. There I met Ana Maria Turner in graduate school. She had the enthusiastic endorsement of Bill, and we asked him to serve as the best man at our wedding in North Carolina on May 15, 1976, but ill health prevented him from making the trip. He died shortly after our wedding.

Chapter 4. How the War Was Run: The Easter Invasion

1. There is a controversy over whether to call this campaign an "offensive" or an "invasion." I use the latter term because, in contrast to the two previous offensives in 1965 and 1968, this one involved attacks by entire North Vietnamese divisions from outside South Vietnam. In 1965 and 1968, the attacking Communist forces had been inside the territory of South Vietnam for some time. I am indebted to my wife, Ana Maria, for the title to this chapter.

2. Stephen P. Randolph, *Powerful and Brutal Weapons: Nixon, Kissinger, and the Easter Offensive* (Cambridge, MA: Harvard University Press, 2007), 38.

3. Lewis Sorley, *A Better War: The Unexamined Victories, and Final Tragedy of America's Last Years in Vietnam* (New York: Harcourt Brace, 1999), 323–325.

4. James H. Willbanks, *Abandoning Vietnam: How America Left and South Vietnam Lost Its War* (Lawrence: University Press of Kansas, 2004), 148.

5. Ibid.; and Randolph, *Powerful and Brutal Weapons*, 146–148.

6. Dale Andrade, *America's Last Vietnam Battle: Halting Hanoi's Easter Offensive* (Lawrence: University Press of Kansas, 2001), 142–143, 162, and 171.

7. Ibid., 165–171; and Randolph, *Powerful and Brutal Weapons*, 253–259.

8. Randolph, *Powerful and Brutal Weapons*, 131–133.

9. Willbanks, *Abandoning Vietnam*, 139–142; and Andrade, *America's Last Vietnam Battle*, 216–227.

10. Willbanks, *Abandoning Vietnam*, 251, 266, and 285–286; and Randolph, *Powerful and Brutal Weapons*, 260–266.

11. Andrade, *America's Last Vietnam Battle*, 321–325. Quote is from 325. Andrade contends that the day of these strikes was May 14. Lewis Sorley claims it was May 12. See Sorley, *A Better War*, 334. In support, Sorley quotes a cable from General Abrams to each of his three MR commanders: "I want to use the three days, 11, 12, and 13 May . . . to inflict as much damage as possible. . . . Therefore, I have decided to allocate the entire B-52 effort to MR-3 on 11 May, to MR-2 on 12 May, and to MR-1 on 13 May." See Sorley, *A Better War*, 334. Direct evidence like this gives the nod to Sorley on this sequence.

12. Andrade, *America's Last Vietnam Battle*, 347–348.

13. Ibid., 349–355.

14. This meant that all three of the Airborne Brigades—ARVN's strategic reserve—were committed to the invasion; one to MR 1, one to MR 2, and now one to MR 3.

15. Andrade, *America's Last Vietnam Battle*, 404–420; and Randolph, *Powerful and Brutal Weapons,*77–79. Andrade intended the "insignificant" title for An Loc as an ironic reference to the classic account of the more "significant" siege of Dienbienphu by Bernard Fall entitled *Hell in a Very Small Place*. See Andrade, *America's Last Vietnam Battle*, 333; and Bernard Fall, *Hell in a Very Small Place* (Philadelphia: J. P. Lippincott, 1967).

16. Sorley, *A Better War,* 334–335.

17. Andrade, *America's Last Vietnam Battle,* 447.

18. Ibid., 461–471.

19. Ibid., 336, 495–496. Surprisingly, in a memorandum to his close advisers Henry Kissinger and Alexander Haig on May 15, Nixon wanted Abrams to amass armored forces for a dramatic American counteroffensive. By this time, all U.S. armored forces had been withdrawn from Vietnam. See Randolph, *Powerful and Brutal Weapons,* 228.

20. Sorley, *A Better War,* 326; and Jeffrey Kimball, *Nixon's Vietnam War* (Lawrence: University Press of Kansas, 1998), 295.

21. Randolph, *Powerful and Brutal Weapons,* 192–197.

22. Ibid., 181, 323; Sorley, *A Better War,* 327; and Andrade, *America's Last Vietnam Battle,* 478.

23. Randolph, *Powerful and Brutal Weapons,* 337–338.

24. Sorley, *A Better War,* 339; and Willbanks, *Abandoning Vietnam,* 152.

25. Andrade, *America's Last Vietnam Battle,* 487.

26. Sorley, *A Better War,* 340.

27. Ibid., 341.

28. For a discussion of these three levels of intelligence, see Robert M. Clark, *Intelligence Analysis: A Target-Centric Approach,* 3rd ed. (Washington, DC: Congressional Quarterly Press, 2010), 50–51.

29. Andrade, *America's Last Vietnam Battle,* 211.

30. For a full discussion of these intelligence sources, see Clark, *Intelligence Analysis,* 87–123.

31. Again, for a full discussion of assessing the validity of intelligence information, see ibid., 124–149.

32. Andrade, *America's Last Vietnam Battle,* 347–348.

33. Interestingly, this problem of shared information within the intelligence community appears to remain unresolved in 2010. See Clark, *Intelligence Analysis,* 2–3.

34. This dominance was reflected all the way down the line in military staffs. The Military Region staffs in Vietnam were "G" level, as were the staffs at divisional headquarters. Headquarters at "sub-unit" levels—battalions and companies—had staffing at the "S" level.

35. Alexander Haig was an Army general. His principal deputy was one Colin Powell, who later became chairman of the Joint Chiefs of Staff and then served as President George W. Bush's Secretary of State.

36. Sorley, *A Better War,* 334–335. The order of strikes and quote from Hollingsworth is from Sorley. The quote of Abrams is my poetic license for the gist of what he said.

37. Marshall L. Michel III, *The Eleven Days of Christmas: America's Last Vietnam Battle* (San Francisco: Encounter Books, 2002), 14–15. For harder targets, a few 2,000-pound bombs might be thrown into the mix. A strategic B-52 bomber carried a payload of four 25-megaton nuclear bombs. For comparison, the explosions over Hiroshima and Nagasaki were in the 10–20 kiloton range. (Michel reports the B-52 target cell as one mile by a half mile. I recall the typical cell as being one kilometer by three kilometers.)

38. Truong Nhu Tang, with David Chanoff and Doan Van Toai, *A Vietcong Memoir: An Inside Account of the Vietnam War and Its Aftermath* (San Diego: Harcourt Brace Jovanovich, 1985), 168, 170–171.

39. Randolph, *Powerful and Brutal Weapons,* 274.

40. This comprised all fixed wing aircraft short of the B-52s, including prop-driven C-47 "Spooky" gunships and AC-130 Specter gunships, as well as such jet fighter bombers as the F-4 Phantoms and F-105 Thunder chiefs.

41. The essentials of the "Lavelle scandal" can be found in Kimball, *Nixon's Vietnam War,* 59–60; and Randolph, *Powerful and Brutal Weapons,* 293–295.

42. Joseph B. Treaster, "Air War Control Tightened by U.S.," *New York Times,* June 27, 1972, 1.

43. Randolph, *Powerful and Brutal Weapons,* 120.

44. Truong Nhu Tang, *A Vietcong Memoir,* 167.

45. Sorley, *A Better War,* 120–122.

46. Randolph, *Powerful and Brutal Weapons,* 119–122.

47. Richard Shultz reported that SOG stood down on April 30, 1972. Kenneth Conboy and Dale Andrade, however, reveal that South Vietnamese units continued these clandestine operations until the signing of the Paris Peace Agreement. See Richard H. Shultz Jr., *The Secret War against Hanoi: The Untold Story of Spies, Saboteurs. and Covert Warriors in North Vietnam* (New York: Perennial Books, 1999), ix; and Kenneth Conboy and Dale Andrade, *Spies and Commandos: How America Lost the Secret War in North Vietnam* (Lawrence: University Press of Kansas, 2000), 260–267. In the maps we used to show the locations of the nominations, there were always a set of boxes that were "no go" zones for aerial targeting. All that happened after April 30 was that the SOG "no go" zones changed the color of their stripes on the maps.

48. Lieutenant Lesser and I were awarded Bronze Stars for "meritorious service" in evaluating and briefing B-52 target nominations that were critical to the success of U.S. military forces in Vietnam. I hasten to add that these awards were pretty much "every man medals" for officers serving in war zone headquarters.

Chapter 5. Life in Saigon and a Trip to Tuy Hoa

1. Allen E. Goodman and Lawrence Franks, "The Dynamics of Migration to Saigon," *Pacific Affairs* 48, no. 2 (Summer 1975): 202.

2. Truong Minh Cac, Tu Uyen, and Vo Liet Nu, "Studies in Family Planning," *East Asia Review* 3, no. 7 (July 1972): 157.

3. Donald E. McQuinn, *Targets* (New York: Tom Doherty Associates, 1980), 57.

4. Ibid., 404.

5. Thomas An, "The Overseas Chinese in South Vietnam: A Note," *Vietnam Perspectives* 2, no. 4 (May 1967): 13. An's figure is for 1959, and it was 12,000. I cite this to confirm the size of this population, but I think the number in 1972 was more like 10,000. In any case, the French presence remained steady after their withdrawal from power in 1954.

6. Frank Snepp reported that Ky was still planning a coup just days before the fall of Saigon in April 1975. See Frank Snepp, *Decent Interval: An Insider's Account of Saigon's Indecent End Told by the CIA's Chief Strategy Analyst in Vietnam* (New York: Random House, 1977), 286–287.

7. An, "Overseas Chinese in South Vietnam," 14.

8. R. W. Apple Jr., "Negro and White Fight Side by Side," *New York Times,* January 3, 1966, 7.

9. In 1969, blacks comprised 58 percent of the inmates at Long Binh, even though they made up only 9 percent of the total U.S. force in Vietnam. See Guenter Lewy, *America in Vietnam* (New York: Oxford University Press, 1978), 154–155.

10. Philip Caputo, *A Rumor of War* (New York: Ballantine Books, 1977), 121.

11. These were the words of the protagonist Paul Bremer, the combat veteran, in Nelson Demille's novel *Up Country* (New York: Warner Books, 2002), 193.

Chapter 6. Peace Talks, Christmas Bombing—and an Indian Interlude

1. It is no small irony that both General Ngo Quang Truong and former President Ngo Dinh Diem were descendants of the first Vietnamese dynasty to throw off Chinese rule, that of Ngo Quyen in 939 A.D. On this first Ngo, see Timothy J. Lomperis, *The War Everyone Lost—And Won: America's Intervention in Viet Nam's Twin Struggles,* rev. ed. (Washington, DC: Congressional Quarterly Press, 1993), 17.

2. Dale Andrade, *America's Last Vietnam Battle: Halting Hanoi's Easter Offensive* (Lawrence: University Press of Kansas, 2001), 176–181.

3. Ibid., 186–192.

4. Stephen P. Randolph, *Powerful and Brutal Weapons: Nixon, Kissinger, and the Easter Offensive* (Cambridge, MA: Harvard University Press, 2007), 324.

5. Andrade, *America's Last Vietnam Battle,* 194–196. Quote is from 196.

6. Marshall L. Michel III, *The Eleven Days of Christmas: America's Last Vietnam Battle* (San Francisco: Encounter Books, 2002), 28.

7. At the time of the eventual ceasefire, U.S. intelligence held PAVN forces in the South as 160,000. See Lewis Sorley, *A Better War: The Unexamined Victories and Final Tragedy of America's Last Years in Vietnam* (New York: Harcourt Brace, 1999), 363. Thieu, however, insisted that these forces numbered at least 300,000. See James H. Willbanks, *Abandoning Vietnam: How America Left and South Vietnam Lost Its War* (Lawrence: University Press of Kansas, 2004), 175. The lower number to the Americans meant that these PAVN forces could be contained. The higher number to Thieu meant that these forces continued to be a real menace to his regime.

8. Again, at the time of the ceasefire, the United States had significant air and naval forces stationed in Thailand and in offshore waters.

9. This arrangement was reminiscent of the "three thirds system" employed by

Mao Zedong with the Guomindang for local government in China during World War II.

10. Willbanks, *Abandoning Vietnam*, 174. It is an unusual gesture of parity to offer one's ally and enemy the same $2 billion.

11. William E. Le Gro, *Vietnam from Cease-Fire to Capitulation* (Washington, DC: U.S. Army Center of Military History, 1981), 17.

12. Willbanks, *Abandoning Vietnam*, 175.

13. Jeffrey C. Clarke, *Advice and Support: The Final Years, 1965–1973* (Washington, DC: U.S. Army Center of Military History, 1988), 489.

14. Dictionary of American History, "Nixon's Letter to Nguyen Van Thieu," 3, http://www.encyclopedia.com/doc/1G2-3401804845.html, accessed April 27, 2010.

15. Michel, *Eleven Days of Christmas*, 42.

16. Allan Goodman, *The Lost Peace: America's Search for a Negotiated Settlement of the Vietnam War* (Stanford, CA: Hoover Institution Press, 1978), 131.

17. Frank Snepp, *Decent Interval: An Insider's Account of Saigon's Indecent End Told by the CIA's Chief Strategy Analyst in Vietnam* (New York: Random House, 1977), 49–50.

18. Goodman, *Lost Peace*, 131–133.

19. Snepp, *Decent Interval*, 50.

20. Andrade, *America's Last Vietnam Battle*, 480.

21. Jeffrey Kimball, *Nixon's Vietnam War* (Lawrence: University Press of Kansas, 1998), 324.

22. Andrade, *America's Last Vietnam Battle*, 480–481.

23. Michel, *Eleven Days of Christmas*, 240.

24. Sorley, *Better War*, 355.

25. Michel, *Eleven Days of Christmas,* 125, 153, and 209.

26. Kimball, *Nixon's Vietnam War*, 367.

27. Sorley, *Better War*, 356.

28. Abrams left Vietnam convinced that ARVN could win after an agreement was signed. See Lewis Sorley, *Thunderbolt: General Creighton Abrams and the Army of His Time* (New York: Simon and Schuster, 1992), 345. Kissinger, on the other hand, often lamented the domestic constraints on U.S. foreign policy as when he wrote, "no foreign policy is stronger than its domestic base." See his *Ending the Vietnam War* (New York: Simon and Schuster, 2003), 457.

29. Kimball, *Nixon's Vietnam War*, 366.

30. Nguyen Tien Hung and Jerrold L. Schecter, *The Palace File* (New York: Harper and Row, 1986), 1. Indeed, the book closes with facsimile reproductions of a file of letters that contain a litany of such American assurances over many years. It goes on for over a hundred pages. See Appendix A, 365–479.

31. Kissinger, *Ending the Vietnam War*, 304–305.

32. About five miles down one of these unimproved "roads" we called *donkas*, there was a temple with a stone tablet inscription testifying to the particulars of Marco Polo's visit. The supervised trip to this temple was the highlight of the retreat for us kids. It also gave an annual opportunity for our local missionary

storyteller, Sam Schmitthenner, to expand on this visit far beyond the bounds of the temple inscription.

33. Despite the obvious danger to his personnel at Camp Davis, in his official protest of this treatment, the senior North Vietnamese delegate, General Tran Van Tra, only complained about "the excessive noise at the compound" and the lack of air conditioning. See Walter Scott Dillard, *Sixty Days to Peace* (Washington, DC: National Defense University, 1982), 121.

Chapter 7. I Spy 1: My Time as an Intelligence Liaison Officer

1. James H. Willbanks, *Abandoning Vietnam: How America Left and South Vietnam Lost Its War* (Lawrence: University Press of Kansas, 2004), 187; Lewis Sorley, *A Better War: The Unexamined Victories and Final Tragedy of America's Last Year in Vietnam* (New York: Harcourt Brace, 1999), 366; William E. Le Gro, *Vietnam from Cease-Fire to Capitulation* (Washington, DC: U.S. Army Center for Military History, 1981), 19; and Frank Snepp, *Decent Interval: An Insider's Account of Saigon's Indecent End Told by the CIA's Chief Strategy Analyst in Vietnam* (New York: Random House, 1977), 78.

2. Le Gro, *Vietnam from Cease-Fire to Capitulation*, 19.

3. When I first arrived in Vietnam, my initial assignment was to CMIC. This was countermanded when I got the interview to work in the Tank. Knowing my ethical "history," I think the Good Lord saved me from more trial than I probably could have withstood.

4. Trung-uy (pronounced "Troong-we") is Vietnamese for "first lieutenant," and was what most of the Vietnamese who worked at MACV called me.

5. I do not believe my little Ho Chi Minh lived much longer after my departure. Though Colonel Lung and Lieutenant Colonel Nho were successfully evacuated in 1975, Colonel Chuong was not.

6. Seventy percent of the Vietnamese population (North and South) have Nguyen for their last name. This was the last Vietnamese dynasty, and most people converted their name for the accrued advantages. Thi is a marker for female, and Huong means flower. Vietnamese girls are commonly named after flowers.

7. The Viet Cong had no love for this Catholic population, and singled out these northern émigré settlements for rocket and mortar attacks.

8. Nguyen Cao Ky, *How We Lost the War* (New York: Stein and Day, 1978), 109.

9. "Corruption Still a Problem in Vietnam," *New York Times*, September 29, 1968, 1.

10. "Corruption Is Taking up to 40% of US Assistance to Vietnam," *New York Times*, November 13, 1966, 1.

11. Felix Belair, "House Committee Charges Mismanagement in Economic Aid to South Vietnam," *New York Times*, November 13, 1966, 7.

12. R. W. Apple Jr., "Vast US AID Loss in Vietnam Denied," *New York Times*, November 18, 1966, 1.

13. "Corruption Is Taking up to 40% of US Assistance to Vietnam," 1.

14. Snepp, *Decent Interval*, 103.

15. James Reston, "Nixon, Drugs, and the War," *New York Times*, June 2, 1971, 41.

16. Alexander B. Woodside, *Community and Revolution in Modern Vietnam* (Boston: Houghton Mifflin, 1978), 289.

17. Jonathan Randal, "Red-Light Limits Opposed in Saigon," *New York Times,* November 14, 1966, 13.

18. Corruption has been a big theme in the writings of Mr. Ky. For one of his more graphic portraits, see his *Twenty Years and Twenty Days* (New York: Stein and Day, 1976), 101–116.

19. Snepp, *Decent Interval,* 117.

20. Edward Van Roy, "On the Theory of Corruption," *Economic Development and Cultural Change* 19, no. 1 (October 1970): 86.

21. Samuel P. Huntington, *Political Order in Changing Societies* (New Haven, CT: Yale University Press, 1968), 59–60.

22. Jon S. T. Quah, "Bureaucratic Corruption in the ASEAN Countries: A Comparative Analysis of their Anti-Corruption Strategies," *Journal of Southeast Asian Studies* 13, no. 1 (March 1982): 164.

23. James C. Scott, *Comparative Political Corruption* (Englewood Cliffs, NJ: Prentice Hall, 1972), 64, 79.

24. "Where the Payoff Is a Way of Life," *New York Times,* January 17, 1969, C63.

25. Quah, "Bureaucratic Corruption in the ASEAN Countries," 155.

26. J. Anthony Lukass, "India's Immunity Offer Fails to Lure Out Illegal Wealth," *New York Times,* June 4, 1965, 6.

27. "Transparency International: Corruption Perception Index 2009," http://www.transparency.org/policy_research/surveys_indices/cpi/2009/cpi_2009_table, accessed February 23, 2010.

28. Perhaps in a belated recognition of this social asymmetry, the Pentagon recently announced "Campaign Continuity" whereby U.S. units in Afghanistan would be redeployed to the same parts of the country as part of its "long war" strategy. See Yochi J. Dreazen, "Pentagon Revamps Afghanistan Deployments: New System Would Return Troops to Same Parts of Country to Develop Better Expertise and Cultivate Local Relationships," *Wall Street Journal,* March 26, 2010, A10. Such a strategy is difficult to square with President Obama's announced 30,000-troop surge into Afghanistan that will be promptly withdrawn in 2011, just eighteen months after the proclamation of this increased commitment.

Chapter 8. I Spy 2: The Order-of-Battle Conference

1. For two full-length works on this trial, see Renata Adler, *Reckless Disregard: Westmoreland vs. CBS et al., Sharon vs. Times* (New York: Alfred A. Knopf, 1986); and Bob Brewin and Sydney Shaw, *Vietnam on Trial: Westmoreland vs. CBS* (New York: Athenaeum, 1987). Interestingly, Westmoreland settled for a symbolic one dollar in damages before the case went to the jury.

2. In this section on the Tet OB Controversy, I am relying on the authoritative coverage of James J. Wirtz, *The Tet Offensive: Intelligence Failure in War* (Ithaca, NY: Cornell University Press, 1991), 247–251.

3. Indeed, in early 1967, some MACV officials were already claiming that the "cross-over point" had been reached. See Guenter Lewy, *America in Vietnam* (New York: Oxford University Press, 1978), 74.

4. As a result of all the controversies over numbers in the Vietnam War, the Pentagon subsequently, in my view, has overreacted on this issue. In the American wars that have followed—Persian Gulf I in 1991, Kosovo in 1998, and both in Iraq and Afghanistan currently—the Pentagon has declined to publicly provide numbers on the size of enemy forces or on their casualties. It has advanced the argument that the provision of such numbers are the responsibility of the enemies involved.

5. Jeffrey J. Clarke, *Advice and Support: The Final Years* (Washington, DC: U.S. Army Center of Military History, 1988), 491. Frank Snepp acknowledged that the CIA admitted to 170,000 North Vietnamese regulars in the South. See Frank Snepp, *Decent Interval: An Insider's Account of Saigon's Indecent End Told by the CIA's Chief Strategy Analyst in Vietnam* (New York: Random House, 1977), 56.

6. Albert E. Palmerlee, Joint United States Public Affairs Office (hereafter JUS-PAO), "Viet Cong Political Geography," *Viet-Nam Documents and Research Notes,* no. 21 (Saigon: U.S. Mission, March 1968), 1–3.

7. The Military History Institute of Vietnam, *Victory in Vietnam: The Official History of the People's Army of Vietnam, 1954–1975,* trans. Merle L. Pribbenow (Lawrence: University Press of Kansas, 2002), 76.

8. Palmerlee, "Viet Cong Political Geography," 1.

9. JUSPAO, "Viet-Cong Political Geography of South Viet-Nam," *Viet-Nam Documents and Research Notes,* no. 93 (Saigon: U.S. Mission, 1971), 12, 13, 24–26. These command arrangements have been confirmed in Hanoi's official account. See Military History Institute of Vietnam, *Victory in Vietnam,* 194.

10. Stanley Karnow, *Vietnam: A History* (New York: Penguin Books, 1997), 558. The quote is Karnow's summary of his interview with this insurgent. Truong Nhu Tang, a high-level Viet Cong defector, wrote his memoir as a saga of this gradual betrayal of the southern Communist movement by Hanoi. For him, the moment of truth came at a victory dinner after the fall of Saigon in which southern participation was a bare token. He wrote, "We knew finally that we had been well and truly sold." See Truong Nhu Tang, with David Chanoff and Doan Van Toai, *A Vietcong Memoir: An Inside Account of the Vietnam War and Its Aftermath* (San Diego: Harcourt Brace Jovanovich, 1985), 270.

11. On the importance of Sihanoukville to the COSVN war effort, see Lewis Sorley, *Thunderbolt, from the Battle of the Bulge to Vietnam and Beyond: General Creighton Abrams and the Army of His Times* (New York: Simon and Schuster, 1992), 290.

12. Snepp, *Decent Interval,* 20.

13. Lewis Sorley, comp. and ed., *Vietnam Chronicles: The Abrams Tapes* (Lubbock: Texas Tech University Press, 2004), 829. Italics in original.

14. To which Ambassador Ellsworth Bunker added, "Absolutely, couldn't agree more." See ibid., 766. Italics in original.

Chapter 9. Civilian Life: The *Kieu* and Tay Ninh

1. This was the basic term in "Nam Speak" for Caucasian women. Unfortunately, this lexicon was full of derogatory terms for the local population, American civilians, and other foreign groups in Saigon that I have tried to refrain from employing in this account.

2. For the story of the *Kieu,* I am relying on Nguyen Du, *The Tale of Kieu,* trans. Huynh Sanh Thong (New York: Random House, 1973).

3. Ibid., 24–25.

4. I have discussed this two-sided face to the Vietnamese concept of political legitimacy in Timothy J. Lomperis, *From People's War to People's Rule: Insurgency, Intervention, and the Lessons of Vietnam* (Chapel Hill: University of North Carolina Press, 1996), 88–97, 111–120.

5. Nguyen Khac Vien, *Traditional Vietnam: Some Historical Stages: Vietnam Studies Number 21* (Hanoi: Foreign Languages Publishing House, 1969), 84, 145.

6. Nguyen Du, *Tale of Kieu,* 142.

7. Graham Greene, *The Quiet American* (London: Penguin Books, 1973 [1955]), 83–114.

8. Ibid., 88.

9. Alexander B. Woodside, *Community and Revolution in Modern Vietnam* (Boston: Houghton Mifflin, 1976), 182–187; and "Cao Dai," http://www.caodai.org/pages/?pageID=2 (accessed April 15, 2010).

10. Woodside, *Community and Revolution,* 188–189.

Chapter 10. The Unraveling: An Overblown Medal

1. Thomas M. Hawley, *The Remains of War: Bodies, Politics, and the Search for American Soldiers Unaccounted for in Southeast Asia* (Durham, NC: Duke University Press, 2005), 47, 61.

2. Allan E. Goodman, *The Lost Peace: America's Search for a Negotiated Settlement of the Vietnam War* (Stanford, CA: Hoover Institute Press, 1978), 154.

3. William E. Le Gro, *Vietnam from Cease-Fire to Capitulation* (Washington, DC: U.S. Army Center of Military History, 1981), 30, 40, 49, 52, and 60.

4. After, of course, the day of my marriage and the birth of our two children. Since this was the culminating and most dramatic event in my service as an intelligence liaison officer for the Defense Attaché Office, I have saved this account for the end of this memoir, despite this violence to the chronology of my employment.

5. Our fears were confirmed by a selection in the memoir of the high-level Viet Cong defector, Truong Nhu Tang. "It was something of a miracle that from 1968 through 1970 the attacks, though they caused significant casualties generally, did not kill a single one of the military or civilian leaders in the headquarters complexes. The luck, though, had a lot to do with accurate advance warning of the raids, which allowed us to move out of the way or take refuge in our bunkers before the bombs began to rain down. B-52s flying out of Okinawa and Guam would be picked up by Soviet intelligence trawlers plying the South China Sea. The planes' headings and air speeds would be computed and relayed to COSVN headquarters, which would then order NLF or Northern elements in the anticipated target zones to move away perpendicularly to the attack trajectory." See Truong Nhu Tang, with David Chanoff and Doan Van Toai, *A Vietcong Memoir: An Inside Account of the Vietnam War and Its Aftermath* (San Diego: Harcourt Brace Jovanovich, 1985), 168.

6. Vann was the subject of a prize-winning biography by Neil Sheehan. See Neil Sheehan, *A Bright Shining Lie: John Paul Vann and America in Vietnam* (New York: Random House, 1988).

7. In Joseph Conrad's novel *Heart of Darkness,* Kurtz had carved out a personal empire of slavery and elephant tusks to the "horror" of Marlow, the novel's narrator, who was charged with finding Kurtz. Francis Ford Coppola used Conrad's novel as the metaphor for his blockbuster movie about Vietnam, *Apocalypse Now.*

8. Neither I nor my superiors at the DAO had paid much attention to reports that after the ceasefire the embassy was determined to reassert its "preeminence" in the in-country chain-of-command. To effect this, CORDS was abolished and was replaced by four U.S. consulates in the former MR Headquarters. The CIA intelligence reporting as well would be filtered through a new cadre of foreign service officers that would head these consulates. Mr. Harrison was the new consular officer for the Mekong Delta. See Joseph B. Treaster, "Civilians Taking over U.S. Task in Vietnam," *New York Times,* February 9, 1973, 3.

Chapter 11. Conclusion: Going Native and Going Home

1. I had applied to both SAIS and Columbia during my senior year of college in 1969, and was accepted by both. Both also said they would honor military deferrals in delayed admittances. Four years later, SAIS honored this commitment. Columbia did not.

2. I received a letter from Phu in 2000 sending me a picture of him and his lovely wife who now live in Portland, Oregon. Margaret lived nearby in Salem, but she has subsequently passed away.

3. Timothy J. Lomperis, *From People's War to People's Rule: Insurgency, Intervention, and the Lessons of Vietnam* (Chapel Hill: University of North Carolina Press, 1996), 109. The $500 million figure is from James H. Willbanks, *Abandoning Vietnam: How America Left and South Vietnam Lost Its War* (Lawrence: University Press of Kansas, 2004), 216.

4. Lewis Sorley, *A Better War: The Unexamined Victories and Final Tragedies of America's Last Years in Vietnam* (New York: Harcourt Brace, 1999), 349.

5. Michael D. Pearlman, *Warmaking and American Democracy* (Lawrence: University Press of Kansas, 1999), 391.

6. James P. Sterba, "'Friendship Pass' No Longer Links Peking to Hanoi," *New York Times,* January 5, 1979, sec. 1, A3; and "China Admits Combat in Vietnam War," *Washington Post,* May 17, 1989, A31. More recently, a Chinese scholar researching provincial archives in China has revealed a massive Chinese commitment to North Vietnam that included the dispatching of 320,000 logistical troops and the guaranteeing of Chinese ground troops in the event of an American invasion of North Vietnam. See Qiang Zhai, *China and the Vietnam Wars, 1950–1975* (Chapel Hill: University of North Carolina Press, 2000), esp. 134–137.

7. William E. Le Gro, *Vietnam from Cease-Fire to Capitulation* (Washington, DC: U.S. Army Center of Military History, 1981), 145.

8. United States embassy intelligence sources also reported that the Soviets urged Hanoi to "go for broke" in this offensive. See "The Vietnam-Cambodia Emergency, 1975, Part III—Vietnam Evacuation: Testimony of Ambassador Graham A. Martin," *Hearing before The Special Subcommittee on Investigations of the Committee on International Relations, House of Representatives, January 27, 1976* (Washington, DC: U.S. Government Printing Office, 1976), 605.

9. Timothy J. Lomperis, *The War Everyone Lost—And Won: America's Intervention in Viet Nam's Twin Struggles,* rev. ed. (Washington, DC: Congressional Quarterly Press, 1993), 96–97.

10. Willbanks, *Abandoning Vietnam,* 233.

11. Just such a Communist attack had been envisioned by Pentagon planners in the 1950s, and they thought they could have broken it up. They certainly could have in 1975 as well. For a fuller discussion of this "stolen strategy," see my "Giap's Dream, Westmoreland's Nightmare," *Parameters* 18 (Summer 1988): 18–33; and Alexander S. Cochran Jr., "American Planning for Ground Combat in Vietnam, 1952–1965," *Parameters* 14 (Summer 1984): 63–65.

12. Quoted in Pearlman, *Warmaking and American Democracy,* 392.

13. Ibid., 345.

14. For full accounts of this last campaign, see Le Gro, *Vietnam from Cease-Fire to Capitulation;* and Willbanks, *Abandoning Vietnam.* The official and triumphant Communist account of this victory is by General Van Tien Dung, *Our Great Spring Victory,* trans. John Spragens (New York: Monthly Review Press, 1977).

15. Nguyen Khanh Toan et al., *The Paris Peace Agreement on Vietnam* (Hanoi, DRV: Institute of Juridicial Sciences, 1973), 304.

16. The argument by some in Congress that sending so much equipment to South Vietnam would be irretrievably lost just as happened to the last-minute military assistance to Chiang Kai-Sheik in China in 1949 falls short on two counts. First, ARVN showed itself fully capable of fending off the North Vietnamese with American fire power support in 1972. As the defense of Xuan Loc in 1975 showed, there was still fight left in ARVN. United States airpower could have made short work of massed forces of Communist troops (though attempts by President Ford in April to gain exceptions against this congressional proscription against the use of American force were also rebuffed by Congress). Second, there is the more fundamental question of a moral obligation. Whatever the merits of our initial intervention in Vietnam, we at least owed it to our trusting Vietnamese clients to give them the wherewithal to defend themselves with our American-provided war machine.

Chapter 12. Epilogue: Secret Mission Revealed—and Its Liberation

1. For a fuller account of Diem's idiosyncratic brand of nationalism, see Denis Warner, *The Last Confucian* (Harmondsworth, UK: Penguin Books, 1963), 13–16, 72, and 256–258.

2. This brief account of the war is a summary of the historical material in Timothy J. Lomperis, *The War Everyone Lost—And Won: America's Intervention in Viet Nam's Twin Struggles,* rev. ed. (Washington, DC: Congressional Quarterly Press, 1993), pt. 1.

3. William Darryl Henderson, *Why the Vietcong Fought: A Study of Motivation and Control in a Modern Army in Combat* (Westport, CT: Greenwood Press, 1979), xv.

4. Guenter Lewy, *America in Vietnam* (New York: Oxford University Press, 1978), 203–204. Nixon's Secretary of State Henry Kissinger confirms this in two subsequent memoirs. In addition to this early April set of proposed raids, he mentions that plans for retaliatory bombing for these violations were being received through June. See Henry Kissinger, *Ending the Vietnam War* (New York: Simon and Schuster,

2003), 464–469. His conclusion was emphatic in an earlier work, where he said, "But for Watergate we surely would have acted in April." See Henry Kissinger, *Years of Upheaval* (Boston: Little, Brown, 1982), 324. Nixon himself acknowledges that from April to June 1973 action against North Vietnam was threatened but never taken because of the weakening of his authority by Watergate. See Richard Nixon, *The Real War* (New York: Simon and Schuster, 1990), 117.

5. Marshall L. Michel III, *The Eleven Days of Christmas: America's Last Vietnam Battle* (San Francisco: Encounter Books, 2002), 234.

6. Joseph S. Nye Jr., *Understanding International Conflicts: An Introduction to Theory and History*, 7th ed. (New York: Pearson Longman, 2009), 52–55, quote is from 52.

7. "Percentage of Public Who Feel Vietnam Was a Mistake," *War rating. if—Powered by Google Docs*, 1, https://mail.goggle.com/a/slu.edu/?ui=2&ik=8a8f29d7 9a&view=att&th=124cc5133353b, accessed November 10, 2009.

8. Joseph Carroll, "The Iraq-Vietnam Comparison," 1, http://pewresearch.org/pubs/579iraq-vietnam, November 10, 2009.

9. Leslie H. Gelb, with Richard K. Betts, *The Irony of Vietnam: The System Worked* (Washington, DC: Brookings Institution, 1978), 332. Genuinely alarmed by this collapse, Walter Scott Dillard attributed the fall of Vietnam to a political paralysis in the United States and warned that America must learn to "toughen its will" to avoid future Vietnams. See Walter Scott Dillard, *Sixty Days to Peace* (Washington, DC: National Defense University, 1982), 185.

10. Peter Braestrup, *Big Story: How the American Press and Television Reported and Interpreted the Crisis of Tet 1968 in Vietnam and Washington*, 2 vols. (Boulder, CO: Westview Press, 1977).

11. William H. Hammond, *United States Army in Vietnam: Public Affairs: The Military and the Media* (Washington, DC: United States Army Center of Military History, 1988), 385–389.

12. Timothy J. Lomperis, *From People's War to People's Rule: Insurgency, Intervention, and the Lessons of Vietnam* (Chapel Hill: University of North Carolina Press, 1996), 130.

13. Kissinger, *Ending the Vietnam War*, 181.

14. Harry G. Summers Jr., *On Strategy: A Critical Analysis of the Vietnam War* (New York: Dell, 1984), 126–132.

15. William C. Westmoreland, *A Soldier Reports* (New York: Doubleday, 1976), 148–153.

16. The Senator Gravel edition, *The Pentagon Papers* (Boston: Beacon Press, 1975), 4:550–555.

17. In NATO, vulnerable U.S. forces in Germany, and particularly in Berlin, served as a guarantee of an American strategic response should Soviet forces have the temerity to launch an attack on West Germany.

18. Indeed, the Russians were alarmed that they might be pulled into a nuclear war with the United States over China's Vietnam policy. See Ilya V. Gaiduk, "The Vietnam War and Soviet-American Relations, 1964–1973: New Russian Evidence," and Qiang Zhai, "Beijing and the Vietnam Conflict, 1964–1965," *Cold War International History Project*, Bulletin 3 (Winter 1995/1996): 232–258. Quote is from 236.

19. George McT. Kahin found numerous references to this fear of the Chinese

258   flashpoint in internal documents of the Johnson administration. See his *Intervention: How America became Involved in Vietnam* (New York: Alfred A. Knopf, 1986), 320,
339, 340, and 384.

20. F. Charles Parker IV, *Vietnam: Strategy for a Stalemate* (New York: Paragon
House, 1989), 122–130, 216–220. As a Hoover Institution scholar, Parker was trying
to show that Mao would not have prevented an American victory in Vietnam. His
own very detailed account of domestic Chinese politics during the chaotic Cultural
Revolution, however, only illustrates the grave risks involved in any determined
U.S. action on this assumption.

21. In the dust jacket to his book, Brokaw proclaimed about this generation,
"They won the war; they saved the world. They came home to joyous and short-
lived celebrations and immediately began the task of rebuilding their lives and the
world they wanted. . . . This book . . . [is] . . . an American family portrait of the
greatest generation." See Tom Brokaw, *The Greatest Generation* (New York: Random
House, 1998).

22. In their prize-winning account, Gelb and Betts argue that U.S. foreign policy
decision makers considered it vital not to lose in Vietnam, and this was reinforced
by a public that supported these stakes while at the same time holding opinions of
constraint that prevented victory until "the consensus . . . changed and the United
States decided to let Vietnam go." See Gelb and Betts, *Irony of Vietnam*, 23–25; quote
is from 24.

23. Since I was a political scientist with no disciplinary axe to grind in English
literature, I was asked to write up the conference report. See Timothy J. Lomperis
with John Clark Pratt, *"Reading the Wind": The Literature of the Vietnam War* (Durham, NC: Duke University Press, 1987).

24. Robert Burns, "Kissinger Sizes up Failures of U.S. Approach to Vietnam," *St.
Louis Post-Dispatch*, September 30, 2010, A22.

25. The usual cycle of historiography on a war is for the opening round of publi-
cations to be written by orthodox, officially sanctioned accounts. These are usually
followed by revisionist, skeptical works. In time, more balanced accounts, called
postrevisionist works, conclude the cycle. In the case of Vietnam, sharply critical
works were often published ahead of more official accounts. Hence, in this war, revisionist works attacked these first critiques, without necessarily subscribing to the
officially sanctioned histories. In my view, the Vietnam War still awaits the definitive postrevisionist work. I intend this volume as a modest such offering.

26. For a fuller discussion of the mortal sin of pride in academic disputes, see
C. S. Lewis, *The Weight of Glory* (San Francisco: HarperCollins, 1980 [1949]), 57–60,
141–158.

27. In the famous love chapter of I Corinthians 13, the King James version of the
Bible renders "love" as "charity."

Index